EP Math

Step 1

Parent's Guide

Welcome to the EP Math Step 1 Parent's Guide!

If you have used other EP Parent's Guides, you'll notice that this one is a bit different. The Step 1 Math Workbook was written with the lesson and examples right on the workbook page so that they can work independently. This book is set up with a lesson a page with a picture of the answer pages right on the Parent's Guide instructions for that day.

I do suggest you read the Parent's Guide as your child goes through the course. You may find that it helps you remember these topics and keeps you fresh so that you will be able to help when your child is stuck. The Parent's Guide will give some different approaches to problems and show the setup for word problems, as well as give a few little notes.

This book offers support for you and for the child that's stuck on something. Step 1 is a different kind of course in EP. It doesn't have 180 days. There are 137 lessons here, divided into sections. That's done because some kids will move slowly through this book, while others will move more quickly. I didn't want to constrain them to a set number of days.

Each lesson has a "Lesson" page and a "Practice" page. A child who gets all of the lesson page correct can skip the practice page and move onto the next lesson. If they got one wrong, see if they can find their mistake without you pointing it out. If not, have them complete a couple of similar problems on the practice page.

If they got a few wrong or just aren't getting it, use the Parent's Guide with them and have them complete maybe half of the Practice page. Half means half of the problems, not the first half of the page. There may be more than one type of problem on the page, and they should try part of each section. (There are *about* 10 problems on the Lesson page and 20 on the Practice page. On the first day you'll see this isn't really true, but it is a general marker.)

If they were getting it the second day, move on to the next lesson and leave the rest of the Practice page blank for review later. However, if they still aren't getting it after using the Lesson and part of the Practice, stay on the lesson. Go over it again, maybe try the YouTube video on EP's Step 1 page for that day, and give it another try. Maybe you'll figure out a way they understand best.

If you know your child is struggling at getting math, you may just want to start with the Parent's Guide each day to see if there are helpful tips for introducing or approaching the topic before they try out the Lesson page.

At the end of the first section, you can have your child go through and complete a couple of problems from each of the practice pages in the section. When you get to the end of the next section, they can start at the beginning and do a couple from each practice page up to that point and so on, until they run out of problems. There are eight sections.

And a little note about the guide: To avoid calling all children "he" or the awkward phrasing of "him or her," I've used the plural pronoun when referring to your child, such as, "Today they are comparing fractions."

Have a great year.

Lee

Lesson 1

LESSON 1 Basic addition

A. You can count to add. Put four coins on the table. Now put three more coins. How many coins are on the table now?

Ⓒ Ⓒ Ⓒ Ⓒ + Ⓒ Ⓒ Ⓒ = 4 + 3 = __7__

B. You can also use a number line to add. Put your finger on 3. Jump four numbers to the right. That adds four. What number are you on now?

0 1 2 3 4 5 6 7 8 9 10   3 + 4 = __7__

C. Add numbers up to 9.

8 + 6 = 14	7 + 7 = 14	6 + 9 = 15
5 + 7 = 12	9 + 1 = 10	5 + 4 = 9
8 + 9 = 17	6 + 2 = 8	4 + 3 = 7
6 + 6 = 12	4 + 9 = 13	8 + 2 = 10
2 + 5 = 7	7 + 3 = 10	3 + 6 = 9
7 + 6 = 13	6 + 4 = 10	9 + 9 = 18
2 + 9 = 11	8 + 8 = 16	7 + 4 = 11
5 + 5 = 10	3 + 5 = 8	4 + 2 = 6
8 + 4 = 12	4 + 4 = 8	3 + 3 = 6
5 + 0 = 5	3 + 2 = 5	7 + 2 = 9
9 + 5 = 14	9 + 7 = 16	5 + 8 = 13
3 + 8 = 11	6 + 5 = 11	9 + 3 = 12
2 + 2 = 4	7 + 8 = 15	0 + 6 = 6

LESSON 1 Practice

A. Add numbers up to 5.

5 + 0 = 5	4 + 0 = 4	1 + 4 = 5
0 + 3 = 3	2 + 1 = 3	3 + 2 = 5
3 + 1 = 4	4 + 1 = 5	0 + 0 = 0
2 + 3 = 5	1 + 2 = 3	2 + 2 = 4
1 + 1 = 2	0 + 5 = 5	1 + 3 = 4

B. Add numbers up to 9.

7 + 9 = 16	6 + 3 = 9	6 + 8 = 14
5 + 6 = 11	9 + 9 = 18	7 + 5 = 12
9 + 6 = 15	4 + 7 = 11	9 + 8 = 17
3 + 7 = 10	2 + 4 = 6	6 + 6 = 12
4 + 6 = 10	9 + 3 = 12	4 + 8 = 12
8 + 8 = 16	6 + 7 = 13	5 + 9 = 14
5 + 3 = 8	9 + 2 = 11	7 + 7 = 14
4 + 4 = 8	5 + 5 = 10	1 + 9 = 10
4 + 5 = 9	8 + 3 = 11	3 + 4 = 7
8 + 7 = 15	0 + 5 = 5	2 + 6 = 8
2 + 8 = 10	2 + 7 = 9	9 + 4 = 13
3 + 3 = 6	5 + 2 = 7	8 + 5 = 13

These they should know by rote memory. While they can use a number line or their fingers, they should keep practicing to just know these facts if they still don't. Use a combination of flashcards, online practice, books, oral quizzing, writing out facts, telling the facts, etc. The goal is repetition until they move into long term memory. If they are struggling to learn these, use them during the day. "We need five more. How many do we need?" Find facts in your daily life and use that for practice. Link the facts to things your child loves to do and have them think about when they might need facts.

You can also help your child see patterns. They should be able to quickly add two on to something, the next odd or even number. The should be able to quickly add nine to something, one less than ten more. The ones digit will be one less than the ones digit you are adding to nine. Ex. $9 + 7 = 16$

They can use the facts they know to find answers, but they need to be able to do it quickly. $6 + 6 = 12$ so $6 + 7 = 13$ All of these kinds of thought processes are beneficial, but the ideal is just knowing the facts without having to think about them.

Lesson 2

LESSON 2 Basic subtraction

A. You can count to subtract. Put seven coins on the table. Now take away four of the coins. How many coins are on the table now?

Ⓒ Ⓒ Ⓒ Ⓒ Ⓒ Ⓒ Ⓒ $7 - 4 = 3$

B. You can also use a number line to subtract. Put your finger on 7. Jump three numbers to the left. That subtracts three. What number are you on now?

0 1 2 3 4 5 6 7 8 9 10 $7 - 3 = 4$

C. Subtract numbers up to 9.

$15 - 9 = 6$	$10 - 1 = 9$	$14 - 6 = 8$
$9 - 4 = 5$	$14 - 7 = 7$	$12 - 7 = 5$
$15 - 8 = 7$	$8 - 2 = 6$	$17 - 9 = 8$
$10 - 2 = 8$	$13 - 9 = 4$	$12 - 6 = 6$
$9 - 6 = 3$	$10 - 4 = 6$	$11 - 8 = 3$
$18 - 9 = 9$	$14 - 5 = 9$	$13 - 6 = 7$
$11 - 4 = 7$	$16 - 8 = 8$	$7 - 3 = 4$
$6 - 2 = 4$	$8 - 5 = 3$	$10 - 5 = 5$
$12 - 3 = 9$	$16 - 7 = 9$	$12 - 4 = 8$
$9 - 7 = 2$	$8 - 4 = 4$	$0 - 0 = 0$
$13 - 8 = 5$	$11 - 2 = 9$	$11 - 6 = 5$
$7 - 2 = 5$	$10 - 3 = 7$	$6 - 3 = 3$
$12 - 5 = 7$	$17 - 8 = 9$	$15 - 7 = 8$

LESSON 2 Practice

A. Subtract numbers up to 5.

$5 - 1 = 4$	$4 - 2 = 2$	$5 - 5 = 0$
$4 - 4 = 0$	$3 - 1 = 2$	$5 - 3 = 2$
$0 - 0 = 0$	$5 - 4 = 1$	$2 - 1 = 1$
$5 - 2 = 3$	$3 - 2 = 1$	$3 - 3 = 0$
$4 - 3 = 1$	$4 - 1 = 3$	$5 - 0 = 5$

B. Subtract numbers up to 9.

$14 - 8 = 6$	$9 - 3 = 6$	$16 - 9 = 7$
$12 - 5 = 7$	$18 - 9 = 9$	$11 - 6 = 5$
$8 - 4 = 4$	$11 - 7 = 4$	$15 - 6 = 9$
$14 - 7 = 7$	$6 - 4 = 2$	$10 - 7 = 3$
$12 - 8 = 4$	$10 - 6 = 4$	$12 - 3 = 9$
$14 - 9 = 5$	$13 - 7 = 6$	$16 - 8 = 8$
$12 - 6 = 6$	$11 - 2 = 9$	$8 - 3 = 5$
$13 - 4 = 9$	$10 - 5 = 5$	$17 - 9 = 8$
$10 - 9 = 1$	$9 - 7 = 2$	$11 - 3 = 8$
$8 - 6 = 2$	$5 - 5 = 0$	$9 - 5 = 4$
$15 - 9 = 6$	$17 - 8 = 9$	$15 - 7 = 8$
$13 - 5 = 8$	$12 - 9 = 3$	$10 - 8 = 2$

Subtraction is finding the difference. You are figuring out how far apart the numbers are. They should be able to see 8 and 6 and see that they are two apart. When they get to negative numbers (soon), they will the difference between the numbers and will need to remember that they are just finding how far apart the numbers are.

If they are stuck on these facts, they should be working on them. While they can use addition facts to help them figure out the answers, it is the goal to learn them independent of addition facts. Ex. $14 - 9 = 5$ The answer is one more in the ones place, the opposite of adding.

Ask your child what are some patterns they can spot. What's an even minus an odd number? What's an odd number minus an odd number? How do they know the answer to a minus nine question?

Lesson 3

LESSON 3 Adding 2-digit numbers without carrying

A. Here are the steps for adding 2-digit numbers without carrying (or regrouping).

$$\begin{array}{r} 2\ 3 \\ +\ 7\ 5 \\ \hline 9\ 8 \end{array}$$

1. Add the ones digits. 3 + 5 = 8
2. Write 8 in the ones column.
3. Add the tens digits. 2 + 7 = 9
4. Write 9 in the tens column.

B. You can also add each place value separately, and then add the sums.

$$\begin{array}{r} 20 + 3 \\ +\ 70 + 5 \\ \hline 90 + 8\ =\ 98 \end{array}$$

1. Think about both numbers in expanded form.
2. Add the tens. 20 + 70 = 90
3. Add the ones. 3 + 5 = 8
4. Add the tens and ones sums. 90 + 8 = 98

C. Add numbers with up to 2-digits.

15	17	6	18	2	24
+ 3	+ 2	+ 13	+ 2	+ 35	+ 4
18	19	19	20	37	28

38	23	24	23	25	37
+ 41	+ 22	+ 64	+ 73	+ 34	+ 60
79	45	88	96	59	97

22	23	56	50	35	63
+ 43	+ 53	+ 31	+ 49	+ 32	+ 26
65	76	87	99	67	89

LESSON 3 Practice

A. Add numbers up to 20.

5 + 14 = 19	13 + 6 = 19	8 + 9 = 17
13 + 3 = 16	5 + 7 = 12	3 + 14 = 17
9 + 6 = 15	14 + 4 = 18	5 + 5 = 10
6 + 12 = 18	8 + 7 = 15	17 + 2 = 19
7 + 6 = 13	3 + 15 = 18	12 + 5 = 17

B. Add the 2-digit numbers.

44	25	53	28	24	42
+ 34	+ 62	+ 33	+ 51	+ 75	+ 14
78	87	86	79	99	56

32	45	73	34	22	60
+ 25	+ 24	+ 25	+ 14	+ 26	+ 39
57	69	98	48	48	99

40	52	52	63	24	42
+ 20	+ 14	+ 37	+ 25	+ 55	+ 45
60	66	89	88	79	87

This page doesn't require regrouping. They shouldn't write out the expanded form of the numbers, such as 20 + 3, but encourage them to try the lesson that way. It's a mental math trick and allows for adding big numbers faster. You add left to right instead of right to left. In this case you would add the tens and then the ones. You think of 23 and 75 as 20 + 70 and 3 + 5. This is much more handy when there is carrying. Right now they get to just add straight down.

When this gets more complicated, they can write their work like this.

$$\begin{array}{r} 45 \\ +\ 32 \\ \hline 70 \\ 7 \\ \hline 77 \end{array} \qquad \begin{array}{r} 5419 \\ +\ 1837 \\ \hline 6000 \\ 1200 \\ 40 \\ 16 \\ \hline 7256 \end{array}$$

When faced with something like 3 + 16, it's easy to think of it in tens and ones turning it into this equation. 10 + 9 = 19

13 + 5 turns in 10 + 8 = 18

12 + 8 turns into 10 + 10 = 20 This can be done in their head, but that's the thought process.

Lesson 4

LESSON 4 Subtracting different ways

A. You can think of subtraction in two ways: taking away and finding the difference.

There are 15 blocks on the table. You take away 8 of them. How many blocks are on the table now?

$15 - 8 = 7$

Mark is 12 years old. His sister Jenny is 9 years old. What is the difference in their ages?

$12 - 9 = 3$

B. Subtraction is the opposite of addition, moving in the opposite direction on a number line. You move to the right to add and to the left to subtract.

$5 + 6 = 11$

$11 - 6 = 5$

C. Write a subtraction fact to match each story.

Alice had 19 candies. She gave 6 candies to her brother. How many candies does Alice have now?

$19 - 6 = 13$

William ate 13 grapes. Ethan ate 8 grapes. How many more grapes did William eat?

$13 - 8 = 5$

Larry needs $12 to buy a gift for his mom, but he only has $7. How much more money does he need?

$12 - 7 = 5$

Sixteen kids were in a room. Nine kids walked out. How many kids are in the room now?

$16 - 9 = 7$

Emma has 15 pencils. Olivia has 6 fewer pencils than Emma. How many pencils does Olivia have?

$15 - 6 = 9$

Fifteen ducks were in the pond. Some swam away and 12 ducks were left. How many ducks swam away?

$15 - 12 = 3$

There are 14 apples in the basket. Eight of them are red and the rest are green. How many apples are green?

$14 - 8 = 6$

Andrew is 11 years old. His brother Peter is 3 years younger than Andrew. How old is Peter?

$11 - 3 = 8$

LESSON 4 Practice

A. Subtract numbers up to 20.

$16 - 8 = 8$	$12 - 6 = 6$	$15 - 6 = 9$
$13 - 4 = 9$	$11 - 7 = 4$	$11 - 6 = 5$
$14 - 8 = 6$	$17 - 9 = 8$	$18 - 9 = 9$
$10 - 2 = 8$	$14 - 5 = 9$	$10 - 5 = 5$
$11 - 5 = 6$	$13 - 8 = 5$	$12 - 9 = 3$
$12 - 7 = 5$	$18 - 5 = 13$	$10 - 4 = 6$
$16 - 14 = 2$	$19 - 14 = 5$	$20 - 15 = 5$
$17 - 12 = 5$	$20 - 10 = 10$	$19 - 13 = 6$

B. Write a subtraction fact to match each story.

Laura is 18 years old. Her brother Daniel is 9 years old. What is the difference in their ages?

$18 - 9 = 9$

Gary has 12 stickers. He gave 8 stickers to Will. How many stickers does Gary have now?

$12 - 8 = 4$

Julia has $14. Hunter has $7. How much more money does Julia have?

$14 - 7 = 7$

Kyle jumped a rope 13 times. Adam jumped 7 times. How many more times did Kyle jump?

$13 - 7 = 6$

A toy car costs $4 less than a fidget spinner. A fidget spinner costs $11. How much does a toy car cost?

$11 - 4 = 7$

Eight children were in the room. Some children walked in. Now 16 children are in the room. How many children walked in?

$16 - 8 = 8$

They don't have to think a lot to complete the assignment since it announces it's a subtraction worksheet. They are to write a subtraction fact, meaning an equation, such as $18 - 9 = 9$.

They can use the same idea of subtracting tens and ones here.
$18 - 5 = 10$ and $8 - 5 = 10 + 3 = 13$

$19 - 14 = 10 - 10$ and $9 - 4 = 0 + 5 = 5$

They don't have to write that out. They should be able to do these in their heads. If they need to write out work, they can use scratch paper for it.

Addition and Subtraction

Lesson 5

LESSON 5 Adding 3-digit numbers with regrouping

A. Here are the steps for adding 3-digit numbers with regrouping.

```
  1 1
  7 8 3
+ 5 6 9
1 3 5 2
```

1. Add the ones digits. 3 + 9 = 12
2. Write 2 in the ones column and carry 1 to the tens column.
3. Add the tens digits. 1 (carryover) + 8 + 6 = 15
4. Write 5 in the tens column and carry 1 to the hundreds column.
5. Add the hundreds digits. 1 (carryover) + 7 + 5 = 13
6. Write 1 in the thousands column and 3 in the hundreds column.

B. You can also add each place value separately, and then add the sums.

```
  700 + 80 + 3
+ 500 + 60 + 9
 1200 + 140 + 12
     = 1352
```

1. Think about both numbers in expanded form.
2. Add the hundreds. 700 + 500 = 1200
3. Add the tens. 80 + 60 = 140
4. Add the ones. 3 + 9 = 12
5. Add the hundreds, tens, and ones sums.
   1200 + 140 + 12 = 1352

C. Add the 3-digit numbers.

353	948	873	214	376
+ 258	+ 675	+ 865	+ 368	+ 385
611	1623	1738	582	761

274	924	965	479	238
+ 554	+ 547	+ 364	+ 677	+ 946
828	1471	1329	1156	1184

LESSON 5 Practice

A. Add numbers up to 100.

83	65	38
+ 19	+ 23	+ 58
102	88	96

45	42	28	59	43	81
+ 89	+ 67	+ 67	+ 49	+ 26	+ 69
134	109	95	108	69	150

B. Add the 3-digit numbers.

547	573
+ 295	+ 459
842	1032

487	524	250	764	746
+ 354	+ 476	+ 594	+ 942	+ 557
841	1000	844	1706	1303

The lesson on the page is for regrouping. On the practice page there is space to write out some of the problems sideways if they want to try that. They can also write the work vertically. Encourage your child to use the method that makes the most sense to them. It may be easiest to just do the "normal" carrying method, but learning this way gives a better concept of what the carrying is doing. I think it gives it more meaning. See if your child can explain what that little one is doing there on top. What does it mean? They should know their place values of ones, tens, hundreds, thousands and know that ten of one place value is one of the next.

```
  49          5419
+ 32        + 1837
  70          6000
  11          1200
  81            40
                16
              7256
```

Lesson 6

LESSON 6 Subtracting 3-digit numbers with regrouping

A. Here are the steps for subtracting 3-digit numbers with regrouping.

```
      13
  8  3̶ 12
  9̶ 4̶ 2̶
- 5 6 7
  3 7 5
```

1. Subtract the ones column. 2 – 7 requires regrouping.
2. Borrow 1 from the tens place. 4 becomes 3. 2 becomes 12.
3. Subtract the ones column again. 12 – 7 = 5
4. Write 5 in the ones column.
5. Subtract the tens column. 3 – 6 requires regrouping.
6. Borrow 1 from the hundreds place. 9 becomes 8. 3 becomes 13.
7. Subtract the tens column again. 13 – 6 = 7
8. Write 7 in the tens column.
9. Subtract the hundreds column. 8 – 5 = 3
10. Write 3 in the hundreds column.

B. Subtract the 3-digit numbers.

923	782	952	834	461
− 832	− 206	− 287	− 562	− 359
91	576	665	272	102

679	831	590	628	472
− 324	− 257	− 453	− 565	− 237
355	574	137	63	235

826	735	942	735	894
− 467	− 597	− 689	− 358	− 338
359	138	253	377	556

Did you know? The first number to contain the letter 'a' is one thousand.

LESSON 6 Practice

A. Subtract numbers up to 100.

74	72	75	63	29	83
− 58	− 27	− 45	− 49	− 25	− 67
16	45	30	14	4	16

84	96	60	95	67	91
− 29	− 56	− 18	− 63	− 30	− 58
55	40	42	32	37	33

75	83	34	63	92	58
− 37	− 50	− 19	− 25	− 38	− 18
38	33	15	38	54	40

B. Subtract the 3-digit numbers.

758	910	679	836	755
− 392	− 447	− 593	− 483	− 257
366	463	86	353	498

527	764	842	534	927
− 235	− 348	− 274	− 419	− 354
292	416	568	115	573

This lesson is on subtracting with borrowing or regrouping. While there are mental math tricks for subtracting, this lesson doesn't teach them. If you didn't check on your child's comprehension of place value in the last lesson, then do it now. This is the opposite, they are taking one away from one place value and it becomes ten of the next place value to the right.

To get these correct, they need to write neatly and cross off numbers that are no longer in use so that they don't get confused. There's no need to cross of the 3 or 2 in the example; they can just add in a 1 to turn them into a 13 and 12.

On the lesson page there is a little "Did you know?" fact. They should always take the time to look at those. They can also appear on the practice page, so they should look for those, as well as any other tidbit added on. Sometimes there is a math riddle they can try to solve.

Just a reminder…There are a lot of questions to solve on the practice page. If they need the practice, have them leave maybe the last line of each section blank. Then you can have that available for review or to try again if they are still getting them wrong.

Lesson 7

LESSON 7 Borrowing & mental subtraction

A. Follow these examples to understand why borrowing works.

$$842 - 64 = \;\;\; 800 + \overset{30}{\cancel{40}} + \overset{12}{\cancel{2}} \;\;\; = \;\;\; \overset{130}{700} + \overset{30}{\cancel{40}} + \overset{12}{\cancel{2}}$$
$$\underline{\quad - 60 - 4 \quad} \;\;\; = \;\;\; \underline{\quad - 60 - 4 \quad}$$

You can't subtract 4 from 2.
You borrow 10 from 40.
40 becomes 40 - 10 = 30.
2 becomes 2 + 10 = 12.
You can subtract 4 from 12.

You can't subtract 60 from 30.
You borrow 100 from 800.
800 becomes 800 - 100 = 700.
30 becomes 30 + 100 = 130.
You can subtract 60 from 130.

B. There are many ways to subtract numbers. The following example illustrates an alternative subtraction method, subtracting from left to right. Complete the example.

$$\begin{array}{r} {}^{1}\\ 9\ 4\ 7\ 2 \\ -\ 5\ 6\ 3\ 9 \\ \hline 3\ 8\ 3\ 3 \end{array}$$

1. Subtract the thousands. 9 - 5 = 4
2. Look at the hundreds column. It needs borrowing. Give 1 to the hundreds column and write 4 - 1 = 3 in the answer.
3. Subtract the hundreds with the borrowed 10. 14 - 6 = 8
4. The tens column doesn't need borrowing, so just write 8.
5. Continue subtracting and borrowing to the next column.

C. Subtract the 4-digit numbers. Use whichever method you like.

6425	8573	5930	7238	8362
− 3798	− 4935	− 2665	− 3693	− 5786
2627	3638	3265	3545	2576

9215	7355	8290	7620	5513
− 4487	− 4636	− 2721	− 6278	− 1878
4728	2719	5569	1342	3635

LESSON 7 Practice

A. Subtract numbers up to 100.

72	97	82	90	75	68
− 39	− 88	− 74	− 59	− 27	− 26
33	9	8	31	48	42

93	84	68	96	62	73
− 55	− 57	− 24	− 68	− 46	− 59
38	27	44	28	16	14

97	65	49	54	83	84
− 49	− 28	− 17	− 29	− 37	− 26
48	37	32	25	46	58

B. Subtract the 4-digit numbers.

8752	9455	7422	8150	6250
− 3434	− 2827	− 4849	− 2587	− 3594
5318	6628	2573	5563	2656

4134	8577	5930	7273	8356
− 1689	− 4939	− 1675	− 3698	− 5762
2445	3638	4255	3575	2594

Remember that the example in part A on the page is for mental math, not for writing out the problem like that. If you are coming from Genesis Curriculum, you know that I would recommend something like this for mental math work.

$$842 - 64 = 800 - 20 - 2 = 780 - 2 = 778$$

I am finding the difference between 40 and 60 which is 20 and seeing that I'm subtracting the larger number so I am subtracting it off. Then I find the difference between 2 and 4 and see that I'm subtracting the larger number, so I have to subtract off that distance. However, if your child hasn't seen negative numbers yet (which they haven't done yet in EP), then don't introduce that method right now.

The point is to understand what you are doing when you subtract. Have your child explain it to you, not the steps, but the what is going on.

Part B has a better way to think through a subtraction problem where you can write out your answer without a lot of fuss. It's subtracting left to right and just noticing if you are subtracting a larger number from a smaller number and need to borrow. I recommend using this method for this lesson and see how it goes. They can switch back tomorrow to the old way if they don't like these ways better.

Lesson 8

LESSON 8 Adding multi-digit numbers

A. You can add any large numbers using regrouping. Complete the example.

```
      1   1
  7 3 5 4 9 8
+ 7 9 8 6 8 6
1 5 3 4 1 8 4
```

1. Add the ones digits. 8 + 6 = 14
2. Write 4 in the ones column and carry 1 to the tens column.
3. Add the tens digits. 1 (carryover) + 9 + 8 = 18
4. Write 8 in the tens column and carry 1 to the hundreds column.
5. Continue adding and carrying to the next column.

B. Add the multi-digit numbers.

9785	6248	6249	4869	4352
+ 3208	+ 6578	+ 3928	+ 7487	+ 6795
12,993	12,826	10,177	12,356	11,147

8347	6265	8465	4392	8927
+ 3607	+ 4953	+ 7453	+ 2358	+ 4937
11,954	11,218	15,918	6,750	13,864

538,532	785,493	1,365,238	4,527,648
+ 207,886	+ 706,346	+ 257,494	+ 936,561
746,418	1,491,839	1,622,732	5,464,209

888 + 88 + 8 + 8 + 8 = 1,000

LESSON 8 Practice

A. Add numbers up to 1000.

753	580	839	237	944
+ 783	+ 847	+ 179	+ 946	+ 986
1536	1427	1018	1183	1930

547	769	542	243	247
+ 628	+ 965	+ 958	+ 632	+ 794
1175	1734	1500	875	1041

462	528	489	539	958
+ 984	+ 785	+ 469	+ 456	+ 373
1446	1313	958	995	1331

B. Add the multi-digit numbers.

3205	9278	8968	7868	4352
+ 8546	+ 6458	+ 7949	+ 4762	+ 5787
11,751	15,736	16,917	12,630	10,139

863,629	437,558	2,468,593	4,699,073
+ 562,760	+ 857,458	+ 958,495	+ 259,546
1,426,389	1,295,016	3,427,088	4,958,619

They are going to add with carrying, or regrouping. They can do this with whatever thought process makes sense to them. Even if they don't write the little ones up top, that's what they are doing.

From the practice page: 547 + 628
Ones: 7 + 8 = 15 They write the 5 down.
Tens: 10 (from 15) + 40 + 20 = 70 They write down the 7.
Hundreds: 5 hundred + 6 hundred = 11 hundred They write down 11.
Answer: 1175

That's the thought process. They are adding the place values. Addition is commutative, which they will be learning this year. That means that 2 + 3 and 3 + 2 equal the same thing. When they are adding, they can add any parts of the numbers together in any order they like. If they add them all together, no matter how, they will get to the answer.

Lesson 9

LESSON 9 Subtracting across zeros

A. Here are the steps for subtracting 3-digit numbers across zeros. Complete the example.

```
      9
  7  10  12
  8   0   2
-  2   3   8
  5   6   4
```

1. Subtract the ones column. 2 – 8 requires regrouping.
2. Borrow 1 from the tens place. But there's nothing to borrow.
3. Borrow 1 from the hundreds place. 8 becomes 7. 0 becomes 10.
4. Now borrow 1 from the tens place. 10 becomes 9. 2 becomes 12.
5. Subtract the ones column. 12 – 2 = 4
6. Write 4 in the ones column.
7. Continue subtracting to the next column.

B. You can also use the box method, as shown below. Complete the example.

```
  5   9   9   13
  6   0   0   3
-  4   7   5   8
  1   2   4   5
```

1. Subtract the ones column. 3 – 8 requires regrouping.
2. There are no tens. Find the first non-zero digit in the columns to the left of the tens place. Draw a box from that digit to the tens place. The first non-zero digit is 6, so the box goes around 600.
3. Take 1 from 600. 600 becomes 599. 3 becomes 13.
4. Subtract as usual from right to left, column by column.

C. Subtract the numbers across zeros.

505	700	802	900	400
− 238	− 482	− 357	− 284	− 318
267	218	445	616	82

900	604	800	502	300
− 529	− 279	− 463	− 236	− 145
371	325	337	266	155

7000	3000	9003	4000	6005
− 1650	− 2350	− 5080	− 2710	− 2980
5350	650	3923	1290	3025

LESSON 9 Practice

A. Subtract numbers up to 1000.

854	713	562	865	931
− 299	− 497	− 229	− 583	− 368
555	216	333	282	563

615	786	980	747	812
− 338	− 547	− 286	− 289	− 367
277	239	694	458	445

934	690	834	753	956
− 568	− 259	− 297	− 376	− 424
366	431	537	377	532

B. Subtract the numbers across zeros.

803	504	900	605	700
− 298	− 276	− 454	− 257	− 319
505	228	446	348	381

900	403	505	802	704
− 393	− 227	− 238	− 445	− 229
507	176	267	357	475

There are two methods shown on the page. Your child can use another tactic normally, but have them look at these and try them out at least for this lesson. Personally, I think the box method is super simple. It works just as well with larger numbers. Here's an example.

```
  699 1
  7000
- 1537
  5463
```

You take one away from 700 instead of borrowing one at a time from each zero. 700 − 1 = 699. Then you can automatically subtract everything straight down.

From the practice page:

```
  89 1
  900
- 454
  446
```

The box goes around the first non-zero digit and all the zeros but the last one. The last one becomes a ten.

Lesson 10

LESSON 10 Word problems: addition and subtraction

A. There are multiple ways to solve word problems. The following examples show just a few of them. It is okay to use your own strategy.

Mia has 90 pennies, nickels, and dimes. Twenty-eight of them are dimes and 45 are nickels. How many pennies does Mia have? **17 pennies**

Solve the problem:
28 dimes + 45 nickels = 73
# of pennies = 90 − 73 = 17

Check your answer:
28 + 45 + 17 = 90

Ryan had some marbles. He lost 19 of them and found 7. If he had 62 after that, how many marbles did Ryan have at first? **74 marbles**

Solve the problem:
Before finding 7 marbles: 62 − 7 = 55
Before losing 19 marbles: 55 + 19 = 74

Check your answer:
74 − 19 + 7 = 62

B. Solve the word problems. Make sure to check your answers.

Sarah has 62 red, blue, and yellow markers. 15 of them are red and 19 are blue. How many markers are yellow? **28 markers**

Laura bought 55 paper cups. After using 48 cups, she bought 25 more cups. How many paper cups did she have in the end? **32 cups**

Ella planted 32 roses, 28 daisies, and 14 violets. Fifty-six of them have bloomed so far. How many flowers have not bloomed yet? **16 flowers**

Ron has $49. Matt has $19 more than Ron. Naomi has $12 less than Matt. How much money do they have altogether? **$173**

There were some ducks swimming in the pond. Fifteen of them flew away, and another 17 ducks flew in. If there were 24 ducks after that, how many ducks were swimming in the pond at first? **22 ducks**

Mom bought some apples. She used 18 of them to make pies and 37 to make jam. If there were 14 apples left, how many apples did Mom buy at first? **69 apples**

Did you know? A paper cannot be folded more than 9 times. Try it yourself!

LESSON 10 Practice

Solve the word problems. Make sure to check your answers.

Ron had 82 stickers. He gave 28 of them to Mark, 26 to Larry, and the rest to Kyle. How many stickers did Kyle get? **28 stickers**

Sam wants to buy three books that cost $15, $12, and $18 each. He has $25. How much more money does Sam need? **$18**

The store had 71 bags of potatoes. It sold 55 bags and brought in 36 more bags. How many bags did the store have in the end? **52 bags**

Angela had some math problems to solve. She solved 28 problems yesterday and 29 today. She still has 11 problems left. How many problems did she have at first? **68 problems**

The pet store had 90 fish. After selling 67 fish, it brought in 55 more fish. How many fish did the store have in the end? **78 fish**

There were some people in the auditorium. Twenty-six of them left, and 15 people entered. If there were 48 people after that, how many people were in the auditorium at first? **59 people**

The pet store had 85 goldfish and 70 angelfish. After selling 57 goldfish, it brought in 32 more angelfish. How many goldfish and angelfish did the store have in the end? **130 fish**

Claire found some seashells on the beach. She used 22 to decorate her room and gave 26 to her sister. If there were 18 seashells left, how many seashells did Clair find at first? **66 seashells**

Kate rode her bike 11 miles to the library and then 14 miles to the park. Later she came home the same way. How many miles did Kate ride altogether? **50 miles**

In the afternoon, Adam took an hour break from his studying. After spending 25 minutes listening to music and 20 minutes watching TV, he went for a walk. How many minutes did he walk during the break? **15 minutes**

They are going to have to think through these word problems. Here are two great strategies for figuring them out. My favorite is to use smaller numbers. Instead of 55, 48, and 25, use 5, 4, and 2. Then it's usually intuitive what the answer is. Then they just have to apply the same thought process and method to figure out the answer with the original numbers. Another technique is to draw the problem. Just using simple lines to show the items being added and taken away can make it clear what's happening and show you if you need to add or subtract.

These are multiple step word problems. They will have to be patient to find the answer. When they do, they should stop and think if their answer makes sense. If the person is supposed to have less than someone else, but the answer is more, they probably did it backwards.

Here's an example from the practice page. I'll do the first and sixth ones.

We start with 82 stickers. He gives away 28 and 26. We need to know what's left over. They can first combine 28 and 26 which is 54. And then subtract that from 82.

There are some people in an auditorium. 26 leave and 15 enter leaving us with 48. They can draw a picture if they need help thinking it through using 2, 1, and 4 as the numbers. They can apply that to the real numbers. Before, those 15 weren't there, so subtract them off. Also before, those 26 were there, so add them back on. That gives you the answer. Does it make sense? It should be bigger than 48 since more people left than came.

Lesson 11

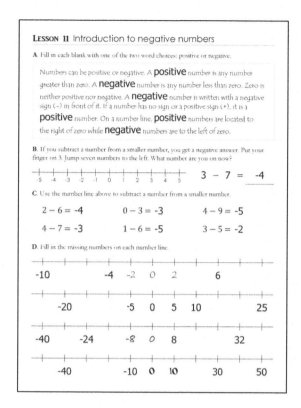

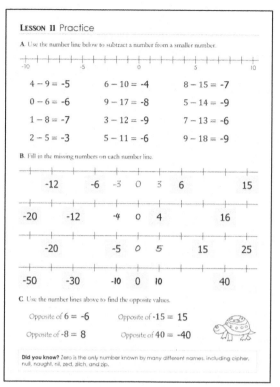

We're starting to work with negative numbers. Negative numbers are like debt. If you spend more money than you have, you have debt. It's not a zero balance. You have a negative balance. You have to pay so much money to get to zero before you have your own money again. You can act this out.

One person owes the other five dollars. They don't have zero dollars, they have negative five dollars. When they pay back one dollar, then they owe four dollars, and have negative four dollars to their name. Keep paying back to get to zero. Then when they get a dollar, they have positive one dollars. They are no longer in debt.

In parts B and C they will use the number line to subtract. They are still just figuring out the distance between the numbers, but now they have to think about what direction the answer is going in. $9 - 4 = 5$ and $4 - 9 = -5$ The difference between 9 and 4 is the same. The direction changed.

In part D they are filling in the number line. This is practicing the direction of the numbers. Each line is worth a different amount in each of the number lines. The first number shows what they are counting by. For instance on the practice page the first one would be -12, -6, 6, 15. Each line represents three.

In part C on the practice page, they are finding the opposite. That's the positive of the negative number and the negative of a postitive number. The opposite of -3 is 3.

Lesson 12

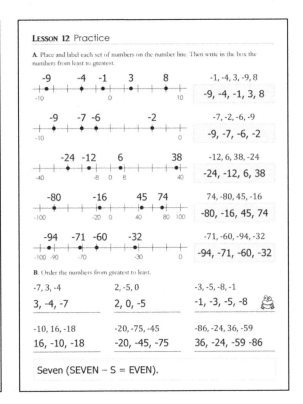

They are ordering numbers in this lesson. They just need to realize that a large negative number is less than a small negative number. −19 is less than −6.

There is an example on the page that you can look at together. It works like a timeline. One hundred BC is more recent than 2000 BC, but 2000 AD is more recent than 100 AD.

For part B they should place dots on the timeline to show about where the numbers go. Then they will write them in order.

For part C, they are ordering the numbers without the benefit of a visual.

Lesson 13

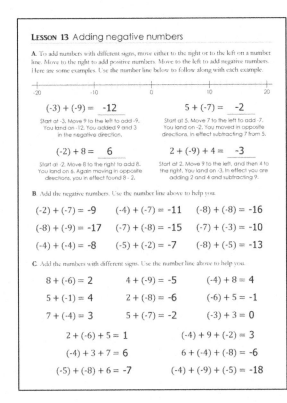

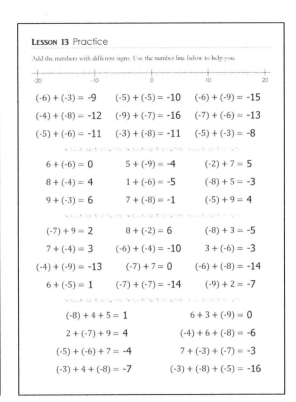

Adding negative numbers is really subtracting a positive number. - 3 (negative three) and –3 (minus three) are the same thing. -3 + (-3) = -3 – 3 It's 3 two times to the left on the number line.

-2 + -2 + -2 = -2 – 2 – 2 = -6 It's 2 + 2 + 2 all in the negative direction. It's starting at -2 and then subtracting two again and again. Encourage them to use a number line as much as they need to until they understand how it works.

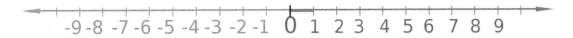

To add a positive and a negative, they just need to think of the negative sign as subtraction. – 3 + 5 = 5 – 3 = 2 You can rearrange addition in any order you like, so you can add the negative number in any order you like.

When there are more than two numbers being added, they should combine all the like signs first. -5 + 4 + -3 + 2 = -8 + 6 = -2

Lesson 14

LESSON 14 Adding and subtracting negative numbers

A. You can use a number line to visualize adding and subtracting numbers with different signs. Move forward (to the right) to add. Move backward (to the left) to subtract. Change the direction when a sign is negative.

$4 + (-7) = 4 - 7 = -3$

Add -7.
= Move forward -7.
= Move backward 7.
= Subtract 7.

Therefore, adding a negative number is the same as subtracting the opposite.

$4 - (-7) = 4 + 7 = 11$

Subtract -7.
= Move backward -7.
= Move forward 7.
= Add 7.

Therefore, subtracting a negative number is the same as adding the opposite.

B. Add and subtract the negative numbers.

$2 + (-9) = -7$ $0 - (-6) = 6$ $(-8) - (-2) = -6$
$7 - (-6) = 13$ $9 - (-3) = 12$ $(-5) - (-7) = 2$
$5 - (-5) = 10$ $4 + (-7) = -3$ $(-4) + (-9) = -13$

C. Add and subtract the numbers with different signs.

$(-2) + 7 = 5$ $8 - (-8) = 16$ $(-7) - (-4) = -3$
$(-5) - 5 = -10$ $(-6) - 3 = -9$ $(-2) - (-5) = 3$
$8 - (-4) = 12$ $(-4) + 4 = 0$ $(-3) + (-3) = -6$
$(-5) + 0 = -5$ $9 + (-6) = 3$ $(-8) + (-2) = -10$
$9 + (-5) = 4$ $5 - (-7) = 12$ $(-5) - (-8) = 3$
$(-3) - 8 = -11$ $7 + (-8) = -1$ $(-9) - (-6) = -3$
$7 - (-5) = 12$ $(-6) + 3 = -3$ $(-2) + (-9) = -11$
$(-4) + 3 = -1$ $2 - (-2) = 4$ $(-1) - (-5) = 4$

LESSON 14 Practice

A. Add the negative numbers.

$8 + (-6) = 2$ $7 + (-7) = 0$ $(-6) + (-9) = -15$
$5 + (-7) = -2$ $9 + (-1) = 8$ $(-5) + (-4) = -9$
$8 + (-9) = -1$ $6 + (-2) = 4$ $(-4) + (-3) = -7$
$6 + (-6) = 0$ $4 + (-9) = -5$ $(-8) + (-2) = -10$
$2 + (-5) = -3$ $7 + (-3) = 4$ $(-3) + (-6) = -9$

B. Subtract the negative numbers.

$7 - (-6) = 13$ $6 - (-4) = 10$ $(-9) - (-9) = 0$
$2 - (-9) = 11$ $8 - (-8) = 16$ $(-7) - (-4) = -3$
$5 - (-5) = 10$ $3 - (-5) = 8$ $(-4) - (-2) = -2$
$8 - (-4) = 12$ $4 - (-4) = 8$ $(-3) - (-3) = 0$
$0 - (-5) = 5$ $9 - (-7) = 16$ $(-7) - (-2) = -5$

C. Add and subtract the numbers with different signs.

$7 + (-9) = -2$ $6 - (-3) = 9$ $(-2) - (-7) = 5$
$(-5) - 6 = -11$ $(-2) + 9 = 7$ $(-8) + (-5) = -13$
$(-9) + 6 = -3$ $(-4) - 7 = -11$ $(-9) - (-4) = -5$
$3 + (-7) = -4$ $(-2) + 4 = 2$ $(-7) + (-7) = -14$
$(-4) - 6 = -10$ $(-6) + 5 = -1$ $(-4) - (-8) = 4$
$(-2) + 8 = 6$ $3 - (-9) = 12$ $(-8) + (-9) = -17$

-9 -8 -7 -6 -5 -4 -3 -2 -1 0 1 2 3 4 5 6 7 8 9

In this lesson they are going to subtract negatives. Walk through the examples at the top of the page which try to explain why adding a negative number is like subtracting, and why subtracting a negative number is like adding.

We've already seen how $5 + -3 = 5 - 3 = 2$ In this lesson we are doing $5 - (-3)$. Subtracting is the opposite of addition, so we're going to do the opposite. $5 - (-3)$ is $5 + 3 = 8$. They can think about taking the two lines - - and putting them together to make an addition sign like this +.

Here are some of the problems from the practice page.

$8 + (-6) = 8 - 6 = 2$
$(-3) + (-6) = -3 - 6 = -9$
$7 - (-6) = 7 + 6 = 13$
$-7 - (-2) = -7 + 2 = -5$ (finding the difference and writing which direction it goes)
         $= 2 - 7 = -5$

Addition and Subtraction

Lesson 15

LESSON 15 Word problems: negative numbers

A. Here are some real word examples of negative numbers. Choose the correct answers.

A thermometer shows temperatures above zero as positive numbers and temperatures below zero as negative numbers. How would 5 degrees Celsius below zero be shown on a thermometer? **b**

Geographers use positive numbers to represent elevation above sea level and negative numbers to represent elevation below sea level. If a submarine dives to 30 feet below sea level, what will be its elevation? **b**

A company uses positive numbers to record earnings and negative numbers to record spending in its bookkeeping. How would a company represent earnings of $5,000? **a**

Banks use positive balances to represent that the bank owes the customer money and negative balances to represent that the customer owes the bank money. If you deposit $50 and later withdraw $35, how would the bank represent your balance? **a**

Credit card companies use negative balances to represent that the customer owes the company money. If a customer spends $100 with the credit card, how would the company represent his or her balance? **b**

B. Solve the word problems.

The temperature yesterday was 5 °C. Today it was 12 degrees colder. What was the temperature today? **-7 °C**

California is 59 feet below sea level. Mt. Everest, the highest mountain on Earth, is 29,028 feet above sea level. What is the difference in elevation between California and Mt. Everest? **29,087 feet**

Stacy had a balance of $248 in her bank account. She wrote a check for $56, deposited a check for $135, and withdrew $210 in cash. What is her final balance? **$117**

Leah has a lemonade stand. Last week she spent $58 and earned $55. This week she spent $35 and earned $60. How much profit did Leah make for two weeks? **$22**

LESSON 15 Practice

A. Express each value as a positive or negative quantity.

Today's temperature is 68 degrees Fahrenheit above zero. **+68**

A shark is swimming 1,000 feet below sea level. **-1,000**

A local store had a profit of $1,200 last month. **+1,200**

Ron lost 5 pounds after going on a diet. **-5**

The number of children in a book club has increased by 18. **+18**

B. Solve the word problems.

The temperature in the morning was 8 °C, but it dropped to -2 °C in the evening. How much did it drop during the day? **10 °C**

A submarine was at -760 feet, then it ascended 235 feet. What is its new depth? **-525 feet**

Jenny had a balance of $67 in her bank account. She withdrew $14 in cash. What is her new balance? **$53**

It is -7 °C in New York and 18 °C in San Francisco. What is the difference in temperature between the two cities? **25 °C**

A submarine was 320 feet below sea level, then it dove another 150 feet. What is its new depth? **-470 feet**

The temperature in the morning was -4 °C. By 3 p.m. it had risen by 8 °C. What was the temperature at 3 p.m.? **4 °C**

Mia had $135 in her bank account. She withdrew $58, wrote a check for $25, and deposited a check for $80. What is her final balance? **$132**

An airplane is 1,150 feet above sea level. A submarine is 520 feet below sea level. What is the distance between the airplane and the submarine? **1,670 feet**

They are solving word problems in this lesson. The first ones have multiple choice answers. They just need to think about whether the answer will be positive or negative.

For the second part they should apply normal word problem techniques like using pictures or smaller numbers to think it through first. They are going to need to use separate paper to solve these.

Here are some from part B on the practice page.

The distance between 8 and -2 is 10. It's eight degrees to get to zero and then two more to get to negative two.

The distance between -760 feet, and 235 feet is 760 + 235. They travel 760 feet to get to the surface and then 235 feet more.

$67 - $14 = $53

The distance between -7 and 18 is 7 + 18 = 25 degrees.

-320 – 150 = - 470 feet

Lesson 16

LESSON 16 Basic multiplication & multiplying up to 9 × 9

A. Multiplication is a fast way to count repeated groups of the same size. The result of a multiplication is called a **product**. Here is an example of counting an array of dots.

There are 4 rows with 9 dots in each row. What is the total number of dots? = $4 \times 9 = 36$

There are 9 columns with 4 dots in each column. What is the total number of dots? = $9 \times 4 = 36$

B. Multiplying a number by 0 means taking the number zero times, so it equals 0. Multiplying a number by 1 means taking the number once, so it equals the number itself.

$1 \times 0 = 0$ $0 \times 489 = 0$ $1 \times 3127 = 3127$

C. Multiply up to 9 × 9.

$6 \times 9 = 54$	$8 \times 6 = 48$	$7 \times 7 = 49$
$5 \times 4 = 20$	$5 \times 7 = 35$	$9 \times 3 = 27$
$4 \times 3 = 12$	$8 \times 9 = 72$	$6 \times 2 = 12$
$8 \times 2 = 16$	$6 \times 1 = 6$	$7 \times 8 = 56$
$3 \times 6 = 18$	$2 \times 5 = 10$	$5 \times 5 = 25$
$9 \times 9 = 81$	$7 \times 6 = 42$	$6 \times 4 = 24$
$7 \times 4 = 28$	$6 \times 5 = 30$	$8 \times 8 = 64$
$5 \times 8 = 40$	$7 \times 3 = 21$	$3 \times 5 = 15$
$3 \times 3 = 9$	$6 \times 6 = 36$	$4 \times 4 = 16$
$7 \times 2 = 14$	$9 \times 5 = 45$	$9 \times 7 = 63$
$0 \times 0 = 0$	$8 \times 4 = 32$	$6 \times 3 = 18$
$4 \times 9 = 36$	$3 \times 8 = 24$	$2 \times 9 = 18$

LESSON 16 Practice

Multiply up to 9 × 9.

$3 \times 7 = 21$	$3 \times 4 = 12$	$9 \times 4 = 36$
$5 \times 2 = 10$	$5 \times 6 = 30$	$8 \times 7 = 56$
$4 \times 4 = 16$	$3 \times 5 = 15$	$2 \times 9 = 18$
$6 \times 7 = 42$	$5 \times 5 = 25$	$5 \times 4 = 20$
$9 \times 3 = 27$	$4 \times 3 = 12$	$4 \times 6 = 24$
$5 \times 8 = 40$	$8 \times 6 = 48$	$8 \times 3 = 24$
$8 \times 4 = 32$	$9 \times 2 = 18$	$2 \times 6 = 12$
$7 \times 2 = 14$	$6 \times 5 = 30$	$7 \times 5 = 35$
$6 \times 8 = 48$	$4 \times 7 = 28$	$6 \times 2 = 12$
$9 \times 7 = 63$	$8 \times 5 = 40$	$9 \times 6 = 54$
$1 \times 6 = 6$	$2 \times 4 = 8$	$4 \times 8 = 32$
$2 \times 8 = 16$	$3 \times 6 = 18$	$9 \times 9 = 81$
$6 \times 3 = 18$	$6 \times 9 = 54$	$2 \times 7 = 14$
$9 \times 5 = 45$	$3 \times 9 = 27$	$7 \times 4 = 28$
$7 \times 3 = 21$	$8 \times 8 = 64$	$8 \times 9 = 72$
$5 \times 9 = 45$	$6 \times 6 = 36$	$7 \times 9 = 63$
$3 \times 3 = 9$	$8 \times 2 = 16$	$0 \times 7 = 0$
$9 \times 8 = 72$	$7 \times 6 = 42$	$4 \times 5 = 20$

This is a simple review, introduction to multiplication. Make sure your child understands the concept of multiplication.

They shouldn't be adding anymore to find the answer to multiplication problems. They need to know these facts by rote memory. Continue to have them working on the facts with online games, flashcards, workbooks, etc. They will be stuck moving forward if they don't know the facts.

You can use the practice page if they aren't fast with the facts yet. You could also print EP's multiplication fact page sheet, the page that's in the Multiplication Facts Workbook. They can complete that every day until they can do it in under a couple of minutes.

Lesson 17

LESSON 17 Multiplying by 10, 11, and 12

A. Complete the multiplication tables for 10, 11, and 12.

$10 \times 0 = 0$	$11 \times 0 = 0$	$12 \times 0 = 0$
$10 \times 1 = 10$	$11 \times 1 = 11$	$12 \times 1 = 12$
$10 \times 2 = 20$	$11 \times 2 = 22$	$12 \times 2 = 24$
$10 \times 3 = 30$	$11 \times 3 = 33$	$12 \times 3 = 36$
$10 \times 4 = 40$	$11 \times 4 = 44$	$12 \times 4 = 48$
$10 \times 5 = 50$	$11 \times 5 = 55$	$12 \times 5 = 60$
$10 \times 6 = 60$	$11 \times 6 = 66$	$12 \times 6 = 72$
$10 \times 7 = 70$	$11 \times 7 = 77$	$12 \times 7 = 84$
$10 \times 8 = 80$	$11 \times 8 = 88$	$12 \times 8 = 96$
$10 \times 9 = 90$	$11 \times 9 = 99$	$12 \times 9 = 108$
$10 \times 10 = 100$	$11 \times 10 = 110$	$12 \times 10 = 120$
$10 \times 11 = 110$	$11 \times 11 = 121$	$12 \times 11 = 132$
$10 \times 12 = 120$	$11 \times 12 = 132$	$12 \times 12 = 144$

B. Complete the multiplication squares.

×	5	12
12	60	144
8	40	96

×	11	3
7	77	21
11	121	33

×	6	9
4	24	36
10	60	90

LESSON 17 Practice

A. Multiply by 11.

$11 \times 7 = 77$	$5 \times 11 = 55$	$11 \times 3 = 33$
$2 \times 11 = 22$	$11 \times 10 = 110$	$11 \times 11 = 121$
$11 \times 12 = 132$	$11 \times 1 = 11$	$9 \times 11 = 99$
$4 \times 11 = 44$	$6 \times 11 = 66$	$11 \times 8 = 88$

B. Multiply by 12.

$5 \times 12 = 60$	$1 \times 12 = 12$	$12 \times 8 = 96$
$12 \times 7 = 84$	$12 \times 9 = 108$	$12 \times 3 = 36$
$12 \times 10 = 120$	$4 \times 12 = 48$	$12 \times 12 = 144$
$2 \times 12 = 24$	$12 \times 11 = 132$	$6 \times 12 = 72$

C. Multiply up to 12×12.

$8 \times 11 = 88$	$7 \times 10 = 70$	$11 \times 2 = 22$
$10 \times 3 = 30$	$3 \times 8 = 24$	$9 \times 8 = 72$
$9 \times 12 = 108$	$4 \times 9 = 36$	$12 \times 5 = 60$
$7 \times 8 = 56$	$11 \times 6 = 66$	$7 \times 6 = 42$
$10 \times 9 = 90$	$6 \times 4 = 24$	$2 \times 9 = 18$
$3 \times 12 = 36$	$8 \times 5 = 40$	$11 \times 4 = 44$
$6 \times 9 = 54$	$7 \times 12 = 84$	$5 \times 10 = 50$
$12 \times 4 = 48$	$11 \times 9 = 99$	$6 \times 6 = 36$

This is an easy page. Talk it through with your child. They probably know that $10 \times 3 = 30$ and $11 \times 4 = 44$ but why?

Look at the breakdowns of these problems. Since you are just mutiplying by 0, 1, and 2, these are simple problems. Personally, I don't think there's any reason to memorize these facts, but many do, but certainly they should be able to quickly solve them in their heads.

$10 \times 3 = 3 \times 10 + 3 \times 0 = 30 + 0 = 30$

$11 \times 3 = 3 \times 10 + 3 \times 1 = 30 + 3 = 33$

$12 \times 3 = 3 \times 10 + 3 \times 2 = 30 + 6 = 36$

When multiplying a two-digit number by ten, you can think how you'll just add a zero. Here's what's happening. $12 \times 10 = 10 \times 10 + 2 \times 10 = 100 + 20 = 120$ $12 \times 10 = 120$

When multiplying a two-digit number by eleven, you can just write the first and last digit with their sum between them.
$12 \times 11 = 132$ This is why. $12 \times 11 = 12 \times 10 + 12 \times 1 = 120 + 12 = 132$

Multiplying by eleven is just multiplying by 1 twice, but the ten moves the place value over one spot.

Lesson 18

LESSON 18 Multiplying by multiples of 10

A. To multiply a number by a multiple of 10, ignore the zeros in the multiple of 10, multiply the rest of the numbers, and then add the zeros at the end of the product.

$$8000 \times 9 = \underline{72{,}000} \qquad 7 \times 1200 = \underline{8{,}400}$$

Find 8 x 9, and add three zeros.   Find 7 x 12, and add two zeros.

B. Multiply by multiples of 10.

$7 \times 50 = 350$	$50 \times 8 = 400$	$11 \times 90 = 990$
$6 \times 60 = 360$	$60 \times 9 = 540$	$70 \times 11 = 770$
$90 \times 9 = 810$	$7 \times 60 = 420$	$12 \times 90 = 1{,}080$
$60 \times 4 = 240$	$6 \times 80 = 480$	$110 \times 5 = 550$
$80 \times 7 = 560$	$50 \times 9 = 450$	$80 \times 12 = 960$
$50 \times 5 = 250$	$40 \times 4 = 160$	$6 \times 120 = 720$
$4 \times 80 = 320$	$90 \times 7 = 630$	$11 \times 80 = 880$
$3 \times 700 = 2{,}100$	$5 \times 600 = 3{,}000$	$7000 \times 7 = 49{,}000$
$900 \times 4 = 3{,}600$	$800 \times 8 = 6{,}400$	$11 \times 600 = 6{,}600$
$12 \times 50 = 600$	$3 \times 120 = 360$	$4 \times 1200 = 4{,}800$

LESSON 18 Practice

A. Multiply by 10, 100, and 1000.

$7 \times 10 = 70$	$100 \times 4 = 400$	$10 \times 5 = 50$
$11 \times 10 = 110$	$12 \times 10 = 120$	$9 \times 10 = 90$
$100 \times 1 = 100$	$100 \times 6 = 600$	$8 \times 100 = 800$
$10 \times 100 = 1{,}000$	$1000 \times 3 = 3{,}000$	$0 \times 1000 = 0$

B. Multiply by multiples of 10.

$80 \times 5 = 400$	$70 \times 9 = 630$	$30 \times 7 = 210$
$90 \times 6 = 540$	$60 \times 5 = 300$	$4 \times 90 = 360$
$6 \times 70 = 420$	$5 \times 70 = 350$	$80 \times 8 = 640$
$40 \times 6 = 240$	$30 \times 5 = 150$	$90 \times 3 = 270$
$70 \times 8 = 560$	$7 \times 70 = 490$	$12 \times 60 = 720$
$50 \times 12 = 600$	$500 \times 5 = 2{,}500$	$6 \times 800 = 4{,}800$
$20 \times 11 = 220$	$9 \times 900 = 8{,}100$	$400 \times 4 = 1{,}600$
$12 \times 80 = 960$	$200 \times 12 = 2{,}400$	$9 \times 1100 = 9{,}900$
$5 \times 110 = 550$	$12 \times 600 = 7{,}200$	$1200 \times 9 = 10{,}800$

The directions at the top of their page are saying to take off the zeros and then add them back onto the answer. This does not mean that the question and answer have the same number of zeros. 5 x 80 = 400 It's 5 x 8 plus the zero tagged on. 5 x 8 = 40, so it already has one zero, but it still needs the 0 from 80 tagged onto the answer.

Ask your child 4000 x 5. It's twenty with three zeros tagged on. 20,000 twenty thousand

Lesson 19

LESSON 19 Basic division

A. Division is splitting a total into equal groups. Divide the total by the size of the groups to find the number of groups. Divide the total by the number of groups to find the size of the groups. Here is an example that shows the relationship between these two quantities.

Divide 36 dots into groups of 9.
How many groups can you make? $= 36 \div 9 = $ __4__

Divide 36 dots into 4 equal groups.
How many dots are in each group? $= 36 \div 4 = $ __9__

B. Sometimes when you divide you have leftovers or **remainders**. You write the remainder after an "r" or "R" in the answer.

Divide 18 dots into groups of 4.
How many dots are remaining? $= 18 \div 4 = $ __4 r 2__

C. Division is the opposite of multiplication, just as addition is the opposite of subtraction.

There are 4 rows of 9 dots in each row.
What is the total number of dots? $= 4 \times 9 = $ __36__

Divide 36 dots into groups of 9.
How many groups can you make? $= 36 \div 9 = $ __4__

D. Divide by 1-digit numbers.

$24 \div 4 = 6$	$28 \div 7 = 4$	$16 \div 2 = 8$
$30 \div 5 = 6$	$32 \div 4 = 8$	$21 \div 3 = 7$
$48 \div 6 = 8$	$63 \div 9 = 7$	$40 \div 8 = 5$

E. Complete the division facts.

$64 \div 8 = 8$	$54 \div 9 = 6$	$27 \div 9 = 3$
$42 \div 6 = 7$	$35 \div 5 = 7$	$81 \div 9 = 9$
$25 \div 5 = 5$	$45 \div 5 = 9$	$20 \div 5 = 4$
$72 \div 8 = 9$	$36 \div 6 = 6$	$56 \div 7 = 8$

LESSON 19 Practice

A. Divide by 1-digit numbers.

$8 \div 4 = 2$	$49 \div 7 = 7$	$40 \div 5 = 8$
$36 \div 6 = 6$	$18 \div 3 = 6$	$27 \div 3 = 9$
$15 \div 5 = 3$	$63 \div 9 = 7$	$48 \div 4 = 12$
$64 \div 8 = 8$	$25 \div 5 = 5$	$35 \div 5 = 7$
$72 \div 9 = 8$	$16 \div 8 = 2$	$42 \div 6 = 7$
$21 \div 7 = 3$	$28 \div 4 = 7$	$60 \div 6 = 10$

B. Complete the division facts.

$9 \div 3 = 3$	$6 \div 3 = 2$	$9 \div 1 = 9$
$24 \div 6 = 4$	$56 \div 8 = 7$	$21 \div 3 = 7$
$36 \div 4 = 9$	$45 \div 9 = 5$	$54 \div 6 = 9$
$16 \div 2 = 8$	$63 \div 7 = 9$	$12 \div 6 = 2$
$81 \div 9 = 9$	$20 \div 4 = 5$	$24 \div 3 = 8$
$14 \div 7 = 2$	$42 \div 7 = 6$	$72 \div 8 = 9$
$12 \div 3 = 4$	$40 \div 8 = 5$	$35 \div 7 = 5$
$48 \div 8 = 6$	$18 \div 2 = 9$	$32 \div 8 = 4$
$10 \div 2 = 5$	$30 \div 6 = 5$	$15 \div 3 = 5$
$8 \div 2 = 4$	$16 \div 4 = 4$	$7 \div 7 = 1$

Have your child go through the motions of circling the groups of dots on the top of the page to find the groups. That's the visual representation of division. You are dividing things into groups with a certain number in each group.

The second one is a visual representation of what a remainder looks like. They won't be finding remainders yet. It's just introducing the idea, which should be a review.

The third example shows the relationship between multiplication and division. The exercise has them using their multiplication facts to determine the missing number in the division problem, but it's important for them to learn their division facts as well. They need to just keep practicing.

Lesson 20

LESSON 20 Introduction to long division

A. Familiarize yourself with three ways to write division problems. Complete the table.

using a division symbol	using a long division symbol	as a fraction
$35 \div 5 = 7$	$5\overline{)35}$ 7	$\dfrac{35}{5} = 7$
$72 \div 8 = 9$	$8\overline{)72}$ 9	$\dfrac{72}{8} = 9$

B. Long division is a way to solve division problems with large numbers. It breaks down a division problem into a series of easier steps: divide, multiply, subtract, bring down, and repeat. This example shows the steps for dividing a 3-digit number by a 1-digit number.

```
      83
7 | 585
    56
    ‾‾
    25
    21
    ‾‾
     4
```

1. **Divide** $58 \div 7 = 8$ r 2 and write 8 on top.
2. **Multiply** $7 \times 8 = 56$ and write 56 underneath 58.
3. **Subtract** $58 - 56 = 2$ and write 2 underneath 56.
4. **Bring down** 5 next to 2 to make 25.
5. **Repeat** the steps 1 through 4 with 25.
   1) Divide $25 \div 7 = 3$ r 4 and write 3 on top.
   2) Multiply $7 \times 3 = 21$ and write 21 underneath 25.
   3) Subtract $25 - 21 = 4$ and write 4 underneath 21.
6. There is no digit to bring down, so $585 \div 7 = 83$ r 4

C. Divide by 1-digit numbers.

114	48	70	18
$8\overline{)912}$	$7\overline{)336}$	$5\overline{)350}$	$9\overline{)162}$

3872	494	1213	1834
$2\overline{)7744}$	$6\overline{)2964}$	$3\overline{)3639}$	$4\overline{)7336}$

LESSON 20 Practice

A. Write each division problem in three different ways.

using a division symbol	using a long division symbol	as a fraction
$21 \div 7 = 3$	$7\overline{)21}$ 3	$\dfrac{21}{7} = 3$
$45 \div 5 = 9$	$5\overline{)45}$ 9	$\dfrac{45}{5} = 9$
$32 \div 4 = 8$	$4\overline{)32}$ 8	$\dfrac{32}{4} = 8$

B. Divide by 1-digit numbers.

82	27	36	81
$7\overline{)574}$	$5\overline{)135}$	$9\overline{)324}$	$3\overline{)243}$

179	94	354	68
$4\overline{)716}$	$6\overline{)564}$	$2\overline{)708}$	$8\overline{)544}$

327	609	579	315
$4\overline{)1308}$	$8\overline{)4872}$	$2\overline{)1158}$	$6\overline{)1890}$

This is the introduction to long division. Let me show you what is happening to try to help your child know what's happening when they do this long division process.

Remember that division is finding a number of groups with a certain number in each group. You are given one number and you need to find the other. You start with the total. Here's the example on the lesson page. 585 divided by 7. You are going to take out groups of seven until you can't any more. That will tell you how many groups of seven there are in 585. You can take out any number of sevens, even one, but that's a slow way to do it. That would just be subtracting 7 over and over again and then counting how many times you subtracted it. Division is repeated subtraction just like multiplication is repeated addition.

You can notice that 8 x 7 = 56 and that's less than 58. When you write the 8 on top in the answer, you are really writing 80. 7 x 80 = 560. You are taking 560 from the total. You are left with 25. 7 goes three times into 25. If you take 7 out three times, that's 21 out of 25. You are left with four and you took out 83 groups of seven.

These problems again don't have remainders to them.

Make sure your child realizes the different ways to write a division problem and that fractions are a way of showing division.

Lesson 21

LESSON 21 Multiplying 2-digit numbers

A. Here are the steps for multiplying a 3-digit number by a 1-digit number with regrouping.

```
  4 6
  2 5 9
×     7
1 8 1 3
```

1. Multiply the ones. 9 x 7 = 63
2. Write 3 in the ones column and carry 6 to the tens column.
3. Multiply the tens and add the carryover. (5 x 7) + 6 = 41
4. Write 1 in the tens column and carry 4 to the hundreds column.
5. Multiply the hundreds and add the carryover. (2 x 7) + 4 = 18
6. Write 1 in the thousands column and 8 in the hundreds column.

B. Here are the steps for multiplying a 2-digit number by a 2-digit number.

```
    7
    3 8
×   2 9
    3 4 2
+ 7 6 0
1 1 0 2
```

1. Multiply 38 x 9 and write the result in the first row.
   1) Multiply the ones. 8 x 9 = 72
   2) Write 2 in the ones column and carry 7 to the tens column.
   3) Multiply the tens and add the carryover. (3 x 9) + 7 = 34
   4) Write 4 in the tens column and 3 in the hundreds column.
2. Multiply 38 x 20 and write the result in the second row.
   1) Write 0 in the ones column.
   2) Multiply 38 x 2 as you did in the step 1. 38 x 2 = 76
3. Add the two products to find the answer. 342 + 760 = 1102

C. Multiply by 1-digit and 2-digit numbers.

```
    87        24       659       523       856
×    4     ×   9     ×   7     ×   5     ×   6
   348       216     4,613     2,615     5,136
```

```
    93        48        73        87        43
×   27     ×  67     ×  57     ×  83     ×  59
 2,511     3,216     4,161     7,221     2,537
```

The letter "E."

LESSON 21 Practice

A. Multiply by 1-digit numbers.

```
   876       428       367       285       579
×    8     ×   9     ×   3     ×   4     ×   5
 7,008     3,852     1,101     1,140     2,895
```

```
   479       859       297       956       392
×    6     ×   3     ×   7     ×   5     ×   4
 2,874     2,577     2,079     4,780     1,568
```

B. Multiply the 2-digit numbers.

```
    52        88        39        63        80
×   26     ×  37     ×  46     ×  35     ×  43
 1,352     3,256     1,794     2,205     3,440
```

```
    10        48        26        29        86
×   72     ×  53     ×  65     ×  75     ×  23
   720     2,544     1,690     2,175     1,978
```

To multiply a two-digit number by a single digit, you multiply the single digit by each place value. For instance, 59 x 7 (from the first example in the book) is 50 x 7 added to 9 x 7.

To multiply hundreds by a single digit, you do the same thing. You multiply the single digit by each place value. From the example: 259 x 7 = 200 x 7 and 50 x 7 and 9 x 7, all added together. That's what you are doing with the carrying in the example. You are just doing it in a different format, adding on that number to the next.

Since multiplication is just adding over and over again, we can break apart the numbers and multiply them in any order and then put them back together by adding.

To multiply two digits by two digits, you multiply each place value. The example on the page is 38 x 29. The answer is 38 x 20 added to 38 x 9. And, of course, 38 x 20 is 38 x 2 with a zero tagged on. That's why there is a zero on the second line of the example answer. There will always be a zero there because you are dealing with the tens place value.

They can use the traditional method of multiplying, but I want them to see and understand what it means and to know it doesn't have to be in that exact format to find the answer.

Lesson 22

LESSON 22 Multiplying multi-digit numbers

A. You can multiply any large numbers using the same technique. Complete the example.

```
      2 2
    5 6 8
  ×   2 9 3
    1 7 0 4
  5 1 1 2 0
+1 1 3 6 0 0
  1 6 6 4 2 4
```

1. Multiply 568 x 3 and write the result in the first row.
2. Multiply 568 x 90 and write the result in the second row.
   1) Write 0 in the ones column.
   2) Multiply 568 x 9 as you did in the step 1.
3. Multiply 568 x 200 and write the result in the third row.
   1) Write 0 in the tens column and ones column.
   2) Multiply 568 x 2 as you did in the step 1.
4. Add the three products to find the answer.

B. Multiply up to 4-digit numbers.

368	540	6180	2510
× 928	× 305	× 90	× 75
341,504	164,700	556,200	188,250

3975	6156	64	78
× 28	× 39	× 5476	× 7963
111,300	240,084	350,464	621,114

LESSON 22 Practice

Multiply up to 4-digit numbers.

258	834	62	89	75
× 9	× 7	× 34	× 73	× 42
2,322	5,838	2,108	6,497	3,150

283	509	329	679
× 576	× 724	× 615	× 309
163,008	368,516	202,335	209,811

4759	7125	56	39
× 60	× 34	× 2716	× 4797
285,540	242,250	152,096	187,083

The example on the page is incomplete. Ask your child how the author knew to put a zero in the second row and two zeros in the third row. The second row is going to be the answer after multiplying the tens place. The third row is going to be the answer after multiplying the hundreds place.

You could have your child fill out the example to make sure they know how to do it. They will be multiplying each digit from the second number by the first number. 568 x 3 and 568 x 90 and 568 x 200. It's 1704 + 51,120 + 113,600 = 166,424.

Here's a worked-through example from the second line.

```
      3975
   x    28
     31800  (3975 x 8)
  + 79500  (3975 x 20)
   111,300
```

Lesson 23

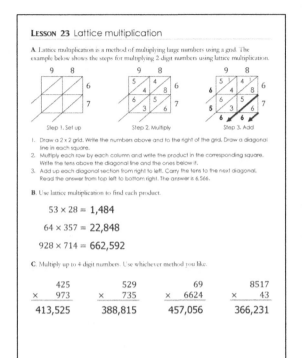

LESSON 23 Lattice multiplication

A. Lattice multiplication is a method of multiplying large numbers using a grid. The example below shows the steps for multiplying 2-digit numbers using lattice multiplication.

Step 1. Set up   Step 2. Multiply   Step 3. Add

1. Draw a 2 x 2 grid. Write the numbers above and to the right of the grid. Draw a diagonal line in each square.
2. Multiply each row by each column and write the product in the corresponding square. Write the tens above the diagonal line and the ones below it.
3. Add up each diagonal section from right to left. Carry the tens to the next diagonal. Read the answer from top left to bottom right. The answer is 6,566.

B. Use lattice multiplication to find each product.

53 × 28 = 1,484

64 × 357 = 22,848

928 × 714 = 662,592

C. Multiply up to 4-digit numbers. Use whichever method you like.

425	529	69	8517
× 973	× 735	× 6624	× 43
413,525	388,815	457,056	366,231

LESSON 23 Practice

Multiply up to 4-digit numbers. Use whichever method you like.

786	851	47	38	62
× 7	× 9	× 81	× 59	× 47
5,502	7,659	3,807	2,242	2,914

998	224	584	290
× 727	× 603	× 322	× 565
725,546	135,072	188,048	163,850

9595	8062	75	83
× 78	× 35	× 4239	× 3704
748,410	282,170	317,925	307,432

This is another multiplication lesson, but it's from a different perspective. Ask your child to look at the example and read the directions that go with it and explain to you why it works. It works because each diagonal represents a place value. It's on a diagonal because 6 is really 60, so the diagonal moves its answer over one place value to the tens place. The box that holds the answer to 9 x 6 is really holding the answer to 90 x 60. The diagonals move the answer over just as adding two zeros would in the traditional method.

Here's a regular solution example from the lesson.

$$
\begin{array}{r}
425 \\
\times\ 973 \\
\hline
1275 \quad (425 \times 3) \\
29750 \quad (425 \times 70) \\
382500 \quad (425 \times 900) \\
\hline
413,525
\end{array}
$$

Lesson 24

LESSON 24 Long division with remainders

A. In division, the number being divided is called the **dividend**. The number dividing the dividend is called the **divisor**. The result of the division is called the **quotient**. The number left over is called the **remainder**. Identify each number in the example by its name.

$89 \div 5 = 17 \text{ r } 4$

Dividend	Divisor	Quotient	Remainder
89	5	17	4

B. You can check your answer to a division problem by using multiplication and addition. Multiply the quotient by the divisor and add the remainder. The result will be the dividend.

$89 \div 5 = 17 \text{ r } 4$ $(17 \times 5) + 4 = 89$

If you divide 89 by groups of 5, you will have 17 groups and 4 left over.   If you have 17 groups of 5 plus 4 extra, the total will be 89.

C. Check whether the answer to the division problem below is correct or not.

$218 \div 4 = 53 \text{ r } 2$ Incorrect: $(53 \times 4) + 2 = 214$

D. Find the quotients and remainders. Make sure to check your answers.

52 r 3   161 r 2   84 r 6   232 r 1
6) 315   4) 646   9) 762   3) 697

2305 r 1   440 r 6   327 r 3   1609 r 1
4) 9221   7) 3086   5) 1638   2) 3219

LESSON 24 Practice

Find the quotients and remainders. Make sure to check your answers.

137 r 5   45 r 6   41 r 3   190 r 1
6) 827   8) 366   7) 290   3) 571

183 r 3   56 r 3   84 r 2   106 r 6
4) 735   7) 395   5) 422   9) 960

1067 r 4   2714 r 2   3820 r 1   590 r 2
9) 9607   3) 8144   2) 7641   7) 4132

546 r 4   267 r 3   1811 r 1   755 r 2
8) 4372   8) 2139   4) 7245   6) 4532

They will be doing long division with remainders today. They have seen these before but haven't practiced them. Here's the first one worked out.

```
    52 r3
6)315
   30
   15
   12
    3
```

Then to check your answer you multiply and add. 52 x 6 + 3.

```
   52
  x 6
  312
  + 3
  315
```
That equals the dividend, so the answer is correct.

They need to write neatly and carefully to fit their work. They could always use scratch paper to check their answers if they don't want to squeeze it in between problems.

Lesson 25

LESSON 25 Word problems: multiplication and division

A. When solving a word problem, it is important to read through the problem and know what is being asked. The example below shows using the strategy of working backwards.

Dylan is baking cookies for the class picnic. Fifty-six people are expected to come. He wants to prepare 3 cookies per person. A recipe calls for 1 egg to make 6 cookies. Eggs are sold in cartons of 12. How many cartons of eggs should Dylan buy?

3 cartons

Work backwards:
# of cartons = # of eggs ÷ 12
# of eggs = # of cookies ÷ 6
# of cookies = # of person × 3

Solve the problem:
# of cookies = 56 × 3 = 168
# of eggs = 168 ÷ 6 = 28
# of cartons = 28 ÷ 12 = 2 r 4

B. Solve the word problems.

There were 12 kids at Olivia's party. Olivia's Mom baked 5 pizzas and sliced each pizza into 8 pieces. Each kid ate 3 pieces. How many pieces were left?

4 pieces

Adam collected 43 stamps. He kept his favorite 7 stamps and then equally divided the remaining stamps among his 4 friends. How many stamps did each of his friends get?

9 stamps

At an apple farm, Kyle picked 18 apples. Orson picked 27 apples. Then they packed all their apples into bags. Each bag held 6 apples. How many bags did they use?

8 bags

Mom bought 56 peaches. She used 28 of them to make jam. Then she baked pies with the remaining peaches. If she used 5 peaches per pie, how many peaches does she have left?

3 peaches

At the bookstore, Ryan bought 5 comic books that all had the same price. Joe bought 4 magazines for $12 each. Ryan spent $7 more than Joe. How much did each comic book cost?

$11

Adam had 20 quarters, 10 dimes, and 25 nickels. He exchanged 5 quarters and 4 dimes for nickels. How many coins did Adam have in the end?

79 coins

Did you know? A baseball diamond is a perfect square.

LESSON 25 Practice

Solve the word problems.

Walter has $14. His weekly allowance is $16. How many weeks will it take him to save for a video game that costs $52?

3 weeks

A group of 27 girls and 32 boys are on a canoe trip. Each canoe can hold 7 people. How many canoes will the group need?

9 canoes

Peter and Sam have $36 in total. Peter has three times more money than Sam. How much money does Peter have?

$27

A recipe calls for 8 apples to make one apple pie. Mom wants to bake 7 pies. Apples are sold in bags of 12. How many bags of apples does she need to buy?

5 bags

Ava spent $82 to order some tickets online. Each ticket cost $12. The shipping cost per order was $10. How many tickets did Ava buy?

6 tickets

This week Kyle set a goal to spend 3 hours on math. He studied 40 minutes per day from Monday to Thursday. How many minutes does he need to study on Friday to meet his goal?

20 minutes

Jessica had 90 beads. She made 14 bracelets with an equal number of beads and had 6 beads left. How many beads were used to make one bracelet?

6 beads

At an apple farm, Mia picked 15 apples. Amy picked 3 times as many apples as Mia. Then they divided all their apples equally into 4 baskets. How many apples were in each basket?

15 apples

Kate had 15 quarters, 15 dimes, and 15 nickels. She exchanged 4 quarters and 8 nickels for dimes. How many coins did Kate have in the end?

47 coins

Emma is planning a birthday party. She has $40. She wants to buy a cake for $15 and spend the rest to buy as many balloons as possible at $4 each. How much money will Emma have left?

$1

This page is on word problems. They will be using multiplication, division, addition, and subtraction. They will need to take multiple steps to find the answer to the question. They could use their word problem strategies like drawing a picture or using smaller numbers to figure out what to do. However, they should start by asking what they need to know to answer the question. That will help them figure out the first step. They will definitely need to work on scratch paper for today.

Here are the first two worked out.

Question: How many pieces left?
Need to know: how many pieces all together and how many were eaten
# of pieces: 5 x 8 = 40
eaten: 12 x 3 = 36
left 40 – 36 = 4 pieces

Question: How many stamps each?
Need to know: how many stamps all together, how many friends
# of stamps: 43 – 7 = 36
# of friends: 4
each: 36/4 = 9 stamps

Lesson 26

LESSON 26 Dividing by multi-digit numbers

A. Here are the steps for dividing a 4-digit number by a 2-digit number.

```
     267
29 | 7761
     58
     196
     174
      221
      203
       18
```

1. Divide 77 ÷ 29 = 2 r 19 and write 2 on top.
2. Multiply 29 x 2 = 58 and write 58 underneath 77.
3. Subtract 77 - 58 = 19 and write 19 underneath 58.
4. Bring down 6 next to 19 to make 196.
5. Repeat the steps 1 through 4 with 196.
   1) Divide 196 ÷ 29 = 6 r 22 and write 6 on top.
   2) Multiply 29 x 6 = 174 and write 174 underneath 196.
   3) Subtract 196 - 174 = 22 and write 22 underneath 174.
   4) Bring down 1 next to 22 to make 221.
6. Repeat the steps 1 through 4 with 221.
7. There is no digit to bring down, so 7761 ÷ 29 = 267 r 18.

B. Find the quotients and remainders. Make sure to check your answers.

27 r 7	13 r 4	6 r 59	24 r 247
12 | 331	36 | 472	75 | 509	376 | 9271
374 r 1	93 r 16	169	33 r 148
17 | 6359	22 | 2062	56 | 9464	235 | 7903

There were only 3 people: grandfather, father, and son.

LESSON 26 Practice

Find the quotients and remainders. Make sure to check your answers.

30 r 11	23 r 9	15 r 3	22 r 309
12 | 371	25 | 584	30 | 453	325 | 7459
19 r 18	16 r 39	18 r 25	36
35 | 683	52 | 871	43 | 799	267 | 9612
121	219 r 16	117 r 24	9 r 153
17 | 2057	41 | 8995	55 | 6459	529 | 4914
314 r 16	147 r 49	308	14 r 281
23 | 7238	56 | 8281	31 | 9548	358 | 5293

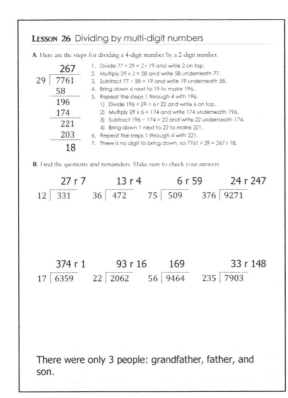

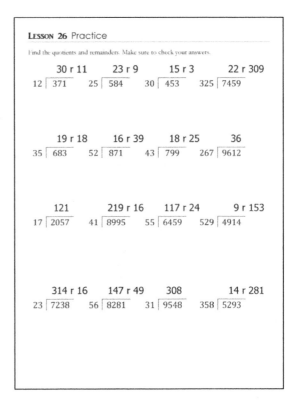

Dividing by two digits is just the same as dividing by one. Encourage your child to use rounding and estimation to figure out how many times the number goes into the dividend. For instance, in trying to figure out how many times 29 goes into 77 (from the example), they can think that 30 two times is 60 and 30 three times is 90, so it's probably going to go in 2 times.

Here's a problem from the page worked out.

```
       24 r 247
376| 9271
      752
     1751
     1504
      247
```

Lesson 27

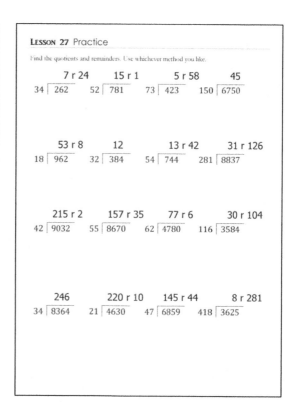

LESSON 27 Partial quotient division

A. Partial quotient division is an alternative division method. It uses easy multiplication facts to find partial quotients, which are then added to find the quotient. Here are the steps for dividing multi-digit numbers using the partial quotient method.

```
        435      Partial
                 Quotients
18 | 7843
     5400        300
     2443
     1800        100
      643
      540         30
      103
       90          5
       13        435
   Remainder    Quotient
```

1. Write some easy multiplication facts.
   18 x 2 = 36; 18 x 3 = 54; 18 x 5 = 90
2. Find a partial quotient.
   1) How many 18s are in 7843? At least 300.
   2) Record 300 in the right column.
   3) Subtract 18 x 300 = 5400 from 7843.
3. Find another partial quotient.
   1) How many 18s are in 2443? At least 100.
   2) Record 100 in the right column.
   3) Subtract 18 x 100 = 1800 from 2443.
4. Repeat and continue finding partial quotients until the remainder is less than 18.
5. Add the partial quotients to find the quotient.
   300 + 100 + 30 + 5 = 435
6. Therefore, 7843 ÷ 18 = 435 r 13

B. Find the quotients and remainders. Use whichever method you like.

```
      18 r 15      28 r 22       5 r 54        36
37 | 681     26 | 750     84 | 474    114 | 4104


      817 r 9       235        118 r 32     11 r 341
12 | 9813    16 | 3760    59 | 6994    650 | 7491
```

LESSON 27 Practice

Find the quotients and remainders. Use whichever method you like.

```
      7 r 24       15 r 1        5 r 58        45
34 | 262     52 | 781     73 | 423    150 | 6750


      53 r 8        12         13 r 42      31 r 126
18 | 962     32 | 384     54 | 744    281 | 8837


      215 r 2      157 r 35      77 r 6      30 r 104
42 | 9032    55 | 8670    62 | 4780    116 | 3584


      246        220 r 10      145 r 44      8 r 281
34 | 8364    21 | 4630    47 | 6859    418 | 3625
```

Your child should take the time to look through the example and use the directions to follow along.

This is another way to look at long division. With this method, they don't have to figure out the highest possible number of times that a number goes into something. In the example, 18 goes into 78 four times, but at first they just use 3 times. They subtract that off and see that it can go in another time.

Here's another way to write the same method.

Groups	Totals
	7843
300	5400 (18 x 300)
	2443
100	1800 (18 x 100)
	643
30	540 (18 x 30)
	103
5	90 (5 x 18)
435	13

Lesson 28

LESSON 28 Word problems: addition and subtraction

Solve the word problems.

Mr. Kim bought a television set for $374. He had $158 left. How much money did Mr. Kim have at first?	$532
The pet store sold 238 goldfish last week and 185 goldfish this week. It has 79 goldfish left. How many goldfish did the store have at first?	502 goldfish
The grocery store had 172 bags of potatoes. It sold 155 bags and brought in 86 more bags. How many bags of potatoes did the store have then?	103 bags
Larry has a 185-page reading assignment. He read 128 pages yesterday and 39 pages today. How many pages does Larry have left to read?	18 pages
Claire found 115 seashells on the beach. Sam found 86 seashells. 37 of them were broken. How many unbroken seashells did they find together?	164 seashells
There were 175 paper cups in the cabinet. Lucy took 36 cups from the cabinet. Carlos took twice as many cups as Lucy. How many paper cups were left in the cabinet?	67 cups
Ron collected 120 flower stamps and 116 bird stamps. He gave 35 of his flower stamps and 28 of his bird stamps to his brother. How many stamps did Ron have then?	173 stamps
The candy store sold 156 candies last week. This week it brought in 200 more candies and sold 182 candies. Now it has 42 candies left. How many candies did the candy store have at first?	180 candies
The library had a book donation campaign. Last month 1,136 fiction books and 523 non-fiction books were donated. This month 147 more fiction books and 78 fewer non-fiction books were donated than last month. How many more fiction books were donated than non-fiction books in all?	1,451 books

---

LESSON 28 Practice

Solve the word problems.

Brian has 55 baseball cards. Matt has 48 more baseball cards than Brian. How many baseball cards does Matt have?	103 cards
Ryan had 33 dimes. His mom gave him some more dimes. Now he has 50 dimes. How many dimes did Ryan get from his mom?	17 dimes
Heather had 72 cents. She spent 44 cents on candies and 15 cents on cookies. How much money does Heather have left?	13 cents
Sam has $25. Clara has $16 more than Sam. Matt has $8 less than Sam. How much money do they have in all?	$83
Ron wants to buy three books that cost $18, $13, and $16 each. He has saved $12 so far. How much more money does Ron need to buy all three books?	$35
Jack solved 32 multiplication problems and 20 division problems. He got 5 multiplication problems and 4 division problems wrong. How many problems did he get correct in all?	43 problems
Julio saved $20 in May. He saved $18 in June and $15 in July. Then Julio spent $28 during summer vacation. How much money does Julio have left?	$25
Jessica has 36 red beads, 65 blue beads, and 42 green beads. She needs 9 beads from each color to make a necklace. How many beads will Jessica have left after making 2 necklaces?	89 beads
This year Mia planted 35 roses. Her sister Heather planted 20 more roses than Mia. Half the roses have bloomed so far. How many roses have not bloomed yet?	45 roses
Our homeschool group included 12 high school students, 27 middle school students, 23 elementary students, 44 parents, and 18 kids in the nursery. How many people were in our homeschool group in all?	124 people

---

This is a page of word problems. They can use word problem strategies like drawing pictures or using smaller numbers. They will need to use scratch paper for today. Here are the first couple of problems worked out and the set up for several others.

$374 + $158 = $532
They could think of this with smaller numbers to figure out what to do. He bought something for $3 and still had $1 leftover. How much did he have at first? $4 (3+1)

238 + 185 + 79 = 502 goldfish
This is another one that using smaller numbers would help. They sold 2 then 1 and had 1 leftover. How many did they have at first? 2 + 1 + 1. They need to add.

172 – 155 + 86 bags

185 – 128 – 39 pages

115 + 86 – 37 seashells

175 – 36 – (2 x 36) cups

120 + 116 – 35 – 28 = 236 – 63 stamps

Lesson 29

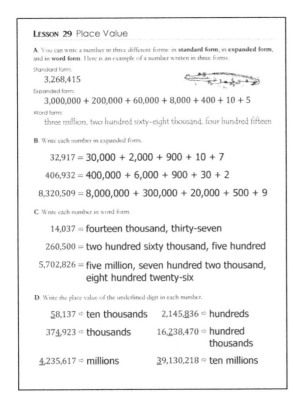

LESSON 29 Place Value

A. You can write a number in three different forms: in **standard form**, in **expanded form**, and in **word form**. Here is an example of a number written in three forms.

Standard form:
3,268,415

Expanded form:
3,000,000 + 200,000 + 60,000 + 8,000 + 400 + 10 + 5

Word form:
three million, two hundred sixty-eight thousand, four hundred fifteen

B. Write each number in expanded form.

32,917 = 30,000 + 2,000 + 900 + 10 + 7

406,932 = 400,000 + 6,000 + 900 + 30 + 2

8,320,509 = 8,000,000 + 300,000 + 20,000 + 500 + 9

C. Write each number in word form.

14,037 = fourteen thousand, thirty-seven

260,500 = two hundred sixty thousand, five hundred

5,702,826 = five million, seven hundred two thousand, eight hundred twenty-six

D. Write the place value of the underlined digit in each number.

5̲8,137 ⇨ ten thousands   2,145,8̲36 ⇨ hundreds

374̲,923 ⇨ thousands   16,2̲38,470 ⇨ hundred thousands

4̲,235,617 ⇨ millions   3̲9,130,218 ⇨ ten millions

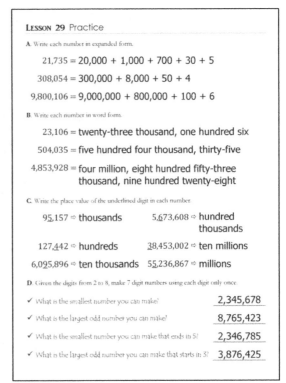

LESSON 29 Practice

A. Write each number in expanded form.

21,735 = 20,000 + 1,000 + 700 + 30 + 5

308,054 = 300,000 + 8,000 + 50 + 4

9,800,106 = 9,000,000 + 800,000 + 100 + 6

B. Write each number in word form.

23,106 = twenty-three thousand, one hundred six

504,035 = five hundred four thousand, thirty-five

4,853,928 = four million, eight hundred fifty-three thousand, nine hundred twenty-eight

C. Write the place value of the underlined digit in each number.

95̲,157 ⇨ thousands   5,6̲73,608 ⇨ hundred thousands

127,4̲42 ⇨ hundreds   3̲8,453,002 ⇨ ten millions

6,09̲5,896 ⇨ ten thousands   55̲,236,867 ⇨ millions

D. Given the digits from 2 to 8, make 7 digit numbers using each digit only once.

✓ What is the smallest number you can make?   2,345,678

✓ What is the largest odd number you can make?   8,765,423

✓ What is the smallest number you can make that ends in 5?   2,346,785

✓ What is the largest odd number you can make that starts in 3?   3,876,425

There is an example on the page of standard form, expanded form, and word form. Have your child read the last number on the page to you.

thirty-nine million, one hundred thirty thousand, two hundred eighteen

Then have your child tell you each place value right to left: ones, tens, hundreds, thousands, ten thousands, hundred thousands, millions, ten millions

Lesson 30

LESSON 30 Rounding whole numbers

A. Rounding is used when we don't need an exact value and an estimate is good enough. To round a number to a given place value, look at the digit to the right of the rounding place. If the digit to the right is 4 or lower, round down by replacing all digits to the right of the rounding place with zeros. If the digit to the right is 5 or greater, round up by adding 1 to the rounding place digit and replacing all digits to the right of it with zeros. Here is an example of rounding a number to the nearest ten, hundred, and thousand.

	Nearest 10	Nearest 100	Nearest 1000
4,752	4,750	4,800	5,000
	The ones digit is 2. Round down!	The tens digit is 5. Round up!	The hundreds digit is 7. Round up!

B. Round each number to the nearest ten, hundred, and thousand.

	Nearest 10	Nearest 100	Nearest 1000
273	270	300	0
4,528	4,530	4,500	5,000
8,374	8,370	8,400	8,000
63,095	63,100	63,100	63,000
89,541	89,540	89,500	90,000
230,487	230,490	230,500	230,000

C. Estimate each product by rounding the top number to the nearest thousand and the bottom number to the nearest ten and then multiplying the first digits.

$$6238 \rightarrow 6000 \qquad 4708 \rightarrow 5000$$
$$\times\ 75 \rightarrow \times\ 80 \qquad \times\ 52 \rightarrow \times\ 50$$

Estimate: 480,000   Estimate: 250,000

Did you know? In Chinese, the word for "4" sounds like the word for "death". That is why many hospitals in China do not have a 4th floor.

LESSON 30 Practice

A. Round each number to the nearest ten.

36	40	1,758	1,760	43,072	43,070
893	890	2,360	2,360	36,399	36,400
495	500	8,107	8,110	59,828	59,830

B. Round each number to the nearest hundred.

72	100	5,359	5,400	52,938	52,900
649	600	2,956	3,000	94,152	94,200
917	900	4,728	4,700	27,560	27,600

C. Round each number to the nearest thousand.

92	0	2,935	3,000	39,938	40,000
298	0	9,486	9,000	15,720	16,000
735	1,000	1,577	2,000	64,163	64,000

D. Use the clues to solve each riddle.

I am a 2-digit number. To the nearest 10, I round to 70. My tens digit is even. The sum of my digits is 11. What number am I? **65**

I am a 3-digit number. I am the smallest possible number that would round to 400 when rounded to the nearest 100. What number am I? **350**

I am a 4-digit number. I am the largest possible number that would round to 8,000 when rounded to the nearest 1,000. What number am I? **8,499**

They are going to be rounding and estimating, so this should be an easy page. They can use the examples to help them.

They will look at the digit to the right of the place value they are rounding to. After the number is rounded, every digit to the right of the place value you are rounding to will be a zero and every number to the left of it will stay the same.

Here's an example from the lesson.

89,541 to the nearest ten: 89,540. You use the ones, the digit to the right of the tens place. Every digit to the right of the tens place becomes a zero. The digits to the left of the tens place, the higher place values, stay the same.

89,541 to the nearest hundred: 89,500 You look at the digit to the right, the tens. The digits to the right become zero and the digits to the left of the hundreds stay the same.

89,541 to the nearest thousand: 90,000 You look to the digit to the right of the thousands, the hundreds. Five will round up. 9,541 is between 9,000 and 10,000. It rounds up to 10,000, so 89,000 becomes 90,000. If your child is stuck on this one, have your child try it smaller. 895 rounded to the nearest ten is 900.

Lesson 31

LESSON 31 Multiplying and dividing negative numbers

A. When multiplying (or dividing) numbers with different signs, ignore the signs and multiply (or divide) as usual. Then determine the sign of the product (or the quotient) using two rules: 1) two like signs become a positive sign, and 2) two unlike signs become a negative sign. Here are some examples.

$9 \times -4 = \underline{-36}$
Positive x Negative = Negative

$-5 \times -7 = \underline{35}$
Negative x Negative = Positive

$-56 \div 7 = \underline{-8}$
Negative ÷ Positive = Negative

$-40 \div -8 = \underline{5}$
Negative ÷ Negative = Positive

B. Multiply the numbers.

$6 \times -9 = -54$ $-8 \times -6 = 48$ $-7 \times 7 = -49$

$-5 \times 4 = -20$ $-5 \times 7 = -35$ $9 \times 3 = 27$

$4 \times -3 = -12$ $8 \times -9 = -72$ $0 \times -1 = 0$

$8 \times 0 = 0$ $-6 \times -6 = 36$ $-7 \times -8 = 56$

$-2 \times -9 = 18$ $4 \times 7 = 28$ $-9 \times 9 = -81$

C. Divide the numbers.

$8 \div -8 = -1$ $54 \div 9 = 6$ $-16 \div 2 = -8$

$-42 \div 6 = -7$ $-36 \div 6 = -6$ $45 \div -5 = -9$

$25 \div 5 = 5$ $40 \div -8 = -5$ $28 \div 7 = 4$

$-72 \div -8 = 9$ $-32 \div -1 = 32$ $-63 \div 9 = -7$

$30 \div -6 = -5$ $-49 \div 7 = -7$ $-24 \div -4 = 6$

Did you know? 18 is the only number that is twice the sum of its digits.

LESSON 31 Practice

A. Multiply the numbers.

$-9 \times 9 = -81$ $7 \times -6 = -42$ $-7 \times 1 = -7$

$7 \times -4 = -28$ $-6 \times -5 = 30$ $-8 \times -8 = 64$

$-5 \times -8 = 40$ $7 \times 3 = 21$ $3 \times -5 = -15$

$3 \times 3 = 9$ $-8 \times 4 = -32$ $-4 \times 0 = 0$

-157	286	-608	935	-427
× 2	× -7	× 8	× 4	× -3
-314	-2,002	-4,864	3,740	1,281

B. Divide the numbers.

$-7 \div 7 = -1$ $-18 \div -6 = 3$ $32 \div -4 = -8$

$48 \div -6 = -8$ $36 \div 4 = 9$ $49 \div 7 = 7$

$-30 \div 5 = -6$ $-24 \div 8 = -3$ $81 \div -9 = -9$

$-16 \div -1 = 16$ $12 \div -6 = -2$ $-20 \div -5 = 4$

$-8 \overline{\smash{)}\,992} = -124$ $-7 \overline{\smash{)}\,-406} = 58$ $5 \overline{\smash{)}\,-285} = -57$ $-9 \overline{\smash{)}\,-405} = 45$

This lesson makes me think of the movie, "Stand and Deliver." The math teacher drills into them, "A negative times a negative equals a positive." They can also think of this like when they subtracted a negative. The two negative signs can form a plus sign.

You could have your child do the first part, Section A, and then check their answers to make sure they got it before they do the rest. They should know all the facts to answer the questions quickly. They just need to determine the sign. If there is one negative, the answer will be negative. If there are two negatives or two positives, the answer will be positive.

Here's one worked out from the practice page. You can ignore the sign and divide normally, but you have to remember the sign in the answer. There is one negative in the problem, so the solution is a negative.

```
        -124
  - 8 | 992
        8
        19
        16
         32
         32
          0
```

Lesson 32

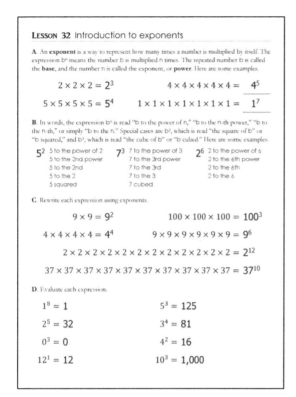

This is an introduction to exponents. They will do more at the end of the course. The idea is that you take the number in the exponent and multiply the base number by itself that many times. Four squared $= 4^2 = 4$ x $4 = 16$

The exponent can be any number. Right now they are just dealing with simple exponents. They can think of exponents as a shortcut. It's the quick and easy way to write out when something needs to be multiplied by itself.

Here are a few examples from their page.

$2^5 = 2$ x 2 x 2 x 2 x $2 = 32$

$5^3 = 5$ x 5 x $5 = 25$ x $5 = 125$

On the practice page it asks you to compare five cubed with six squared. We just figured five cubed was 125. Six squared is just 36. Five cubed is bigger.

They basically all can be figured out without multiplying. If the exponents are the same, the larger base number will be the greater one. If the base numbers are the same, the one with the larger exponent will be greater.

Lesson 33

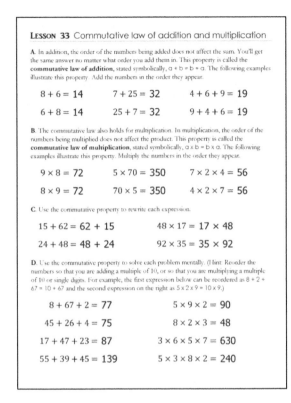

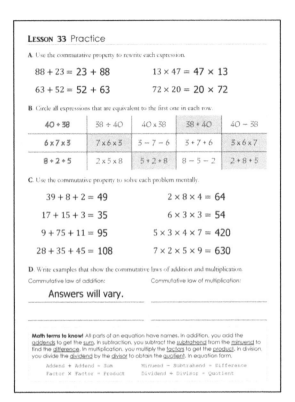

This next section is easy math, but all new concepts. That means lots of new vocabulary. If you know that your child learns best by hearing, read the lesson to them. If they learn best by writing things out, have them make flashcards with these new terms.

Today is the commutative property. They can remember this one by thinking of the word commute. Someone's commute is their drive to work. When someone is commuting back and forth, they are traveling back and forth.

That's what is happening in their math. They already know this; it just puts a name to it.

It's saying that $2 + 3 = 3 + 2$ and $2 \times 3 = 3 \times 2$.

The last section on the page shows the value of this. Sometimes it will make their work easier to reorder the numbers, and who wouldn't want to make their work easier?

They don't have to write out the steps in Section D. I'm just showing the thought process for some of them (below). They should also read the "Math terms" on the practice page.

$8 + 67 + 2 = 8 + 2 + 67 = 10 + 67$ $5 \times 9 \times 2 = 5 \times 2 \times 9 = 10 \times 9 = 90$

$45 + 26 + 4 = 45 + 30$ $8 \times 2 \times 3 = 8 \times 6$

$17 + 47 + 23 = 17 + 70 \text{ or } 40 + 47$ $3 \times 6 \times 5 \times 7 = 30 \times 21$

Lesson 34

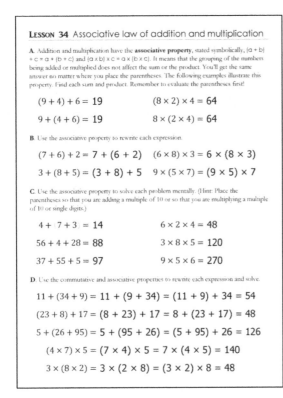

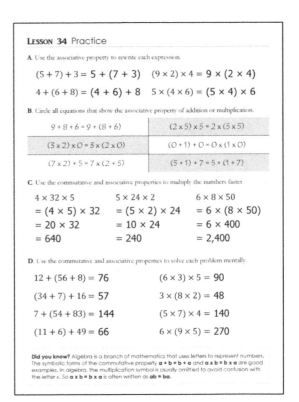

This is called the associative property. They can remember this because people who associate with each other hang out in a group. The parentheses puts together the numbers that are grouped together, that are associating together.

Right now it doesn't make much sense to have parentheses in the equations, but it's best to start in this simple way before things become complicated. In math we solve what's inside the parenthesis before we do what it says outside of the parenthesis. They should follow that rule as they solve these and add and multiply what's inside first.

Like the commutative law, this only works with addition and multiplication. However, subtraction can be written as adding a negative and division can be written as multiplying a fraction, so these tricks will be able to be applied in lots of ways.

You can remind your child that these serve a purpose. These laws, when learned and applied, will make their work easier, which means faster as well.

Here are examples from the lesson.

$(11 + 9) + 34 = 20 + 34$ $(4 \times 5) \times 7 = 20 \times 7$

$(23 + 17) + 8 = 40 + 8$ $(3 \times 2) \times 8 = 6 \times 8$

Lesson 35

LESSON 35 Distributive law of multiplication

A. Multiplication distributes over addition, meaning that multiplying a sum by a factor is equivalent to multiplying each addend by the factor separately and adding the products. This property is called the **distributive law of multiplication**, stated symbolically, $a(b + c) = ab + ac$. Multiplication distributes over subtraction as well, so $a(b - c) = ab - ac$ also holds true. The examples below illustrate this property. Complete the second example.

$4 \times (10 + 7) = (4 \times 10) + (4 \times 7) = 40 + 28 = 68$

Distribute 4 to 10 and 7. This form is easier to solve than 4 x 17.

$6 \times (20 - 5) = (6 \times 20) - (6 \times 5) = 120 - 30 = 90$

B. You can use the distributive property in reverse. This process is called factoring because you are rewriting the expression as a multiplication of factors. Here is an example.

$56 + 24 = (8 \times 7) + (8 \times 3) = 8 \times (7 + 3)$

Take out (or factor out) the common factor 8.

C. Use the distributive property to rewrite each expression and solve.

$7 \times (5 + 4) = (7 \times 5) + (7 \times 4) = 35 + 28 = 63$

$4 \times (8 - 3) = (4 \times 8) - (4 \times 3) = 32 - 12 = 20$

$9 \times (10 + 6) = (9 \times 10) + (9 \times 6) = 90 + 54 = 144$

$8 \times (20 - 5) = (8 \times 20) - (8 \times 5) = 160 - 40 = 120$

D. Use the distributive property in reverse to rewrite each expression in $a(b + c)$ or $a(b - c)$ form, where a, b, and c represent positive whole numbers.

$56 + 24 = 8 \times (7 + 3)$

$30 + 42 = 6 \times (5 + 7)$

$81 - 45 = 9 \times (9 - 5)$

$28 - 16 = 4 \times (7 - 4)$

LESSON 35 Practice

A. Use the distributive property to rewrite each expression and solve.

$4 \times (9 + 3) = (4 \times 9) + (4 \times 3) = 36 + 12 = 48$

$7 \times (6 - 4) = (7 \times 6) - (7 \times 4) = 42 - 28 = 14$

$9 \times (8 + 2) = (9 \times 8) + (9 \times 2) = 72 + 18 = 90$

$8 \times (9 - 4) = (8 \times 9) - (8 \times 4) = 72 - 32 = 40$

$2 \times (30 + 6) = (2 \times 30) + (2 \times 6) = 60 + 12 = 72$

$5 \times (10 - 2) = (5 \times 10) - (5 \times 2) = 50 - 10 = 40$

$3 \times (70 + 5) = (3 \times 70) + (3 \times 5) = 210 + 15 = 225$

$6 \times (40 - 6) = (6 \times 40) - (6 \times 6) = 240 - 36 = 204$

B. Use the distributive property in reverse to rewrite each expression in $a(b + c)$ or $a(b - c)$ form, where a, b, and c represent positive whole numbers.

$9 + 15 = 3 \times (3 + 5)$

$18 - 12 = 6 \times (3 - 2)$

$49 + 35 = 7 \times (7 + 5)$

$35 - 20 = 5 \times (7 - 4)$

$28 + 40 = 4 \times (7 + 10)$

$64 - 24 = 8 \times (8 - 3)$

$55 + 88 = 11 \times (5 + 8)$

$90 - 50 = 10 \times (9 - 5)$

Today's law is the distributive law of multiplication. This one is a little more complicated than the ones they've been looking at. You do just like the name says, you distribute the number. When you distribute something, you are giving it out. If you are in charge of distributing programs at a show, you give one out to each person.

This is the example problem. $4 \times (10 + 7)$ I would write this $4(10+7)$. They could solve what's in the parentheses first which would leave them with 4×17. But, if they distributed the four first, it would become $(4 \times 10) + (4 \times 7)$ or $40 + 28$. Make sure your child sees these are the same thing. $4 \times 17 = 68 = 40 + 28$

You can draw little arrows from the four to the ten and to the seven to diagram how the four is being distributed. The four is being multiplied by each thing in the parentheses. It's not 4×10; it's 4×17, which is 4×10 and 4×7 together.

The first problem in their lesson is $7 \times (5 + 4)$ or $7(5 + 4)$ and will become $(7 \times 5) + (7 \times 4) = 35 + 28 = 63$. The seven is distributed across each number in the parentheses because everything in the parentheses is being multiplied by seven. The problem becomes 7 times 5 and 7 times 4. Again, this may not seem worth it now, but it will make their lives easier in the future, so they should practice it now with these easier questions.

The last section asks them to do this in reverse, to pull out what each number is being multiplied by. 12 and 27 are both multiples of 3. We can write: $12 + 27 = 3 \times (4 + 9)$

Here are some hints. First one: $7 \times 8 = 56$ Second one: $6 \times 7 = 42$ Third one: $9 \times 5 = 45$

Lesson 36

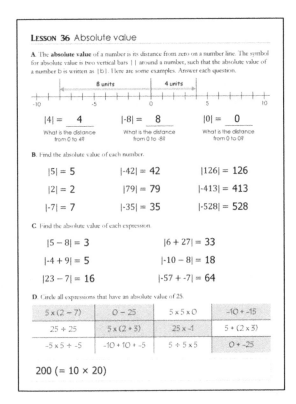

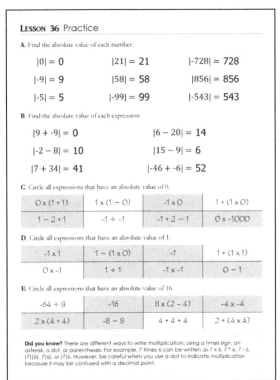

After the distributive property, today's lesson is simple to find the answer. It's absolute value. The end of it is that you just take the negative sign off of any negative number to find its absolute value.

Here is the why. They can think of this as distance. On their page is a number line. The absolute value is the distance traveled to get to the number on the number line from zero. To get to negative three on the number line, you travel three. The absolute value of negative three is three. We write it like this $|-3| = 3$.

They can also treat the absolute value sign like parentheses, so the absolute value of $5 - 8$ is three as well. $|5 - 8| = |-3| = 3$ They should solve whatever is in the absolute value sign first, and then find the absolute value of it.

Lesson 37

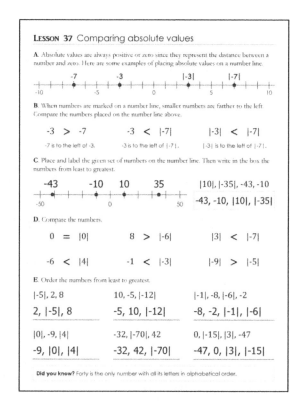

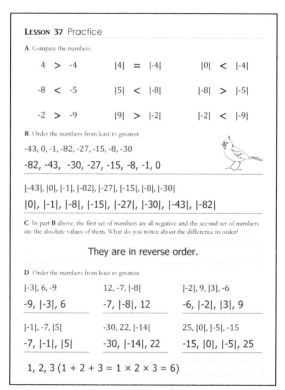

This is a simple lesson if they will let it be. I suggest writing in the answers to the absolute values right above the number, so they can keep straight in their heads what numbers they are comparing.

They are comparing numbers like -25 and |-45|. Those are -25 and 45, so 45 is greater. The answer looks like this: -25 < |-45|

Lesson 38

LESSON 38 Identity property of 0 and 1

A. In addition, when you add 0 to any number, the sum equals the number itself. This property is called the **identity property of 0** (also called the **identity property of addition**), stated symbolically, $a + 0 = 0 + a = a$. The number 0 is called the **additive identity**. The following examples illustrate the property. Find each sum.

$1 + 0 = 1$ $-508 + 0 = -508$ $0 + 3127 = 3,127$

B. In multiplication, when you multiply any number by 1, the product equals the number itself. This property is called the **identity property of 1** (also called the **identity property of multiplication**), stated symbolically, $a \cdot 1 = 1 \cdot a = a$. The number 1 is called the **multiplicative identity**. The examples below illustrate this property. Find each product.

$1 \times 1 = 1$ $1 \times -508 = -508$ $3127 \times 1 = 3,127$

C. In multiplication, when you multiply any number by 0, the product always equals 0. This property is called the **zero product property**, stated symbolically, $a \cdot 0 = 0 \cdot a = 0$.

D. Use the number properties to solve each expression mentally.

$-6 \times (1 + 0) = -6$ $85 + (0 \times -9) = 85$

$-125 + |0| = -125$ $419 \times 27 \times 0 = 0$

$0 + 17 + -17 = 0$ $1 \times |-1| \times 35 = 35$

E. Evaluate each expression mentally. To evaluate expressions, replace letters (also called variables) with the given numbers. Note that multiplication symbols are omitted.

✓ Evaluate $539a$ when $a = -1$. -539

✓ Evaluate $0 + a + (-8)$ when $a = 8$. 0

✓ Evaluate $41ab$ when $a = 20$ and $b = 0$. 0

✓ Evaluate $a + 76 + b$ when $a = 45$ and $b = -45$. 76

✓ Evaluate $|a| - |b|$ when $a = 100$ and $b = -100$. 0

LESSON 38 Practice

A. Write two examples that show the identity property of 0.

   Answers will vary.

B. Write two examples that show the identity property of 1.

   Answers will vary.

C. Write two examples that show the zero product property.

   Answers will vary.

D. Evaluate each expression mentally.

$1,245 \times 1 = 1,245$ $(24 + 38) \times 0 = 0$

$-8 \times (1 + 0) = -8$ $49 + 54 + -49 = 54$

$|0 + -836| = 836$ $1 \times -1 \times 1 \times -1 = 1$

$-98 + 0 + 98 = 0$ $1,324 \times 0 \times 15 = 0$

$1 \times (512 + 0) = 512$ $(8 \times 1) - (8 \times 0) = 8$

E. Evaluate each expression mentally.

✓ Evaluate $745a$ when $a = 1$. 745

✓ Evaluate $0 + -95 + b$ when $b = 0$. -95

✓ Evaluate $256ab$ when $a = -1$ and $b = 1$. -256

✓ Evaluate $50abc$ when $a = 3$, $b = -7$ and $c = 0$. 0

✓ Evaluate $8 + a + 12 + b$ when $a = 0$ and $b = 0$. 20

Today's lesson is the identity property. Numbers are going to keep their identity. You can ask your child what they can add to a number so that it doesn't change. It's zero. Anything plus zero is just that number. You can do the same with multiplication and ask what number you can multiply by to get the same number. It's one. Any number times one is itself. They keep their identity. That's what today's lesson is.

We use this property when we find equivalent fractions. It's why one fourth equals two eighths. When we multiply one fourth by two halves, we are really just multiplying by one and the number doesn't change.

The lesson will ask them to apply some of the other things they've been learning. They will also be multiplying by zero, which they already know is always zero. That's the zero product property. A product is the answer to a multiplication question.

In part E, they will substitute in numbers. The first one is 539a. That means 539 times a. It tells you that a = -1. So it's 539 x -1 = -539. All they have to do is rewrite the equation with the number given in place of the letter.

On the practice page, here are some examples for A, B, and C.

A. $6 + 0 = 6$ B. $8 \times 1 = 8$ C. $4 \times 0 = 0$

Lesson 39

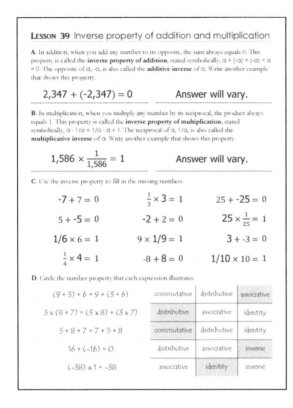

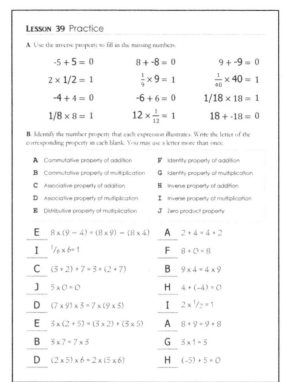

Today's lesson is the inverse property of addition and multiplication. The inverse is the opposite. We are going to add and multiply by the opposite.

What's the opposite of 1? -1 What happens when we add one and negative one? We get zero. And that's the property. That any number plus its opposite will give us zero.

What do you need to add to -546 to get zero? 546, its opposite

For multiplication, the property states that any number multiplied by its opposite will give the answer of one. Let's see it at work.

The opposite of a whole number is its reciprocal. $4 \times \frac{1}{4} = \frac{4}{4} = 1$

They don't have to do this with fractions, but this is what it would look like.

$$\frac{4}{5} \times \frac{5}{4} = \frac{20}{20} = 1$$

Today's lesson is also a review of the different properties they have learned. They can turn back in their book to help them if need be.

Lesson 40

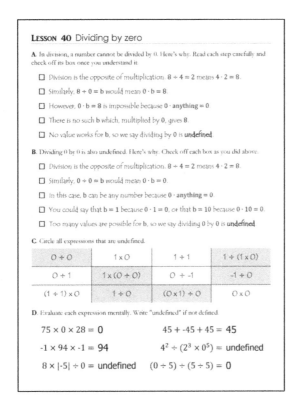

Today's lesson is on dividing by zero. The answer is undefined. Let me explain why a couple of different ways.

If you had a barrel with ten toys in it and you took out two at a time, how many times could you take out toys? five times

That's ten divided by two equals five. Now what if I asked you to take out zero toys at a time, how many times could you take out toys? There's no answer.

Here's another way to show you can't divide by zero. We have fact families. 3 x 9 = 27 and 9 x 3 = 27 and 27 ÷ 3 = 9 and 27 ÷ 9 = 3 We can't say that 10 ÷ 0 = something and that something times zero equals ten. It can't happen. We already know that anything times zero equals zero. That's how it is explained on their page.

They will also be practicing their other properties.

Lesson 41

LESSON 41 Word problems: multiplication and division

Solve the word problems.

Dana can solve 12 addition problems per minute. How many addition problems can she solve in 5 minutes?	60 problems
The librarian puts 400 books equally on 25 shelves. How many books are on each shelf?	16 books
Jack recycles 28 cans each month. How many cans does he recycle in a year?	336 cans
Max read a 180-page book. He read the same number of pages for 15 days. How many pages did he read each day?	12 pages
Lucy is on a 72-mile hike. She hiked 15 miles per day for 4 days. How many miles does Lucy have left?	12 miles
The teacher divides 132 students into groups of 12. How many groups will be made?	11 groups
Adam has $16. Sam has 3 times more Adam but only half of Abby. How much money does Abby have?	$96
Kyle bought 7 pounds of candies. He paid with $50 and received $8 as change. What was the price per pound?	$6
Derek spent $120 to order some tickets online. Each ticket cost $14. The shipping cost was $8. How many tickets did Derek buy?	8 tickets
There are 5 boys and 5 girls. Each boy has 11 stickers and each girl has 19 stickers. How many stickers do they have in all?	150 stickers
Leah has 15 pennies. Kate has 6 times as many pennies as Leah. Matt has 5 times as many pennies as Kate. How many pennies does Matt have?	450 pennies
Monica solved 8 worksheets. Each worksheet had 6 rows of 5 problems in each row. Eighty of the problems were division problems. How many problems were not division problems?	160 problems

LESSON 41 Practice

Solve the word problems.

A worksheet has 6 rows with 6 problems in each row. How many problems are in the worksheet?	36 problems
Rebekah learns 5 new words every day. How many words will she learn in 4 weeks?	140 words
Kyle read a 90-page book. He read 18 pages per day. How many days did it take him to finish the book?	5 days
Stacy has 90 cents. She wants to buy 7 candy bars. Each candy bar costs 12 cents. How much money will Stacy have left?	6 cents
Emma baked 112 cookies for a bake sale. She put them equally into 8 boxes. How many cookies does each box have?	14 cookies
Larry has 11 dimes. Ava has 6 times as many dimes as Larry but half as many dimes as Marie. How many dimes does Marie have?	132 dimes
Brian has $14. His weekly allowance is $9. How many weeks will it take him to save for a video game that costs $50?	4 weeks
Twelve friends bought movie tickets. They paid $108 in total. How much did each ticket cost?	$9
A recipe calls for 8 apples to make 1 apple pie. Angela has 60 apples. After baking 7 pies, how many apples will she have left?	4 apples
Jim and Tom have $54. Tom has half as much money as Jim. How much money does Tom have?	$18
Laura has 5 stickers. Daniel has 3 times as many stickers as Laura. Ron has 8 times as many stickers as Daniel. How many stickers does Ron have?	120 stickers
At a grocery, Tina bought 7 bags of apples and 7 jars of apple jam. Each bag of apples cost $4. Each jar of jam cost $6. How much did Tina spend in all?	$70

Today's lesson is word problems. They will need to use multiplication and division. They can use techniques like drawing pictures and using smaller numbers to help them figure out what they need to do.

Here is the set up for most of the questions.

Max: 180/15 (15 x 2 = 30 and 6 x 30 = 180) pages

Lucy: 72 – (15 x 4) miles

The teacher: 132/12 students

Adam: 2 x (16 x 3) dollars

Kyle: (50 – 8) / 7 dollars

Derek: (120 – 8) / 14 tickets

Boys and girls: (11 x 5) + (12 x 5) stickers

Leah: (15 x 6) x 5 pennies

Monica: (8 x 6 x 5) – 80 problems

Lesson 42

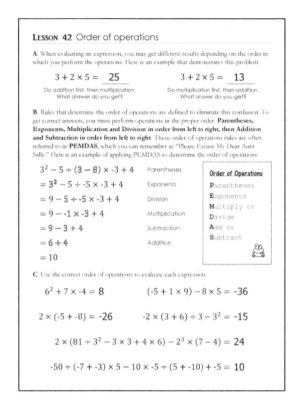

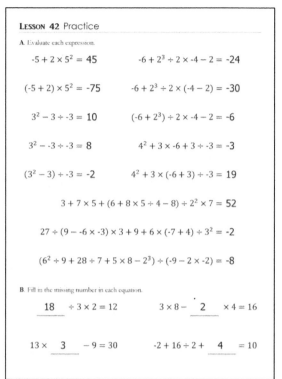

Today's lesson is on order of operations. Their page explains the pneumonic, "Please Excuse My Dear Aunt Sally." It reminds us of the order we should solve equations: parentheses, exponents, multiplication and division, addition and subtraction.

For addition and subtraction we work left to right, same with multiplication and division. However, you could also rewrite subtraction as addition and division as multiplication and then you could use the communitive property to do them in any order you like. We can do that because all subtraction is just adding a negative number. It's just a form of addition. And all division is just multiplying by the reciprocal, so all division is really just a form of multiplication. But, they would have to change the problem first because you can't subtract and divide in any order you like. They don't commute.

But this lesson is about plain order of operations, so they don't need to think like that unless they find it fun to manipulate the numbers and make the problems as easy as possible.

For the first of the two long ones, they would solve $7 - 4$ and then 81 divided by 9 first, as well as 3 x 3 and 4 x 6. Then they would solve the whole parentheses. Then they would multiply the two parts. Then finally, they would subtract.

Lesson 43

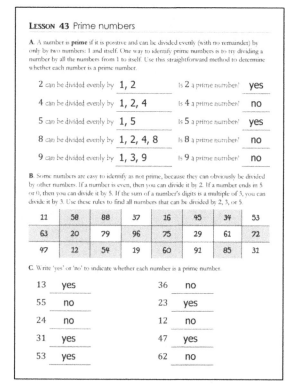

Today's lesson is on prime numbers. A prime number is a positive number that can be divided evenly by only itself and the number one.

The number one is not prime because it can't be divided by one **and** itself because it is one. Two is the first prime number and the only even one. All other even numbers are not prime because they can be divided by two.

They have to think about whether or not the number can be divided by anything, but really, they are given tricks on the page for a short cut.

* Even numbers can be divided by two.
* Numbers ending in 0 or 5 are divisible by five.
* Numbers whose digits add up to a multiple of 3 (such as 9, 12, 18…) will be divisible by three. Example: 126 1 + 2 + 6 = 9 and 9 is divisible by 3

All of the numbers on the page fall under these tricks or are prime. There are other non-prime numbers; for instance, 49 doesn't meet any of those tricks but is divisible by 7. Forty-nine is on the practice page.

Lesson 44

LESSON 44 Recognizing prime numbers

A. A number is **composite** if it is positive and can be divided evenly by one, itself, and at least one other positive integer. In other words, a composite number is a positive integer that can be formed by multiplying two smaller positive integers. Make three composite numbers out of prime numbers less than 10.

Prime x Prime = Composite   Prime x Prime = Composite

$2 \times 5 = 10$ **Answers will vary.**

B. Every positive integer is prime, composite, or one. One is neither prime nor composite. Write 'prime' or 'composite' for each number. If the number is composite, write at least one division fact showing it can be divided by a number other than one and itself. (Hint: Find composite numbers first! There are 6 prime numbers.)

80	composite	$80 \div 2 = 40, 80 \div 5 = 16, 80 \div 8 = 10$
73	prime	
97	prime	
77	composite	$7 \times 11 = 77$
49	composite	$7 \times 7 = 49$
67	prime	
83	prime	
69	composite	$3 \times 23 = 69$
89	prime	
75	composite	$3 \times 25 = 75, 5 \times 15 = 75$
31	prime	

LESSON 44 Practice

A. Circle all prime numbers. (Hint: Eliminate composite numbers first! There are 25 prime numbers between 1 and 100.)

1	2	3	4	5	6	7	8	9	10
11	12	13	14	15	16	17	18	19	20
21	22	23	24	25	26	27	28	29	30
31	32	33	34	35	36	37	38	39	40
41	42	43	44	45	46	47	48	49	50
51	52	53	54	55	56	57	58	59	60
61	62	63	64	65	66	67	68	69	70
71	72	73	74	75	76	77	78	79	80
81	82	83	84	85	86	87	88	89	90
91	92	93	94	95	96	97	98	99	100

B. Where are prime numbers used in real life? Here's one example.

Prime numbers are important in Internet security. For example, when people shop online, their credit card numbers are encrypted (converted into a secure format) by a process that involves multiplying very large prime numbers. Only someone who has the secret key consisting of those prime numbers can decrypt the information. Even if an encrypted message is stolen, without the key it is nearly impossible to figure out which prime numbers were multiplied. How big are the prime numbers used for encryption? One of the most popular encryption algorithms uses more than 100-digit prime numbers!

Today's lesson is on composite numbers, basically, the positive numbers that are not prime.

The top of the page asks them to multiply together two small prime numbers. That will automatically get them a composite number.

For the next section they are to look for numbers they can divide by. It tells them how many are prime to help them out. They should start by looking for ones they know for sure are composite, such as 95 since it ends with 5, and 77 because it can obviously be divided by 11.

On the practice page they can eliminate whole columns, every even-number column and the columns that end with 5 and 0. Then they can go through and cross of every third number because those are all multiples of three and so are divisible by three.

Lesson 45

LESSON 45 Divisibility rules

A. When a number *a* can be evenly divided by another number *b*, we say '*a* is divisible by *b*' and the number *b* is called a **divisor** or **factor** of *a*. A straightforward way to determine divisibility is to actually do the division and see if there is any remainder.

B. However, mathematicians have found that the numbers divisible by certain divisors follow interesting patterns. For those certain divisors, you can determine divisibility by simply checking for those patterns, without doing any actual division. Those number patterns are called divisibility rules. Here are the divisibility rules for 2, 3, 4, 5, 6, 9, and 10.

An integer is divisible by

2 if it ends in 0, 2, 4, 6, or 8.　　6 if it is divisible by both 2 and 3.

3 if the sum of its digits is divisible by 3.　　9 if the sum of its digits is divisible by 9.

4 if its last 2 digits are divisible by 4.　　10 if it ends in 0.

5 if it ends in 0 or 5.

C. Determine whether each number is divisible by 2, 3, 4, 5, 6, 9, or 10. If so, list below.

48	54	80
2, 3, 4, 6	2, 3, 6, 9	2, 4, 5, 10
456	570	216
2, 3, 4, 6	2, 3, 5, 6, 10	2, 3, 4, 6, 9
6,345	9,216	1,890
3, 5, 9	2, 3, 4, 6, 9	2, 3, 5, 6, 9, 10
25,380	45,550	83,320
2, 3, 4, 5, 6, 9, 10	2, 5, 10	2, 4, 5, 10

LESSON 45 Practice

A. Determine whether each number is divisible by 2, 3, 4, 5, 6, 9, or 10. If so, list below.

32	45	72
2, 4	3, 5, 9	2, 3, 4, 6, 9
240	816	140
2, 3, 4, 5, 6, 10	2, 3, 4, 6	2, 4, 5, 10
6,410	4,425	9,000
2, 5, 10	3, 5	2, 3, 4, 5, 6, 9, 10
11,133	55,590	36,594
3, 9	2, 3, 5, 6, 10	2, 3, 6, 9

B. Circle all numbers divisible by both 3 and 4.

531	756	592	315	304	752	888	192
396	669	103	228	702	552	257	464

C. Circle all numbers divisible by both 5 and 9.

160	990	333	954	405	855	587	729
419	585	420	180	605	234	125	270

Did you know? The mathematics and science writer Martin Gardner explained and popularized the divisibility rules in his September 1962 "Mathematical Games" column in Scientific American.

Today's lesson is on divisibility rules. These will come in handy and make their lives easier in solving bigger equations and in things like reducing fractions, so it's worth their time and effort to try to learn these.

We've already talked about how even numbers are divisible by two and numbers that end in zero and five are divisible by five. The rules for other numbers are on their page.

Here are some of the lesson questions worked out.

456 is divisible by:
　　2 because it's even
　　3 because $4 + 5 + 6 = 15$ and $5 \times 3 = 15$
　　4 because $56 \div 4 = 14$　$56 - 40$ (4×10) $= 16$ and $16/4 = 4$ (I took away an easy amount, 10×4, to get to a smaller number that I know is divisible by four.)
　　6 because it's divisible by two and three
　　Not 5 or 10 because it doesn't end in 5 or 0

6,345 is divisible by:
　　3 because $6 + 3 + 4 + 5 = 18$　$18/3 = 6$
　　5 because it ends in 5
　　9 because $18/9 = 2$
　　Not 2 because it's not even, so not 6 as well
　　Not 4 because $45 \div 4$ has a remainder

Lesson 46

LESSON 46 Finding factor pairs

A. A **factor pair** is two integers that when multiplied together equal a given number. Here are the steps for finding all factor pairs of a number.

36	To find all factor pairs of 36:
1 × 36	1. The first pair is always 1 and the number itself. List 1 x 36.
2 × 18	2. Test 2. Is the number divisible by 2? If so, find the other factor that pairs with 2 and list the pair. 36 is even, so it is divisible by 2. The other factor is 36 ÷ 2 = 18. List 2 x 18.
3 × 12	3. Test 3 in the same way. 3 + 6 = 9, so 36 is divisible by 3. The other factor is 36 ÷ 3 = 12. List 3 x 12.
4 × 9	
6 × 6	4. Continue until you have no more numbers to test. In our example, you can stop at 6 since the factors larger than 6 are already found.
9 × 4	

B. List all factor pairs of each number.

16	55	63	21
1 × 16	1 × 55	1 × 63	1 × 21
2 × 8	5 × 11	3 × 21	3 × 7
4 × 4		7 × 9	

30	88	92	70
1 × 30	1 × 88	1 × 92	1 × 70
2 × 15	2 × 44	2 × 46	2 × 35
3 × 10	4 × 22	4 × 23	5 × 14
5 × 6	8 × 11		7 × 10

80	56	48	64
1 × 80	1 × 56	1 × 48	1 × 64
2 × 40	2 × 28	2 × 24	2 × 32
4 × 20	4 × 14	3 × 16	4 × 16
5 × 16	7 × 8	4 × 12	8 × 8
8 × 10		6 × 8	

LESSON 46 Practice

List all factor pairs of each number.

18	49	32	54
1 × 18	1 × 49	1 × 32	1 × 54
2 × 9	7 × 7	2 × 16	2 × 27
3 × 6		4 × 8	3 × 18
			6 × 9

66	75	40	98
1 × 66	1 × 75	1 × 40	1 × 98
2 × 33	3 × 25	2 × 20	2 × 49
3 × 22	5 × 15	4 × 10	7 × 14
6 × 11		5 × 8	

52	42	28	24
1 × 52	1 × 42	1 × 28	1 × 24
2 × 26	2 × 21	2 × 14	2 × 12
4 × 13	3 × 14	4 × 7	3 × 8
	6 × 7		4 × 6

90	60	72	84
1 × 90	1 × 60	1 × 72	1 × 84
2 × 45	2 × 30	2 × 36	2 × 42
3 × 30	3 × 20	3 × 24	3 × 28
5 × 18	4 × 15	4 × 18	4 × 21
6 × 15	5 × 12	6 × 12	6 × 14
9 × 10	6 × 10	8 × 9	7 × 12

Today's lesson is on finding factor pairs. They will use those divisibility rules to help them do this more quickly. A factor divides evenly into a given number. They will be looking for all the multiplication facts that will give a certain answer. Each number used will be a factor of the number.

They don't need to list the second version of a pair, only 2 x 3 not 3 x 2 as well. They will start with 1, move to 2, but once the first number is larger than the second number (example: 3 x 2), they can stop. They will have already found all the factors.

Lesson 47

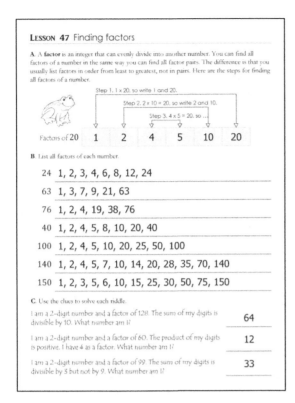

LESSON 47 Finding factors

A. A **factor** is an integer that can evenly divide into another number. You can find all factors of a number in the same way you can find all factor pairs. The difference is that you usually list factors in order from least to greatest, not in pairs. Here are the steps for finding all factors of a number.

Step 1. 1 x 20, so write 1 and 20.

Step 2. 2 x 10 = 20, so write 2 and 10.

Step 3. 4 x 5 = 20, so ...

Factors of 20   1   2   4   5   10   20

B. List all factors of each number.

24	1, 2, 3, 4, 6, 8, 12, 24
63	1, 3, 7, 9, 21, 63
76	1, 2, 4, 19, 38, 76
40	1, 2, 4, 5, 8, 10, 20, 40
100	1, 2, 4, 5, 10, 20, 25, 50, 100
140	1, 2, 4, 5, 7, 10, 14, 20, 28, 35, 70, 140
150	1, 2, 3, 5, 6, 10, 15, 25, 30, 50, 75, 150

C. Use the clues to solve each riddle.

I am a 2-digit number and a factor of 128. The sum of my digits is divisible by 10. What number am I? — **64**

I am a 2-digit number and a factor of 60. The product of my digits is positive. I have 4 as a factor. What number am I? — **12**

I am a 2-digit number and a factor of 99. The sum of my digits is divisible by 3 but not by 9. What number am I? — **33**

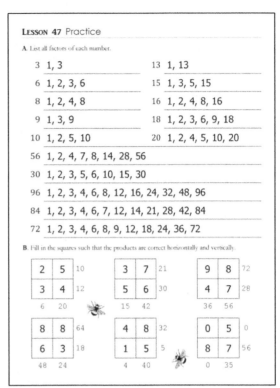

LESSON 47 Practice

A. List all factors of each number.

3	1, 3	13	1, 13
6	1, 2, 3, 6	15	1, 3, 5, 15
8	1, 2, 4, 8	16	1, 2, 4, 8, 16
9	1, 3, 9	18	1, 2, 3, 6, 9, 18
10	1, 2, 5, 10	20	1, 2, 4, 5, 10, 20
56	1, 2, 4, 7, 8, 14, 28, 56		
30	1, 2, 3, 5, 6, 10, 15, 30		
96	1, 2, 3, 4, 6, 8, 12, 16, 24, 32, 48, 96		
84	1, 2, 3, 4, 6, 7, 12, 14, 21, 28, 42, 84		
72	1, 2, 3, 4, 6, 8, 9, 12, 18, 24, 36, 72		

B. Fill in the squares such that the products are correct horizontally and vertically.

2	5	10
3	4	12
6	20	

3	7	21
5	6	30
15	42	

9	8	72
4	7	28
36	56	

8	8	64
6	3	18
48	24	

4	8	32
1	5	5
4	40	

0	5	0
8	7	56
0	35	

Today's lesson is on finding factor pairs as well. They are just asked to write their answers in a different format. They are going to list the factors of the number instead of writing them like a multiplication fact. Everything still applies. This is the same activity with just a different format.

At the bottom of the page there are some riddles. They will need to use scratch paper to work on these. They aren't as hard as they might seem at first glance. They just need to start finding factors and the answer will become obvious.

On the practice page there is a different sort of puzzle. They are finding factors by looking for numbers that multiply together to give a certain answer. Don't let them skip any of these types of things just because at first glance it might seem harder. It's good for them to think in different ways and to have to approach problems in different ways.

Lesson 48

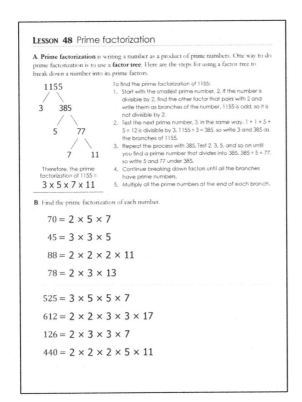

LESSON 48 Prime factorization

A. Prime factorization is writing a number as a product of prime numbers. One way to do prime factorization is to use a factor tree. Here are the steps for using a factor tree to break down a number into its prime factors.

1155

3   385

5   77

7   11

Therefore, the prime factorization of 1155 =

3 × 5 × 7 × 11

To find the prime factorization of 1155:
1. Start with the smallest prime number, 2. If the number is divisible by 2, find the other factor that pairs with 2 and write them as branches of the number. 1155 is odd, so it is not divisible by 2.
2. Test the next prime number, 3, in the same way. 1 + 1 + 5 + 5 = 12 is divisible by 3. 1155 ÷ 3 = 385, so write 3 and 385 as the branches of 1155.
3. Repeat the process with 385. Test 2, 3, 5, and so on until you find a prime number that divides into 385. 385 ÷ 5 = 77, so write 5 and 77 under 385.
4. Continue breaking down factors until all the branches have prime numbers.
5. Multiply all the prime numbers at the end of each branch.

B. Find the prime factorization of each number.

70 = 2 × 5 × 7

45 = 3 × 3 × 5

88 = 2 × 2 × 2 × 11

78 = 2 × 3 × 13

525 = 3 × 5 × 5 × 7

612 = 2 × 2 × 3 × 3 × 17

126 = 2 × 3 × 3 × 7

440 = 2 × 2 × 2 × 5 × 11

LESSON 48 Practice

Find the prime factorization of each number.

35 = 5 × 7

18 = 2 × 3 × 3

52 = 2 × 2 × 13

66 = 2 × 3 × 11

44 = 2 × 2 × 11

75 = 3 × 5 × 5

85 = 5 × 17

60 = 2 × 2 × 3 × 5

546 = 2 × 3 × 7 × 13

245 = 5 × 7 × 7

375 = 3 × 5 × 5 × 5

510 = 2 × 3 × 5 × 17

924 = 2 × 2 × 3 × 7 × 11

882 = 2 × 3 × 3 × 7 × 7

294 = 2 × 3 × 7 × 7

780 = 2 × 2 × 3 × 5 × 13

They are still finding factors today, but of a different sort. This is called prime factorization. Every number can be broken down into multiples of prime numbers.

First they will need to know what prime numbers are, numbers that can only be evenly divided by one and itself. They will be breaking down numbers into digits like 2, 3, 5, 7, and 11. They will just keep breaking apart numbers into factors until they get there. So this time they aren't just looking for factors of the main number, but of each factor itself, until they are all prime.

They will write the answer as a multiplication problem of all prime numbers.

For instance 2 and 4 are factors of 8 apart from eight and one themselves. Two is already a prime number. We would break down four into 2 x 2 and write the prime factorization of 8 as 2 x 2 x 2.

They will figure these out as little trees. They can see the example on their page.

Factors and Multiples

Lesson 49

LESSON 49 Least common multiple (LCM)

A. A **multiple** is a number you get when you multiply by an integer. The times tables are good example of multiples. All answers in the 7 times table are multiples of 7.

B. The **least common multiple (LCM)** of two integers is the smallest positive integer that is a multiple of both integers. One way to find the LCM is to list the multiples of each number until you find the first one in common. Here is an example. Fill in the blanks.

| Multiples of 6 | 6, 12, 18, 24, 30, 36, 42, 48, ... | LCM(6, 8) = |
| Multiples of 8 | 8, 16, 24, 32, 40, 48, 56, ... | 24 |

C. Another method to find the LCM is to use prime factorization. This method works better than the listing method when numbers are large. Here are the steps for using the prime factorization method to find the LCM of two numbers.

```
12 = 2 × 2 × 3
30 = 2 ×     3 × 5
LCM = 2 × 2 × 3 × 5
    = 60
```

To find the LCM of 12 and 30:
1. Write the prime factorization of each number, aligning the common factors vertically.
2. Bring down the factors in each column.
3. Multiply the factors to get the LCM.

D. Find the least common multiple for each number pair.

4 6	12	2 9	18	5 8	40
7 11	77	12 20	60	14 21	42
16 24	48	10 25	50	18 27	54

LESSON 49 Practice

Find the least common multiple for each number pair.

5 7	35	3 9	9	4 13	52
8 12	24	6 14	42	2 28	28
17 51	51	16 40	80	12 21	84
16 22	176	10 15	30	11 20	220
15 35	105	13 17	221	27 36	108
30 80	240	35 42	210	25 60	300

Today we are going to work the other way and multiply instead of divide. This will also help them when they need to work with fractions, which is coming soon.

They are going to find the Least Common Multiple (LCM). A multiple is a product of the number. Multiples of 5 are the answers to 1 x 5, 2 x 5, 3 x 5, etc.

They will use this when they need to add together two fractions or to compare two fractions.

A hint for doing this would be to list the multiples for the biggest number and then look for ones that you know the smaller number divides into. There is also an example on the page of how to use prime factorization to find the LCM.

Sometimes the LCM of two numbers will just be the two numbers multiplied by each other. For instance, the LCM of 6 and 7 is just 6 x 7 = 42. That number will always be a multiple of both numbers, but it's not always the least, and it's easier to work with smaller numbers, which is why they have to think about the LEAST common multiple. It will make their other work easier if they can find it.

Lesson 50

LESSON 50 Greatest common divisor (GCD)

A. The **greatest common divisor (GCD)** of two integers is the largest positive integer that evenly divides both integers. One way to find the GCD is to list all the divisors of each number and find the greatest one in common. Here is an example. Fill in the blanks.

Divisors of 24   1, 2, 3, 4, 6, 8, 12, 24   GCD(24, 36) =

Divisors of 36   1, 2, 3, 4, 6, 9, 12, 18, 36   12

B. Another method to find the GCD is to use prime factorization. This method works better than the listing method when numbers are large. Here are the steps for using the prime factorization method to find the GCD of two numbers.

$$30 = 2 \times 3 \times 5$$
$$70 = 2 \times 5 \times 7$$
$$GCD = 2 \times 5$$
$$= 10$$

To find the GCD of 30 and 70:
1. Write the prime factorization of each number, aligning the common factors vertically.
2. Bring down the common factors only.
3. Multiply the factors to get the GCD.

C. Find the greatest common divisor for each number pair.

6 / 8	2	3 / 9	3	5 / 7	1
4 / 10	2	8 / 44	4	6 / 15	3
12 / 18	6	21 / 35	7	20 / 30	10

3 minutes.

LESSON 50 Practice

Find the greatest common divisor for each number pair.

4 / 6	2	2 / 8	2	6 / 9	3
5 / 20	5	9 / 12	3	4 / 18	2
9 / 33	3	7 / 21	7	8 / 36	4
20 / 35	5	42 / 63	21	12 / 56	4
16 / 52	4	14 / 49	7	28 / 70	14
25 / 30	5	16 / 27	1	45 / 75	15

Today they are flipping back again to finding divisors, numbers that divide evenly into a number. They will be finding factors of the numbers and looking for the highest number they have in common. This is called the Greatest Common Divisor (GCD).

Again, there is a method on their page that shows them how to use prime factorization to find the GCD.

They just need to be careful to find the greatest, the highest number possible and not just any common factor.

They will be using this to reduce fractions which will make their math easier. As such, the goal would be able to look at numbers and see what they have in common, what you could divide both numbers by. They could even see maybe that both could be divided by five and divide them, and then see that they could be divided by three. That would mean that fifteen was the greatest common divisor. It's okay to get at it however works best for your child. The most important thing is to understand what they are doing.

Lesson 51

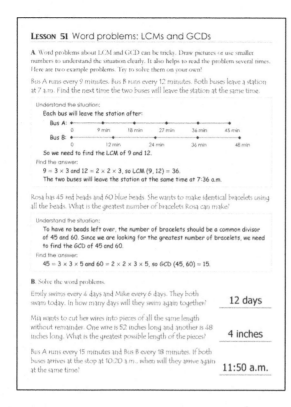

LESSON 51 Word problems: LCMs and GCDs

A. Word problems about LCM and GCD can be tricky. Draw pictures or use smaller numbers to understand the situation clearly. It also helps to read the problem several times. Here are two example problems. Try to solve them on your own!

Bus A runs every 9 minutes. Bus B runs every 12 minutes. Both buses leave a station at 7 a.m. Find the next time the two buses will leave the station at the same time.

Understand the situation:
Each bus will leave the station after:

Bus A: 0, 9 min, 18 min, 27 min, 36 min, 45 min
Bus B: 0, 12 min, 24 min, 36 min, 48 min

So we need to find the LCM of 9 and 12.
Find the answer:
$9 = 3 \times 3$ and $12 = 2 \times 2 \times 3$, so LCM (9, 12) = 36.
The two buses will leave the station at the same time at 7:36 a.m.

Rosa has 45 red beads and 60 blue beads. She wants to make identical bracelets using all the beads. What is the greatest number of bracelets Rosa can make?

Understand the situation:
To have no beads left over, the number of bracelets should be a common divisor of 45 and 60. Since we are looking for the greatest number of bracelets, we need to find the GCD of 45 and 60.
Find the answer:
$45 = 3 \times 3 \times 5$ and $60 = 2 \times 2 \times 3 \times 5$, so GCD (45, 60) = 15.

B. Solve the word problems.

Emily swims every 4 days and Mike every 6 days. They both swam today. In how many days will they swim again together? — **12 days**

Mia wants to cut her wires into pieces of all the same length without remainder. One wire is 52 inches long and another is 48 inches long. What is the greatest possible length of the pieces? — **4 inches**

Bus A runs every 15 minutes and Bus B every 18 minutes. If both buses arrives at the stop at 10:20 a.m., when will they arrive again at the same time? — **11:50 a.m.**

LESSON 51 Practice

Solve the word problems.

Matt runs a mile every 8 minutes. Jake runs a mile every 6 minutes. They start running around a 1-mile track. How long will it be before they meet at the starting point? — **24 minutes**

Sam wants to make a game board using square tiles. The board is 18 inches by 24 inches. If he uses the largest tile possible, how many tiles will he use? — **12 tiles**

A gear with 40 teeth is engaged with another gear with 30 teeth. How many turns must the first gear make for the two gears to return to their original positions? — **3 turns**

In the United States, representatives are elected every 2 years. The president is elected every 4 years. Both were elected in 2016. When is the next year after 2016 that both will be elected? — **2020**

Dana is making fruit baskets using 21 apples and 14 peaches. She wants to make identical baskets with no fruit left over. If she makes the greatest number of fruit baskets possible, how many peaches will be in each basket? — **2 peaches**

A store had a grand opening event. Every 50th customer received $100. Every 30th customer received free movie tickets. How many customers had to arrive before one of them received both $100 and free tickets? — **150 customers**

Jerry is making treat bags for his friends. He has 36 cookies and 24 candies, and he wants to use them all. If he makes the greatest number of identical bags possible, how many cookies will be in each bag? — **3 cookies**

The teacher divides 25 boys and 35 girls into groups of the same size, and each group has the same number of boys and the same number of girls. If the teacher makes the greatest number of groups possible, how many girls will be in each group? — **7 girls**

They are going to be using LCM and GCD to solve word problems. They need to look for clues. If they are being asked to find the largest number of something, they should find the greatest common divisor for the numbers. If they are being asked to find the next time something will happen, they are asking for the lowest number possible, the least common multiple.

They will look for the clues largest or greatest to know to find the greatest common denominator, and in the others they will find the least common multiple. They should always read the question after they find the answer to see if their answer makes sense.

Each of their three word problems on the lesson page will match up to one of the examples on the page.

Lesson 52

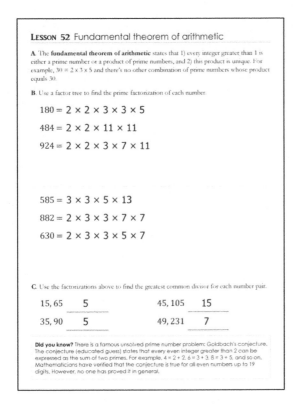

LESSON 52 Fundamental theorem of arithmetic

A. The **fundamental theorem of arithmetic** states that 1) every integer greater than 1 is either a prime number or a product of prime numbers, and 2) this product is unique. For example, $30 = 2 \times 3 \times 5$ and there's no other combination of prime numbers whose product equals 30.

B. Use a factor tree to find the prime factorization of each number.

$$180 = 2 \times 2 \times 3 \times 3 \times 5$$
$$484 = 2 \times 2 \times 11 \times 11$$
$$924 = 2 \times 2 \times 3 \times 7 \times 11$$

$$585 = 3 \times 3 \times 5 \times 13$$
$$882 = 2 \times 3 \times 3 \times 7 \times 7$$
$$630 = 2 \times 3 \times 3 \times 5 \times 7$$

C. Use the factorizations above to find the greatest common divisor for each number pair.

15, 65	5	45, 105	15
35, 90	5	49, 231	7

Did you know? There is a famous unsolved prime number problem: Goldbach's conjecture. The conjecture (educated guess) states that every even integer greater than 2 can be expressed as the sum of two primes. For example, $4 = 2 + 2$, $6 = 3 + 3$, $8 = 3 + 5$, and so on. Mathematicians have verified that the conjecture is true for all even numbers up to 19 digits. However, no one has proved it in general.

LESSON 52 Practice

A. Use a factor tree to find the prime factorization of each number.

$$126 = 2 \times 3 \times 3 \times 7$$
$$140 = 2 \times 2 \times 5 \times 7$$
$$351 = 3 \times 3 \times 3 \times 13$$

$$975 = 3 \times 5 \times 5 \times 13$$
$$308 = 2 \times 2 \times 7 \times 11$$
$$665 = 5 \times 7 \times 19$$

$$243 = 3 \times 3 \times 3 \times 3 \times 3$$
$$200 = 2 \times 2 \times 2 \times 5 \times 5$$
$$726 = 2 \times 3 \times 11 \times 11$$

B. Use the factorizations above to find the greatest common divisor for each number pair.

35, 65	5	50, 140	10
27, 39	3	77, 121	11
19, 81	1	126, 154	14

Today they will be using prime factorization again, but they should first read the top of the page about the fundamental theorem of arithmetic. It says that each prime factorization is unique, every number has a unique factorization.

A theorem in math is a proven statement. It's been proven to always be true. In high school math they will learn to prove things, to use math to show that something is true. In college it took me a couple of pages to prove that $1 + 1 = 2$. It's trickier than you might think! At the bottom of their page it talks about a math hypothesis. Everyone is pretty sure it is true, but it's never been proven. In science we prove something true by just doing it a bunch of times and getting the same result. That doesn't work for math. It's much more rigorous. They would prove it with things like $a + b = c$, to show that it would work for any number. By the way, sometimes scientific theories are later proven wrong. While math ideas have been wrong, theorems are never later found false, they truly prove themselves.

Lesson 53

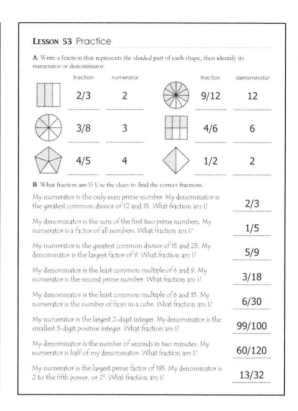

They are starting a new section today, fractions. These don't have to be hard. They are starting simple, just like they started with 1 + 1 in the addition section. With any new subject, getting the vocabulary is half the battle. Use the terms numerator and denominator instead of top and bottom number to help your child get comfortable with them.

The denominator is the total number of parts. The numerator is the number of parts we're working with. I searched online for the root word meanings of these vocabulary words, and this is what I found at http://mathforum.org/dr.math/. The definitions below are from *The Words of Mathematics*, by Steven Schwartzman.

A numerator is literally "a numberer." In arithmetic, the numerator of a fraction gives the number of parts being considered, where each part is an equal fraction of the whole. Since the numerator tells you how many parts you have, when you add fractions you add only numerators, never denominators...

Denominator [is] from Latin de and nomen, "name,"... In arithmetic the denominator of a fraction names the kind of thing you're dealing with. In the fraction 3/5, for example, you have three fifths, just the way you could have three sheep or three apples or three of any other thing... Since the denominator names the sort of a thing you're dealing with, you must have a common denominator when you add fractions; otherwise it's like trying to add sheep and apples...

Lesson 54

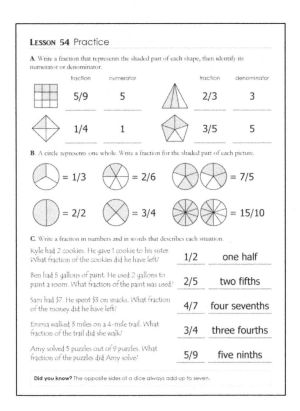

LESSON 54 Identifying fraction parts

A. Fractions are used in daily life to express information about wholes and parts. Read each situation below and write a fraction that describes the situation.

A pizza was cut into 8 equal pieces. Jerry ate 3 pieces of the pizza for dinner. What fraction of the pizza did Jerry eat? **3/8**

Elizabeth went for a run on a 5-mile trail. She ran 3 miles and walked the rest. What fraction of the trail did Elizabeth walk? **2/5**

Matthew solved 10 fraction problems and got 9 correct. What fraction of the problems did Matthew get correct? **9/10**

Eighteen people were expected to come to Olivia's party. Fifteen people came. What fraction of the people missed the party? **3/18**

There are 15 children in Paul's book club. Eight of them are boys. What fraction of the children are girls? **7/15**

There are 7 milk chocolates and 9 dark chocolates in a box. What fraction of the chocolates in the box are dark chocolates? **9/16**

B. When you read fractions, you first read the numerator as a whole number and then read the denominator as an ordinal number. If the numerator is greater than 1, the ordinal number becomes plural. Exceptions are the denominators 2 and 4. The denominator 2 is read "half" instead of "second." The denominator 4 is read "quarter" as well as "fourth." Here are some examples. Say each fraction out loud.

$\frac{1}{3}$ one third $\frac{2}{5}$ two fifths $\frac{1}{2}$ one half $\frac{3}{4}$ three fourths / three quarters

C. Write each fraction in numbers or in words.

two thirds = 2/3   five sixths = 5/6 $\frac{3}{10}$ = three tenths

five halves = 5/2   six eighths = 6/8   1/7 = one seventh

one fourth = 1/4   four fifths = 4/5 $^2/_9$ = two ninths

LESSON 54 Practice

A. Write a fraction that represents the shaded part of each shape, then identify its numerator or denominator.

fraction	numerator	fraction	denominator
5/9	5	2/3	3
1/4	1	3/5	5

B. A circle represents one whole. Write a fraction for the shaded part of each picture.

= 1/3   = 2/6   = 7/5

= 2/2   = 3/4   = 15/10

C. Write a fraction in numbers and in words that describes each situation.

Kyle had 2 cookies. He gave 1 cookie to his sister. What fraction of the cookies did he have left? **1/2 one half**

Ben had 5 gallons of paint. He used 2 gallons to paint a room. What fraction of the paint was used? **2/5 two fifths**

Sam had $7. He spent $3 on snacks. What fraction of the money did he have left? **4/7 four sevenths**

Emma walked 3 miles on a 4-mile trail. What fraction of the trail did she walk? **3/4 three fourths**

Amy solved 5 puzzles out of 9 puzzles. What fraction of the puzzles did Amy solve? **5/9 five ninths**

Did you know? The opposite sides of a dice always add up to seven.

They are identifying the numerator and denominator today. This is practice for setting up word problems, which in turn is practice for solving problems they will face in the real world.

There is also practice for using fraction words. They are supposed to read some out loud and they will have to write some.

Sometimes you'll see fractions hyphenated. In a sentence like, "You'll need two-thirds cup of flour," the fraction acts as an adjective and is hyphenated just as you would others such as, puppy-dog eyes.

Lesson 55

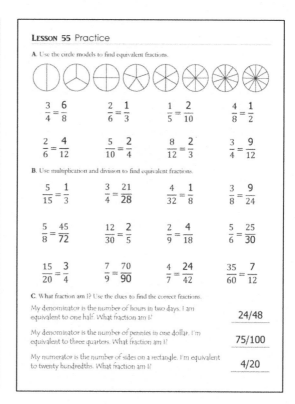

LESSON 55 Equivalent fractions

A. Fractions are **equivalent** if they represent the same amount. One way to find equivalent fractions is to use visual models (draw pictures). Here are some examples. Compare the rectangular strips and find the equal fraction in each example.

$$\frac{1}{2} = \frac{2}{4} \qquad \frac{2}{3} = \frac{4}{6}$$

B. Another way to find equivalent fractions is to use multiplication or division. You multiply or divide the numerator and the denominator by the same number. Here are some examples of using this method to find equal fractions. Complete the examples.

$$\frac{3}{4} = \frac{3 \times 5}{4 \times 5} = \frac{15}{20} \qquad \frac{6}{18} = \frac{6 \div 6}{18 \div 6} = \frac{1}{3}$$

C. Find an equivalent fraction for each fraction.

$$\frac{1}{2} = \frac{4}{8} \qquad \frac{3}{7} = \frac{9}{21} \qquad \frac{12}{20} = \frac{6}{10} \qquad \frac{3}{4} = \frac{12}{16}$$

$$\frac{18}{24} = \frac{3}{4} \qquad \frac{2}{3} = \frac{6}{9} \qquad \frac{3}{9} = \frac{24}{72} \qquad \frac{10}{60} = \frac{1}{6}$$

$$\frac{5}{6} = \frac{15}{18} \qquad \frac{9}{18} = \frac{3}{6} \qquad \frac{35}{56} = \frac{5}{8} \qquad \frac{4}{5} = \frac{20}{25}$$

D. Write at least three equivalent fractions for each fraction.

$$\frac{3}{5} \qquad \text{Answers will vary.} \qquad \frac{20}{40}$$

$$\frac{2}{7} \qquad\qquad \frac{60}{90}$$

LESSON 55 Practice

A. Use the circle models to find equivalent fractions.

$$\frac{3}{4} = \frac{6}{8} \qquad \frac{2}{6} = \frac{1}{3} \qquad \frac{1}{5} = \frac{2}{10} \qquad \frac{4}{8} = \frac{1}{2}$$

$$\frac{2}{6} = \frac{4}{12} \qquad \frac{5}{10} = \frac{2}{4} \qquad \frac{8}{12} = \frac{2}{3} \qquad \frac{3}{4} = \frac{9}{12}$$

B. Use multiplication and division to find equivalent fractions.

$$\frac{5}{15} = \frac{1}{3} \qquad \frac{3}{4} = \frac{21}{28} \qquad \frac{4}{32} = \frac{1}{8} \qquad \frac{3}{8} = \frac{9}{24}$$

$$\frac{5}{8} = \frac{45}{72} \qquad \frac{12}{30} = \frac{2}{5} \qquad \frac{2}{9} = \frac{4}{18} \qquad \frac{5}{6} = \frac{25}{30}$$

$$\frac{15}{20} = \frac{3}{4} \qquad \frac{7}{9} = \frac{70}{90} \qquad \frac{4}{7} = \frac{24}{42} \qquad \frac{35}{60} = \frac{7}{12}$$

C. What fraction am I? Use the clues to find the correct fractions.

My denominator is the number of hours in two days. I am equivalent to one half. What fraction am I? 24/48

My denominator is the number of pennies in one dollar. I'm equivalent to three quarters. What fraction am I? 75/100

My numerator is the number of sides on a rectangle. I'm equivalent to twenty hundredths. What fraction am I? 4/20

They are going to start manipulating the fractions today by finding equivalent fractions. See if your child can find the root of the word equivalent and figure out what it is related to. Equivalent is related to the word equal. They should have seen these before. Equivalent fractions are equal fractions. Knowing their multiplication and division facts will come in handy!

There are two examples at the top of their page. You can make sure they understand what the pictures are showing. The two bars on the left both show one half. One is divided into two parts with one part shaded. The other is divided into four parts with two parts shaded. However, they both have half of the bar colored in. You can easily see that the amounts are the same. The second example on the right is similar with two thirds and four sixths.

To find an equivalent fraction, you multiply or divide the numerator and denominator by the same number. Let me tell you why. You can have them color in the rest of the ½ bar at the top of the page. Now how much is colored in? Two out of two, the whole thing, one whole. Any fraction where the numerator and denominator are the same equals one. Make sure your child knows that. Then ask what does any number times one equal or divided by one equal? It's just the number. It doesn't change.

That's what's happening when they find an equivalent fraction. They are just multiplying or dividing by one. It doesn't change the amount. The answer will be equal. The numbers will change, but by multiplying the numerator and denominator by the same number, they are really just multiplying by one, giving them an equal, equivalent fraction.

Lesson 56

LESSON 56 Word problems: equivalent fractions

A. To solve word problems involving fractions, first identify the relationship among the given numbers. Which number represents a whole? Which number represents part of a whole? Which fractions should be equivalent? Use this information to solve the problems. Below is an example problem. Try to solve it on your own before reading the solution.

Jenny has $50. She wants to donate one fifth of her money to charity. How many dollars should she donate? $10

Identify the relationship among the numbers:
  A whole = The money Jenny has
  Part of a whole = The money Jenny wants to donate
  The fraction of the money Jenny wants to donate is 1/5. That is,

$$\frac{The\ amount\ of\ the\ money\ Jenny\ wants\ to\ donate}{The\ amount\ of\ the\ money\ Jenny\ has} = \frac{1}{5}$$

Now all we have to do is find a fraction equivalent to 1/5 whose denominator is 50. The numerator of that fraction is our answer.

Find the answer:
$\frac{a}{50} = \frac{1}{5}$, and $a = 10$. Therefore, Jenny should donate $10.

B. Solve the word problems.

Ray has $36. He wants to save one fourth of his money for a trip. How many dollars should he save? $9

Sarah had $48. She spent one sixth of her money to buy a magazine. How many dollars did she spend? $8

Wendy had 39 candies. She wants to give one third of the candies to her sister. How many candies should she give?   13 candies

Sam made a fruit basket using 16 pieces of fruit. Three quarters of the fruits were apples. How many apples were in the basket?   12 apples

Mark has a 49-foot rope. He needs two sevenths of the rope for his art project. How many feet of rope should he cut?   14 feet

Leo collected 110 stamps. Two fifths of the stamps were from other countries. How many stamps were from other countries?   44 stamps

LESSON 56 Practice

A. What fraction am I? Use the clues to find the correct fractions.

I'm equivalent to 2/3. My denominator is 15. What fraction am I?   10/15

I'm equivalent to 1/2. My numerator is 9. What fraction am I?   9/18

I'm equivalent to 3/5. My numerator is 12. What fraction am I?   12/20

I'm equivalent to 7/3. My denominator is 33. What fraction am I?   77/33

I'm equivalent to 8/5. My numerator is 80. What fraction am I?   80/50

B. Circle all fractions that are equivalent to the first one in each row.

$\frac{9}{15}$	$\frac{7}{10}$	$\frac{45}{75}$	$\frac{18}{45}$	$\frac{3}{5}$	$\frac{12}{30}$	$\frac{27}{45}$	$\frac{45}{60}$	$\frac{18}{30}$
$\frac{6}{12}$	$\frac{3}{6}$	$\frac{15}{21}$	$\frac{1}{2}$	$\frac{30}{60}$	$\frac{12}{24}$	$\frac{4}{9}$	$\frac{18}{36}$	$\frac{12}{18}$
$\frac{45}{60}$	$\frac{9}{12}$	$\frac{60}{150}$	$\frac{3}{4}$	$\frac{90}{120}$	$\frac{30}{90}$	$\frac{15}{20}$	$\frac{20}{30}$	$\frac{135}{180}$

C. Solve the word problems.

A toy car is on sale. The regular price is $15, and the sale price is one third of the regular price. What is the sale price? Adam had $20, and he bought three toy cars at the sale price. What fraction of his money did he spend? $5   15/20

The math class lasts five sixths of an hour, and Danny spent three tenths of the class solving fraction problems. How many minutes long is the math class? How many minutes did Danny spent solving fraction problems?   50 minutes   15 minutes

This is a page of fraction word problems. They will start like they did for lesson two, with identifying the parts of the fraction. Then they will find an equivalent fraction to find the answer. There is an example on their page that they should take the time to walk through.

Here is the set up for the word problems on the lesson page.

¼ = 9/36 because 4 x 9 = 36 and 1 x 9 = 9

1/6 = 8/48 because 6 x 8 = 48 and 1 x 8 = 8 Really, they could just divide 48 by 6.

1/3 = 13/39 because 3 x 13 = 39 and 1 x 13 = 13

¾ = 12/16 because 4 x 4 = 16 and 3 x 4 = 12

2/7 = 14/49 because 7 x 7 = 49 and 2 x 7 = 14

2/5 = 44/110 because 5 x 22 = 110 and 2 x 22 = 44

Fractions

Lesson 57

LESSON 57 Comparing fractions

A. To compare fractions with like denominators, compare the numerators. When the denominators are the same, the fraction with the larger numerator is the larger fraction. The following examples demonstrate this visually. Compare the fractions using <, >, or =.

$\frac{1}{3} < \frac{2}{3}$ $\frac{4}{5} > \frac{3}{5}$

B. To compare fractions with like numerators, compare the denominators. When the numerators are the same, the fraction with the smaller denominator is the larger fraction. The following examples demonstrate this visually. Compare the fractions using <, >, or =.

$\frac{3}{8} < \frac{3}{5}$ $\frac{1}{2} > \frac{1}{10}$

C. Equivalent fractions have the same value, which means you can compare fractions by comparing their equivalent fractions. The following example compares fractions with unlike numerators and denominators using equivalent fractions. Complete the example.

$\frac{28}{49}$? $\frac{15}{35}$ ⟹ $\frac{28 \div 7}{49 \div 7}$ and $\frac{15 \div 5}{35 \div 5}$ ⟹ $\frac{4}{7} > \frac{3}{7}$

D. Compare the fractions. Find and compare equivalent fractions if necessary.

$\frac{2}{3} > \frac{1}{3}$ $\frac{2}{6} > \frac{2}{9}$ $\frac{15}{21} = \frac{10}{14}$

$\frac{1}{4} = \frac{2}{8}$ $\frac{3}{8} < \frac{5}{8}$ $\frac{18}{12} > \frac{12}{16}$

$\frac{4}{9} < \frac{7}{9}$ $\frac{3}{2} > \frac{3}{8}$ $\frac{25}{35} > \frac{20}{36}$

LESSON 57 Practice

A. Find an equivalent fraction for each fraction.

$\frac{3}{7} = \frac{6}{14}$ $\frac{15}{40} = \frac{3}{8}$ $\frac{5}{8} = \frac{15}{24}$ $\frac{3}{4} = \frac{9}{12}$

$\frac{18}{27} = \frac{6}{9}$ $\frac{2}{5} = \frac{12}{30}$ $\frac{20}{28} = \frac{10}{14}$ $\frac{36}{63} = \frac{12}{21}$

B. Compare the fractions. Find and compare equivalent fractions if necessary.

$\frac{3}{5} > \frac{3}{8}$ $\frac{2}{3} = \frac{4}{6}$ $\frac{9}{21} < \frac{20}{35}$

$\frac{5}{7} < \frac{9}{7}$ $\frac{3}{4} > \frac{3}{5}$ $\frac{9}{15} > \frac{18}{45}$

$\frac{1}{2} < \frac{5}{8}$ $\frac{4}{8} < \frac{3}{4}$ $\frac{40}{16} = \frac{30}{12}$

$\frac{7}{9} < \frac{7}{8}$ $\frac{1}{6} < \frac{2}{6}$ $\frac{11}{12} > \frac{11}{15}$

$\frac{2}{4} > \frac{2}{7}$ $\frac{3}{9} = \frac{1}{3}$ $\frac{17}{15} = \frac{34}{30}$

Today they are comparing fractions using the greater than and less than symbols and the equal sign. > < = The big end opens to the bigger number!

They can see in the top line that when the denominators are the same, the fraction with the greater numerator is greater. That should make perfect sense. It's just like someone eating more slices of pizza than someone else.

In the second line of pictures they can see that when the numerators are equal, whichever denominator is smaller, that fraction is the greatest. That should make sense too. One jumbo slice is more than one little-kid slice of pizza.

Whenever the fractions have the same numerator or denominator, they should be able to think their way to the answer without doing anything. Otherwise, they can find equivalent fractions to give them equal denominators (or numerators) to be able to compare them.

It's great to find equivalent fractions, but it's just as great if they can think their way to the answers without doing the math. Don't force the math. Figuring it out (not guessing) shows that they understand the numbers they are looking at, and that is a good thing. For instance, 3/2 is greater than one so any fraction less than one will be less than three halves. The last one in the corner has 35 and 36 as the denominators. They are large and close together. The pieces aren't that different in size. The smaller denominator has the larger numerator, so that's going to be the larger number. If they don't use math, have them explain how they know the answer.

Lesson 58

LESSON 58 Simplifying fractions

A. Simplifying fractions means to make the fraction as simple as possible. It is also called reducing since you make the numerator and denominator as small as possible without changing the value of the fraction. In other words, simplifying a fraction is finding an equivalent fraction with the smallest possible numerator and denominator. This equivalent fraction is called the simplest form, simplest terms, or lowest terms.

B. To simplify fractions, divide the numerator and denominator by their greatest common divisor (GCD). Here is an example of using this method. Complete the example.

$$\frac{60}{84} \Rightarrow \begin{matrix} 60 = 2 \times 2 \times 3 \times 5 \\ 84 = 2 \times 2 \times 3 \times 7 \\ GCD = 2 \times 2 \times 3 = 12 \end{matrix} \Rightarrow \frac{60 \div 12}{84 \div 12} = \frac{5}{7}$$

C. Another way to simplify fractions is to keep dividing the numerator and denominator by a common divisor until you can't divide them any further. Here is an example of reducing a fraction through this process. Complete the example.

$$\frac{42}{210} \Rightarrow \frac{42 \div 3}{210 \div 3} = \frac{14 \div 7}{70 \div 7} = \frac{2 \div 2}{10 \div 2} = \frac{1}{5}$$

D. Simplify (or reduce) each fraction to its lowest terms.

$$\frac{16}{22} = \frac{8}{11} \qquad \frac{12}{16} = \frac{3}{4} \qquad \frac{18}{30} = \frac{3}{5}$$

$$\frac{40}{72} = \frac{5}{9} \qquad \frac{36}{28} = \frac{9}{7} \qquad \frac{15}{45} = \frac{1}{3}$$

$$\frac{24}{108} = \frac{2}{9}$$

$$\frac{315}{405} = \frac{7}{9}$$

LESSON 58 Practice

Write each fraction in its simplest form.

$$\frac{8}{18} = \frac{4}{9} \qquad \frac{10}{14} = \frac{5}{7} \qquad \frac{16}{20} = \frac{4}{5}$$

$$\frac{9}{15} = \frac{3}{5} \qquad \frac{12}{27} = \frac{4}{9} \qquad \frac{35}{40} = \frac{7}{8}$$

$$\frac{6}{20} = \frac{3}{10} \qquad \frac{28}{32} = \frac{7}{8} \qquad \frac{21}{28} = \frac{3}{4}$$

$$\frac{9}{36} = \frac{1}{4} \qquad \frac{25}{45} = \frac{5}{9} \qquad \frac{13}{39} = \frac{1}{3}$$

$$\frac{7}{42} = \frac{1}{6} \qquad \frac{14}{49} = \frac{2}{7} \qquad \frac{48}{80} = \frac{3}{5}$$

$$\frac{90}{315} = \frac{2}{7}$$

$$\frac{64}{200} = \frac{8}{25}$$

$$\frac{140}{448} = \frac{5}{16}$$

They are going to be reducing fractions, finding an equivalent fraction with the smallest denominator.

There are two examples on the page. They found the greatest common divisor before. The first example uses prime factorization to find the GCD to divide by. I really don't expect anyone to write all that out unless that really helps your child think this through. They should still look at the example though, a little review.

Again, knowing their facts is the best way to make this as easy as possible. If your child doesn't know their facts, let them use a calculator to work on these. It won't change anything. They will still need to figure it out for themselves.

The second example shows dividing by what you can until you know the answer. That's how they would use a calculator.

Lesson 59

LESSON 59 Comparing fractions

A. To compare fractions with unlike denominators, make the denominators the same and then compare the numerators. One way to make the denominators the same is to use the least common multiple (LCM) as the new denominator. The following examples find the LCM by listing multiples and by using prime factorization. Complete the examples.

$$\frac{2}{6} \; ? \; \frac{4}{9} \implies \begin{array}{l} \text{Multiples of 6: 12, 18, 24, ...} \\ \text{Multiples of 9: 18, 27, 36, ...} \\ \text{Common Multiples: 18, 36, 54, ...} \end{array} \implies \frac{6}{18} < \frac{8}{18}$$

$$\frac{1}{12} \; ? \; \frac{3}{25} \implies \begin{array}{l} 12 = 2 \times 2 \times 3 \\ 25 = 5 \times 5 \\ \text{LCM} = 2 \times 2 \times 3 \times 5 \times 5 \end{array} \implies \frac{25}{300} < \frac{36}{300}$$

B. When you make the denominators the same, you can actually use any common multiple as a new denominator. The following example finds a new denominator by simply multiplying two denominators. Complete the example.

$$\frac{2}{6} \; ? \; \frac{4}{9} \implies \frac{2 \times 9}{6 \times 9} \; \text{and} \; \frac{4 \times 6}{9 \times 6} \implies \frac{18}{54} < \frac{24}{54}$$

D. Compare the fractions.

$$\frac{1}{3} < \frac{2}{5} \qquad \frac{4}{5} > \frac{2}{9} \qquad \frac{8}{12} < \frac{12}{16}$$

$$\frac{4}{7} < \frac{5}{6} \qquad \frac{3}{8} < \frac{5}{6} \qquad \frac{7}{15} > \frac{6}{21}$$

$$\frac{1}{2} = \frac{4}{8} \qquad \frac{2}{3} > \frac{4}{7} \qquad \frac{5}{18} > \frac{7}{30}$$

LESSON 59 Practice

Compare the fractions.

$$\frac{4}{5} > \frac{5}{8} \qquad \frac{3}{4} = \frac{6}{8} \qquad \frac{5}{25} < \frac{3}{10}$$

$$\frac{2}{3} = \frac{6}{9} \qquad \frac{2}{5} < \frac{2}{3} \qquad \frac{6}{18} = \frac{5}{15}$$

$$\frac{4}{7} > \frac{1}{2} \qquad \frac{3}{5} > \frac{4}{7} \qquad \frac{9}{14} > \frac{11}{35}$$

$$\frac{2}{4} = \frac{3}{6} \qquad \frac{4}{9} < \frac{3}{5} \qquad \frac{7}{40} > \frac{8}{50}$$

$$\frac{1}{3} < \frac{2}{5} \qquad \frac{3}{8} > \frac{2}{6} \qquad \frac{5}{12} > \frac{7}{22}$$

$$\frac{7}{9} > \frac{3}{4} \qquad \frac{1}{4} > \frac{2}{9} \qquad \frac{20}{45} = \frac{16}{36}$$

They will be comparing fractions again today, but this time they will need to find equivalent fractions to be sure of the answer.

The two examples on the page are the same example done two different ways. One uses the LCM, the least common multiple, to make equivalent fractions with the smallest denominator possible. This is the best practice, though they don't need to use prime factorization to find it. They should just think about what the denominators are both multiples of. 6 => 12, 18   9 => 18 They both have 18 as a multiple. Eighteen is the least common multiple.

When they will be using equivalent fractions to solve math problems, they will want to be working with the smallest numbers possible. It will make it easier. The LCM will give that to them. For today, however, they are just needing to compare the numbers. The second example on the page shows how you can always just cross multiply and multiply the numerators by the opposite denominator. Multiplying the two denominators together will always give you a multiple of each.

Lesson 60

LESSON 60 Ordering fractions

A. When ordering fractions with like denominators, order them by their numerators. Here is an example. Order the fractions from least to greatest.

$$\frac{4}{11}, \frac{1}{11}, \frac{7}{11}, \frac{2}{11}, \frac{9}{11} \Rightarrow \frac{1}{11} < \frac{2}{11} < \frac{4}{11} < \frac{7}{11} < \frac{9}{11}$$

B. When ordering fractions with unlike denominators, use the least common multiple (LCM) to find equivalent fractions with like denominators. Then compare the equivalent fractions to order the original fractions. Here is an example of using this method. Follow the steps to complete the example.

First, find the LCM of the denominators using prime factorization:

$$\frac{5}{6}, \frac{3}{4}, \frac{7}{15}, \frac{9}{10}, \frac{5}{12} \Rightarrow$$

$6 = 2 \times 3 \qquad 10 = 2 \times 5$
$4 = 2 \times 2 \qquad 12 = 2 \times 2 \times 3$
$15 = 3 \times 5 \qquad \text{LCM} = 2 \times 2 \times 3 \times 5 = 60$

Second, find equivalent fractions and use them to order the original fractions:

$$\frac{50}{60}, \frac{45}{60}, \frac{28}{60}, \frac{54}{60}, \frac{25}{60} \Rightarrow \frac{5}{12} < \frac{7}{15} < \frac{3}{4} < \frac{5}{6} < \frac{9}{10}$$

C. Order each set of fractions from least to greatest.

$\frac{1}{2}, \frac{2}{5}, \frac{5}{6}$ $\frac{2}{5}, \frac{1}{2}, \frac{5}{6}$ $\frac{3}{4}, \frac{1}{2}, \frac{5}{8}$ $\frac{1}{2}, \frac{5}{8}, \frac{3}{4}$

$\frac{1}{3}, \frac{2}{9}, \frac{1}{4}$ $\frac{2}{9}, \frac{1}{4}, \frac{1}{3}$ $\frac{3}{7}, \frac{1}{3}, \frac{5}{6}$ $\frac{1}{3}, \frac{3}{7}, \frac{5}{6}$

$\frac{1}{2}, \frac{3}{5}, \frac{4}{10}$ $\frac{4}{10}, \frac{1}{2}, \frac{3}{5}$ $\frac{4}{9}, \frac{7}{12}, \frac{5}{18}$ $\frac{5}{18}, \frac{4}{9}, \frac{7}{12}$

LESSON 60 Practice

Order each set of fractions from least to greatest.

$\frac{1}{9}, \frac{8}{9}, \frac{5}{9}$ $\frac{1}{9}, \frac{5}{9}, \frac{8}{9}$ $\frac{2}{5}, \frac{2}{4}, \frac{2}{7}$ $\frac{2}{7}, \frac{2}{5}, \frac{2}{4}$

$\frac{4}{7}, \frac{1}{2}, \frac{5}{8}$ $\frac{1}{2}, \frac{4}{7}, \frac{5}{8}$ $\frac{4}{5}, \frac{1}{2}, \frac{1}{3}$ $\frac{1}{3}, \frac{1}{2}, \frac{4}{5}$

$\frac{2}{3}, \frac{3}{4}, \frac{5}{9}$ $\frac{5}{9}, \frac{2}{3}, \frac{3}{4}$ $\frac{3}{8}, \frac{5}{7}, \frac{1}{4}$ $\frac{1}{4}, \frac{3}{8}, \frac{5}{7}$

$\frac{2}{6}, \frac{3}{8}, \frac{1}{4}$ $\frac{1}{4}, \frac{2}{6}, \frac{3}{8}$ $\frac{4}{9}, \frac{2}{3}, \frac{5}{12}$ $\frac{5}{12}, \frac{4}{9}, \frac{2}{3}$

$\frac{4}{5}, \frac{5}{6}, \frac{23}{30}$ $\frac{23}{30}, \frac{4}{5}, \frac{5}{6}$ $\frac{3}{5}, \frac{13}{15}, \frac{11}{20}$ $\frac{11}{20}, \frac{3}{5}, \frac{13}{15}$

$\frac{7}{12}, \frac{10}{18}, \frac{3}{4}$ $\frac{10}{18}, \frac{7}{12}, \frac{3}{4}$ $\frac{7}{9}, \frac{11}{12}, \frac{13}{15}$ $\frac{7}{9}, \frac{13}{15}, \frac{11}{12}$

They are comparing fractions in a different way today. They are going to be putting them in order from least to greatest.

The example shows finding the LCM of all of the fractions. Another way to think of it would be to just find multiples of the largest number and see if the other numbers divide into them. They can use their math fact knowledge and the divisibility rules to help them here.

They don't have to follow the example to get the answer, and that is okay. For instance, the first one compares one half, two fifths, and five sixths. You don't have to put them all over a denominator of 30 to compare them. They can find equivalents of one half. Two fours would be one half, so two fifths is less than one half. Three sixths would be one half, so five sixths is greater than one half. There's the order: two fifths, one half, five sixths.

If they don't show any math to figure out the answer, have them explain their thinking. Guessing is not allowed. If they can't tell you why, have them show you the work.

Fractions

Lesson 61

LESSON 61 Types of fractions

A. There are three types of fractions: proper, improper, and mixed fractions. A **proper fraction** is a fraction where the numerator is less than the denominator. An **improper fraction** is a fraction where the numerator is greater than or equal to the denominator. A mixed fraction, or a **mixed number**, is a whole number and a proper fraction combined.

B. To read a mixed number, you use the word "and" between the whole number part and the fraction part. Here are some examples. Say each fraction out loud.

$5\frac{1}{3}$ five and one third $2\frac{3}{5}$ two and three fifths $4\frac{5}{6}$ four and five sixths $1\frac{6}{10}$ one and six tenths

C. The **reciprocal** of a fraction is the fraction turned upside down. The reciprocal of a whole number (except 0) is 1 over the number. Write the reciprocal of each fraction.

$\frac{7}{15}$ $\frac{15}{7}$ $\frac{4}{9}$ $\frac{9}{4}$ 15 $\frac{1}{15}$ $\frac{11}{2}$ $\frac{2}{11}$

D. Classify each fraction as proper, improper, or mixed. Write P for proper fractions, I for improper fractions, and M for mixed fractions.

$\frac{4}{11}$ P	$\frac{14}{9}$ I	$\frac{5}{8}$ P	$\frac{25}{15}$ I
$\frac{16}{16}$ I	$8\frac{1}{2}$ M	$4\frac{7}{9}$ M	$\frac{29}{30}$ P
$1\frac{2}{14}$ M	$\frac{13}{15}$ P	$\frac{16}{12}$ I	$2\frac{3}{5}$ M

E. Circle the fractions whose reciprocal is a proper fraction.

$\frac{12}{10}$ | $\frac{3}{3}$ | $\frac{5}{4}$ | $\frac{21}{10}$ | $\frac{1}{9}$ | $\frac{6}{3}$ | $\frac{15}{60}$ | $\frac{8}{7}$

'1' is most frequent and '0' is least frequent.

LESSON 61 Practice

A. Circle all proper fractions.

$\frac{4}{2}$	$\frac{2}{5}$	$\frac{8}{6}$	$\frac{11}{11}$	$\frac{5}{7}$	$\frac{3}{9}$	$\frac{15}{10}$	$\frac{1}{6}$
$\frac{12}{16}$	$\frac{7}{3}$	$\frac{20}{10}$	$\frac{2}{4}$	$\frac{30}{15}$	$\frac{4}{6}$	$\frac{8}{8}$	$\frac{9}{15}$

B. Circle all improper fractions.

$\frac{6}{5}$	$\frac{2}{3}$	$\frac{2}{10}$	$\frac{15}{9}$	$\frac{2}{8}$	$\frac{8}{7}$	$\frac{15}{15}$	$\frac{4}{6}$
$\frac{4}{2}$	$\frac{8}{8}$	$\frac{1}{5}$	$\frac{5}{7}$	$\frac{12}{6}$	$\frac{3}{4}$	$\frac{7}{10}$	$\frac{5}{3}$

C. Circle all mixed numbers.

$1\frac{7}{3}$	$4\frac{1}{2}$	$\frac{6}{8}$	$1\frac{7}{10}$	$5\frac{3}{4}$	$\frac{11}{9}$	$3\frac{2}{7}$	$2\frac{9}{8}$
$8\frac{2}{5}$	$\frac{3}{21}$	$2\frac{7}{4}$	$5\frac{3}{3}$	$6\frac{7}{9}$	$4\frac{2}{3}$	$\frac{12}{5}$	$1\frac{1}{6}$

D. Write the reciprocal of each fraction.

$\frac{36}{9}$ $\frac{9}{36}$	23 $\frac{1}{23}$	$\frac{10}{6}$ $\frac{6}{10}$	$\frac{14}{12}$ $\frac{12}{14}$
$\frac{8}{16}$ $\frac{16}{8}$	$\frac{21}{7}$ $\frac{7}{21}$	17 $\frac{1}{17}$	$\frac{9}{42}$ $\frac{42}{9}$

8 (7 × 7 = 49, 4 × 9 = 36, 3 × 6 = 18, 1 × 8 = 8)

This is another vocabulary lesson. Use these words when you talk about math. The words are proper fractions, improper fractions, mixed fractions or mixed numbers, and reciprocals.

Proper fractions are the regular ones.

Improper fractions are where the numerator is not less than the denominator. So two halves is an improper fraction.

A mixed number has a whole number and a fraction.

A reciprocal is a fraction upside-down. It's the inverse. The inverse of two is one half. There's an invisible 1 under every whole number. We don't need to write it because two over one just equals two, but we could write it there without changing the value of two. That's just like we could write 2.0000000. It's still equal to two. We just don't because that would be more work. Despite what your child might think, mathematicians like to keep things simple.

Lesson 62

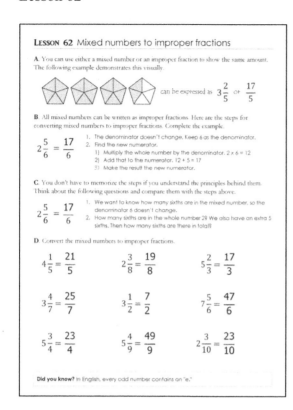

LESSON 62 Mixed numbers to improper fractions

A. You can use either a mixed number or an improper fraction to show the same amount. The following example demonstrates this visually.

can be expressed as $3\frac{2}{5}$ or $\frac{17}{5}$

B. All mixed numbers can be written as improper fractions. Here are the steps for converting mixed numbers to improper fractions. Complete the example.

$2\frac{5}{6} = \frac{17}{6}$

1. The denominator doesn't change. Keep 6 as the denominator.
2. Find the new numerator.
   1) Multiply the whole number by the denominator. 2 x 6 = 12
   2) Add that to the numerator. 12 + 5 = 17
   3) Make the result the new numerator.

C. You don't have to memorize the steps if you understand the principles behind them. Think about the following questions and compare them with the steps above.

$2\frac{5}{6} = \frac{17}{6}$

1. We want to know how many sixths are in the mixed number, so the denominator 6 doesn't change.
2. How many sixths are in the whole number 2? We also have an extra 5 sixths. Then how many sixths are there in total?

D. Convert the mixed numbers to improper fractions.

$4\frac{1}{5} = \frac{21}{5}$ $2\frac{3}{8} = \frac{19}{8}$ $5\frac{2}{3} = \frac{17}{3}$

$3\frac{4}{7} = \frac{25}{7}$ $3\frac{1}{2} = \frac{7}{2}$ $7\frac{5}{6} = \frac{47}{6}$

$5\frac{3}{4} = \frac{23}{4}$ $5\frac{4}{9} = \frac{49}{9}$ $2\frac{3}{10} = \frac{23}{10}$

Did you know? In English, every odd number contains an "e."

LESSON 62 Practice

Convert the mixed numbers to improper fractions.

$7\frac{1}{4} = \frac{29}{4}$ $4\frac{5}{7} = \frac{33}{7}$ $9\frac{1}{3} = \frac{28}{3}$

$8\frac{4}{6} = \frac{52}{6}$ $5\frac{1}{2} = \frac{11}{2}$ $5\frac{7}{8} = \frac{47}{8}$

$3\frac{7}{9} = \frac{34}{9}$ $1\frac{2}{5} = \frac{7}{5}$ $9\frac{6}{7} = \frac{69}{7}$

$6\frac{3}{5} = \frac{33}{5}$ $5\frac{1}{10} = \frac{51}{10}$ $3\frac{7}{11} = \frac{40}{11}$

$2\frac{1}{9} = \frac{19}{9}$ $3\frac{17}{20} = \frac{77}{20}$

$4\frac{5}{8} = \frac{37}{8}$ $5\frac{15}{16} = \frac{95}{16}$

$7\frac{2}{3} = \frac{23}{3}$ $4\frac{22}{25} = \frac{122}{25}$

$9\frac{3}{4} = \frac{39}{4}$ $8\frac{11}{15} = \frac{131}{15}$

Take a look at the example on the top of the page. Have your child count up the little triangles to show that three and two fifths equals seventeen fifths.

The next example, in part B, walks through the math to figure it out. You multiply the denominator and whole number together and add the numerator. They should read through part C. After that, have them look at the drawing and explain how you convert that mixed number into an improper fraction. They can see the three fives there, the three groups of five triangles. They will multiply three by five to save having to count them up. Then there are two more triangles to add on. That's all they are doing.

By the way, the reason to do this is for the sake of future math problems. They will use improper fractions to help them multiply and divide fractions. "Simplest form" means changing an improper fraction into a mixed number, but sometimes an improper fraction is really the simplest form to work with when solving a math problem.

Lesson 63

LESSON 63 Improper fractions to mixed numbers

A. Improper fractions can also be written as mixed numbers. Here are the steps for converting improper fractions to mixed numbers. Complete the example.

$$\frac{17}{5} = 3\frac{2}{5}$$

1. The denominator doesn't change. Keep 5 as the denominator.
2. Find the new whole number and new numerator.
   1) Divide the numerator by the denominator. 17 ÷ 5 = 3 r 2
   2) Make the whole number quotient the new whole number.
   3) Make the remainder the new numerator.

B. As before, you don't have to memorize the steps if you understand the principles behind them. Think about the following questions and compare them with the steps above.

$$\frac{17}{5} = 3\frac{2}{5}$$

1. We want to know how many wholes and fifths are in the improper fraction, so the denominator 5 doesn't change.
2. How many fifths are in one whole? How many wholes are in 17 fifths? How many parts are left over?

C. Convert the improper fractions to mixed numbers.

$$\frac{16}{7} = 2\frac{2}{7} \qquad \frac{13}{2} = 6\frac{1}{2} \qquad \frac{39}{5} = 7\frac{4}{5}$$

$$\frac{45}{6} = 7\frac{3}{6} \qquad \frac{30}{8} = 3\frac{6}{8} \qquad \frac{46}{3} = 15\frac{1}{3}$$

$$\frac{27}{4} = 6\frac{3}{4} \qquad \frac{52}{9} = 5\frac{7}{9} \qquad \frac{37}{10} = 3\frac{7}{10}$$

$$\frac{149}{12} = 12\frac{5}{12}$$

$$\frac{458}{35} = 13\frac{3}{35}$$

LESSON 63 Practice

Convert the improper fractions to mixed numbers.

$$\frac{37}{4} = 9\frac{1}{4} \qquad \frac{23}{2} = 11\frac{1}{2} \qquad \frac{42}{8} = 5\frac{2}{8}$$

$$\frac{48}{9} = 5\frac{3}{9} \qquad \frac{51}{7} = 7\frac{2}{7} \qquad \frac{22}{5} = 4\frac{2}{5}$$

$$\frac{64}{3} = 21\frac{1}{3} \qquad \frac{39}{6} = 6\frac{3}{6} \qquad \frac{43}{4} = 10\frac{3}{4}$$

$$\frac{26}{7} = 3\frac{5}{7} \qquad \frac{19}{12} = 1\frac{7}{12} \qquad \frac{30}{16} = 1\frac{14}{16}$$

$$\frac{29}{8} = 3\frac{5}{8} \qquad \frac{101}{15} = 6\frac{11}{15}$$

$$\frac{17}{2} = 8\frac{1}{2} \qquad \frac{319}{25} = 12\frac{19}{25}$$

$$\frac{43}{5} = 8\frac{3}{5} \qquad \frac{475}{20} = 23\frac{15}{20}$$

$$\frac{80}{9} = 8\frac{8}{9} \qquad \frac{232}{16} = 14\frac{8}{16}$$

Today's lesson is the opposite of Day 62's lesson. They are going to be reversing the steps basically. Instead of multiplying, they will be dividing. Instead of adding, they will be subtracting.

While they can just follow the steps to divide and then place the remainder as the numerator, it's better to understand what's happening. Understanding starts with knowing that a fraction where the numerator and denominator are the same equals one.

To find the answer they can subtract off those "ones," or they can use long division to solve them more "mathematically."

Lesson 64

LESSON 64 Comparing mixed numbers

A. To compare mixed numbers, compare the whole number parts first. The fraction with the larger whole number is the larger fraction. When the whole numbers are the same, compare the fraction parts. The following examples demonstrate this visually. Compare the fractions using <, >, or =.

$2\frac{1}{3} > 1\frac{3}{4}$

$2\frac{2}{3} > 2\frac{1}{4}$

B. Another way to compare mixed numbers is to convert them to improper fractions before comparing. Here is an example of using this method. Complete the example.

$1\frac{3}{4} < 1\frac{4}{5} \Rightarrow \frac{7}{4} < \frac{9}{5} \Rightarrow \frac{35}{20} < \frac{36}{20}$

C. Compare the mixed numbers.

$2\frac{1}{4} < 2\frac{1}{3}$ $5\frac{1}{2} = 5\frac{3}{6}$ $1\frac{2}{5} < 1\frac{3}{5}$

$3\frac{2}{7} > 3\frac{2}{9}$ $1\frac{4}{6} = 1\frac{6}{9}$ $4\frac{7}{8} < 6\frac{1}{8}$

$4\frac{5}{6} > 4\frac{3}{4}$ $6\frac{2}{4} > 2\frac{5}{9}$ $8\frac{6}{7} > 8\frac{4}{5}$

LESSON 64 Practice

Compare the mixed numbers.

$2\frac{3}{8} > 2\frac{1}{3}$ $1\frac{3}{5} < 2\frac{5}{9}$ $3\frac{5}{7} < 3\frac{4}{5}$

$5\frac{3}{4} < 5\frac{5}{6}$ $2\frac{4}{7} > 2\frac{4}{8}$ $1\frac{5}{9} < 1\frac{5}{6}$

$7\frac{2}{5} < 7\frac{2}{4}$ $3\frac{1}{2} < 5\frac{1}{3}$ $4\frac{2}{3} > 4\frac{4}{7}$

$2\frac{2}{3} = 2\frac{4}{6}$ $1\frac{1}{4} > 1\frac{1}{9}$ $7\frac{4}{5} < 8\frac{1}{5}$

$6\frac{1}{7} > 5\frac{3}{7}$ $3\frac{6}{9} > 3\frac{5}{8}$ $2\frac{5}{6} > 2\frac{4}{9}$

$7\frac{1}{2} < 7\frac{3}{5}$ $6\frac{1}{9} < 6\frac{1}{3}$ $5\frac{1}{2} = 5\frac{4}{8}$

This lesson is on comparing mixed numbers. They should be able to spot the answer to the first example easily. If the whole number of one mixed number is greater than the other, then it doesn't matter what the fraction is.

When the whole numbers are the same, then they will be comparing the fractions. They can use their techniques for finding a common denominator. They can also use their brains and figure out which is greater. If the denominators are the same, then they already have a common denominator, and so the numerators can be compared. If the numerators are the same, they can compare the denominators to figure out which is greater. Even though that doesn't use "math," it's more important to understand what the fractions represent and be able to see the comparative size, than to be able to blindly find an answer without understanding.

Lesson 65

LESSON 65 Comparing mixed and improper fractions

A. One way to compare a mixed number to an improper fraction is to convert the mixed number to an improper fraction and compare two improper fractions. Here is an example of using this method. Complete the example.

$$2\frac{1}{4} < \frac{17}{6} \Rightarrow \frac{9}{4} < \frac{17}{6} \Rightarrow \frac{27}{12} < \frac{34}{12}$$

B. Another way to compare a mixed number to an improper fraction is to convert the improper fraction to a mixed number and compare two mixed numbers. This method helps you avoid dealing with large numbers. Complete the example below.

$$2\frac{1}{5} > \frac{17}{8} \Rightarrow 2\frac{1}{5} > 2\frac{1}{8} \Rightarrow \text{The whole number parts are the same, so } \frac{1}{5} > \frac{1}{8}$$

C. Compare the fractions.

$$1\frac{3}{4} > \frac{11}{8} \qquad \frac{19}{4} > 3\frac{5}{6} \qquad 5\frac{2}{3} = \frac{68}{12}$$

$$2\frac{2}{5} < \frac{35}{11} \qquad \frac{15}{5} < 3\frac{1}{8} \qquad 3\frac{5}{9} > \frac{35}{12}$$

$$\frac{29}{13} < 3\frac{1}{7} \qquad 2\frac{1}{5} = \frac{44}{20} \qquad \frac{18}{10} > 1\frac{2}{5}$$

$$4\frac{1}{2} = \frac{27}{6} \qquad \frac{59}{9} < 6\frac{7}{8} \qquad 3\frac{3}{4} > \frac{26}{7}$$

LESSON 65 Practice

Compare the fractions.

$$2\frac{4}{5} < \frac{20}{3} \qquad 2\frac{1}{4} > \frac{13}{6} \qquad \frac{39}{12} = 3\frac{1}{4}$$

$$\frac{24}{7} > 2\frac{5}{6} \qquad 1\frac{8}{9} < \frac{10}{3} \qquad 6\frac{3}{5} > \frac{61}{12}$$

$$1\frac{9}{10} > \frac{17}{9} \qquad 1\frac{3}{9} = \frac{40}{30} \qquad \frac{37}{9} < 4\frac{1}{5}$$

$$\frac{75}{11} < 9\frac{1}{7} \qquad 3\frac{4}{5} > \frac{24}{9} \qquad 4\frac{3}{8} > \frac{13}{3}$$

$$5\frac{8}{12} = \frac{51}{9} \qquad 1\frac{5}{8} < \frac{27}{15} \qquad \frac{45}{7} < 7\frac{3}{6}$$

$$\frac{85}{9} > 6\frac{2}{5} \qquad \frac{60}{7} > 2\frac{11}{14} \qquad \frac{96}{21} = 4\frac{4}{7}$$

This lesson is on comparing mixed numbers and improper fractions. The lesson examples show two different ways to go about it, converting to improper fractions or converting to mixed numbers.

You can encourage them to think about which way would be easier. I think that converting the improper fraction into a mixed number is the easiest way to go about it because if they can figure out that the whole numbers are different, then they don't have worry about the fractions.

When thinking about converting an improper fraction into a mixed number, they can think about doubling the denominator and finding multiples of the denominator, instead of dividing, to figure out the whole number. Here are examples.

Thirty-five elevenths equals three and two elevenths. Eleven three times is thirty-three and 33 + 2 = 35.

Twenty-seven sixths equals four and three sixths. 6 + 6 = 12, 12 + 12 = 24, 24 + 3 = 27.

Lesson 66

LESSON 66 Adding fractions with like denominators

A. To add fractions with like denominators, add the numerators and keep the same denominator. Then simplify the result and convert it to a mixed number, if possible. The following example shows this visually. Complete the example.

$$\frac{2}{9}+\frac{4}{9}=\frac{2+4}{9}=\frac{6}{9}=\frac{2}{3}$$

B. Add the fractions. Simplify and convert your answers to mixed numbers, if possible.

$$\frac{1}{4}+\frac{3}{4}=1 \qquad \frac{2}{15}+\frac{10}{15}=\frac{4}{5}$$

$$\frac{3}{8}+\frac{7}{8}=1\frac{1}{4} \qquad \frac{8}{12}+\frac{6}{12}=1\frac{1}{6}$$

$$\frac{5}{6}+\frac{4}{6}=1\frac{1}{2} \qquad \frac{17}{24}+\frac{9}{24}=1\frac{1}{12}$$

$$\frac{4}{9}+\frac{8}{9}=1\frac{1}{3} \qquad \frac{15}{18}+\frac{12}{18}=1\frac{1}{2}$$

$$\frac{3}{5}+\frac{3}{5}=1\frac{1}{5} \qquad \frac{11}{30}+\frac{14}{30}=\frac{5}{6}$$

$$\frac{3}{28}+\frac{15}{28}+\frac{17}{28}=1\frac{1}{4}$$

$$\frac{34}{45}+\frac{42}{45}+\frac{20}{45}=2\frac{2}{15}$$

LESSON 66 Practice

Add the fractions. Simplify and convert your answers to mixed numbers, if possible.

$$\frac{5}{6}+\frac{5}{6}=1\frac{2}{3} \qquad \frac{9}{16}+\frac{3}{16}=\frac{3}{4}$$

$$\frac{5}{9}+\frac{7}{9}=1\frac{1}{3} \qquad \frac{5}{12}+\frac{11}{12}=1\frac{1}{3}$$

$$\frac{1}{4}+\frac{1}{4}=\frac{1}{2} \qquad \frac{9}{11}+\frac{10}{11}=1\frac{8}{11}$$

$$\frac{6}{7}+\frac{3}{7}=1\frac{2}{7} \qquad \frac{12}{21}+\frac{6}{21}=\frac{6}{7}$$

$$\frac{2}{3}+\frac{2}{3}=1\frac{1}{3} \qquad \frac{17}{60}+\frac{23}{60}=\frac{2}{3}$$

$$\frac{7}{8}+\frac{5}{8}=1\frac{1}{2} \qquad \frac{15}{48}+\frac{37}{48}=1\frac{1}{12}$$

$$\frac{2}{5}+\frac{3}{5}=1 \qquad \frac{17}{32}+\frac{23}{32}=1\frac{1}{4}$$

$$\frac{8}{9}+\frac{7}{9}=1\frac{2}{3} \qquad \frac{24}{25}+\frac{11}{25}=1\frac{2}{5}$$

Today's a simple lesson on adding with a common denominator. There's a picture on the page to help them visualize. While the math is simple to add fractions with like denominators, they should understand why the denominators stay the same. Adding one fifth and one fifth is like adding one apple and one apple. You get two apples, or two fifths. The fifths part is just describing what it is. Here's one more picture. One fifth is like one finger. That's one out of the five fingers on a hand. Holding up a second finger is two fifths, two of the five fingers. The number of fingers on your hand doesn't change.

While they just have to add the numerators, they will still need to simplify their answer. If it's an improper fraction, they need to turn it into a mixed number. They should also reduce the fractions if they can. They can use the divisibility rules to check to see if they can divide the numerator and denominator to make them as low as possible.

Fractions

Lesson 67

LESSON 67 Subtracting fractions with like denominators

A. To subtract fractions with like denominators, subtract the numerators and keep the same denominator. Then simplify the result, if possible. The following example shows this visually. Complete the example.

$$\frac{5}{9} - \frac{2}{9} = \frac{5-2}{9} = \frac{3}{9} = \frac{1}{3}$$

B. Subtract the fractions. Simplify your answers to the lowest terms.

$$\frac{2}{6} - \frac{0}{6} = \frac{1}{3}$$

$$\frac{4}{5} - \frac{2}{5} = \frac{2}{5}$$

$$\frac{6}{7} - \frac{4}{7} = \frac{2}{7}$$

$$\frac{4}{9} - \frac{1}{9} = \frac{1}{3}$$

$$\frac{1}{2} - \frac{1}{2} = 0$$

$$\frac{7}{8} - \frac{3}{8} = \frac{1}{2}$$

$$\frac{5}{6} - \frac{2}{6} = \frac{1}{2}$$

$$\frac{9}{10} - \frac{1}{10} = \frac{4}{5}$$

$$\frac{14}{18} - \frac{8}{18} = \frac{1}{3}$$

$$\frac{14}{15} - \frac{5}{15} = \frac{3}{5}$$

$$\frac{11}{12} - \frac{7}{12} = \frac{1}{3}$$

$$\frac{19}{24} - \frac{9}{24} = \frac{5}{12}$$

$$\frac{28}{45} - \frac{16}{45} = \frac{4}{15}$$

$$\frac{27}{36} - \frac{15}{36} = \frac{1}{3}$$

LESSON 67 Practice

Subtract the fractions. Simplify your answers to the lowest terms.

$$\frac{8}{9} - \frac{3}{9} = \frac{5}{9}$$

$$\frac{4}{6} - \frac{1}{6} = \frac{1}{2}$$

$$\frac{7}{8} - \frac{5}{8} = \frac{1}{4}$$

$$\frac{3}{5} - \frac{2}{5} = \frac{1}{5}$$

$$\frac{5}{7} - \frac{0}{7} = \frac{5}{7}$$

$$\frac{3}{4} - \frac{1}{4} = \frac{1}{2}$$

$$\frac{5}{9} - \frac{2}{9} = \frac{1}{3}$$

$$\frac{4}{8} - \frac{4}{8} = 0$$

$$\frac{10}{12} - \frac{7}{12} = \frac{1}{4}$$

$$\frac{11}{15} - \frac{2}{15} = \frac{3}{5}$$

$$\frac{17}{18} - \frac{8}{18} = \frac{1}{2}$$

$$\frac{13}{14} - \frac{6}{14} = \frac{1}{2}$$

$$\frac{14}{16} - \frac{8}{16} = \frac{3}{8}$$

$$\frac{17}{20} - \frac{5}{20} = \frac{3}{5}$$

$$\frac{29}{33} - \frac{14}{33} = \frac{5}{11}$$

$$\frac{67}{84} - \frac{46}{84} = \frac{1}{4}$$

There is a similar lesson today; they are going to be subtracting fractions with a common denominator. There is an example on the page they should complete to make sure they know what to do.

Just like with addition, the denominator will not change; it's just telling them what they are adding together, like adding apples to apples.

They need to take the time to check to see if they can reduce their answer. The simplest way is to check to see if both the numerator and denominator are even.

One of the lesson equations is one half minus one half. Fractions work just the same as other numbers. If you are subtracting the same number, the answer is zero.

Lesson 68

<table>
<tr><td colspan="2">

LESSON 68 Finding the least common multiple

A. A **multiple** is a number you get when you multiply by an integer. For example, the multiples of 3 are 3, 6, 9, 12, and so on. Circle the numbers below that are multiples of 6.

12	24	46	18	30	52	16	48	32	20

B. The **least common multiple (LCM)** of two integers is the smallest positive integer that is a multiple of both integers. We have already learned two methods for finding the LCM: the listing method and the prime factorization method. Find the LCM of 9 and 12 using one of the two methods. Show your steps. Review Lesson 49 if needed.

See Day 49, Part B and C.

The LCM of 9 and 12 = 36

C. Find the least common multiple for each number pair.

$\frac{6}{8}$	24	$\frac{4}{9}$	36	$\frac{3}{7}$	21
$\frac{5}{10}$	10	$\frac{8}{12}$	24	$\frac{9}{15}$	45
$\frac{16}{28}$	112	$\frac{12}{30}$	60	$\frac{15}{25}$	75
$\frac{24}{28}$	168	$\frac{36}{45}$	180	$\frac{64}{96}$	192

</td>
<td colspan="2">

LESSON 68 Practice

Find the least common multiple for each number pair.

$\frac{2}{3}$	6	$\frac{6}{9}$	18	$\frac{7}{8}$	56
$\frac{4}{10}$	20	$\frac{9}{12}$	36	$\frac{6}{11}$	66
$\frac{12}{15}$	60	$\frac{13}{39}$	39	$\frac{18}{21}$	126
$\frac{10}{55}$	110	$\frac{14}{42}$	42	$\frac{11}{30}$	330
$\frac{27}{42}$	378	$\frac{25}{35}$	175	$\frac{32}{40}$	160
$\frac{49}{56}$	392	$\frac{36}{54}$	108	$\frac{48}{88}$	528

</td></tr>
</table>

Today they're finding the least common multiple. This will be first step when they get to adding fractions with unlike dominators. That's important because if their fractions don't have common denominators, they can't be added or subtracted. Adding fractions with unlike denominators is like trying to add oranges and apples together. One orange and one apple is just one orange and one apple, but it's two pieces of fruit. You can only add them if you find what they have in common. You do that by finding a common multiple.

On their page it shows multiples of three. They are to find multiples of six. A multiple of six is any answer to six times something. Six hundred, six thousand, and six million are all multiples of six.

Then they are to find the least common multiple, the lowest multiple they have in common. We do that just to make the numbers smaller and easier to work with. They should start with the larger number and see if the other divides into it. If not, they can find the next multiple of the larger number and check that. The larger number will never divide into the smaller number, so they only need to check multiples of the largest number.

Examples: one sixth and one twelfth   You can divide six into twelve, so you only need to multiply two halves by one sixth.

one eighth and one twelfth   Eight does not go into twelve, so you can multiply twelve by two to get twenty-four. Eight does go into twenty-four.

Fractions

Lesson 69

LESSON 69 Finding common denominators

A. When two or more fractions have the same denominator, we say they have **common denominators**. Fractions with common denominators are easy to add, subtract, and compare because we can simply add, subtract, and compare their numerators. That is why, when we deal with fractions with different denominators, we rewrite them as equivalent fractions with common denominators.

B. When rewriting fractions, you can use any of their common denominators. Use the easiest one to work with. Here is an example of rewriting fractions with three different common denominators. Complete the example.

$$\frac{4}{5} \ \& \ \frac{7}{10} \iff \frac{8}{10} \ \& \ \frac{7}{10} \iff \frac{16}{20} \ \& \ \frac{14}{20} \iff \frac{40}{50} \ \& \ \frac{35}{50}$$

C. The least common denominator (LCD) is often used as a common denominator because it is easier to work with smaller numbers. The least common denominator is the least common multiple (LCM) of the denominators. Here is an example of rewriting fractions with the least common denominator. Complete the example.

$$\frac{2}{6} \ \& \ \frac{4}{15} \Rightarrow \quad \begin{matrix} 6 = 6, 12, 18, \dots \\ 15 = 15, 30, 45, \dots \\ LCM = 30, 60, 90, \dots \end{matrix} \ OR \ \begin{matrix} 6 = 2 \times 3 \\ 15 = 3 \times 5 \\ LCM = 2 \times 3 \times 5 = 30 \end{matrix} \Rightarrow \frac{10}{30} \ \& \ \frac{8}{30}$$

D. Rewrite each pair of fractions with the least common denominator.

$\frac{7}{9}, \frac{9}{12}$ $\frac{28}{36}, \frac{27}{36}$ $\frac{7}{15}, \frac{3}{10}$ $\frac{14}{30}, \frac{9}{30}$

$\frac{3}{8}, \frac{5}{20}$ $\frac{15}{40}, \frac{10}{40}$ $\frac{5}{16}, \frac{9}{24}$ $\frac{15}{48}, \frac{18}{48}$

$\frac{5}{6}, \frac{10}{21}$ $\frac{35}{42}, \frac{20}{42}$ $\frac{11}{12}, \frac{13}{30}$ $\frac{55}{60}, \frac{26}{60}$

LESSON 69 Practice

A. Rewrite each pair of fractions with two different common denominators.

$\frac{1}{2}, \frac{4}{5}$ Answers will vary. $\frac{2}{3}, \frac{4}{15}$

$\frac{3}{4}, \frac{5}{6}$ $\frac{3}{4}, \frac{7}{10}$

$\frac{2}{5}, \frac{3}{7}$ $\frac{1}{9}, \frac{5}{12}$

B. Rewrite each pair of fractions with the least common denominator.

$\frac{2}{3}, \frac{6}{7}$ $\frac{14}{21}, \frac{18}{21}$ $\frac{7}{12}, \frac{11}{18}$ $\frac{21}{36}, \frac{22}{36}$

$\frac{1}{4}, \frac{5}{18}$ $\frac{9}{36}, \frac{10}{36}$ $\frac{9}{14}, \frac{13}{35}$ $\frac{45}{70}, \frac{26}{70}$

$\frac{7}{6}, \frac{9}{15}$ $\frac{35}{30}, \frac{18}{30}$ $\frac{16}{27}, \frac{37}{54}$ $\frac{32}{54}, \frac{37}{54}$

$\frac{4}{9}, \frac{5}{16}$ $\frac{64}{144}, \frac{45}{144}$ $\frac{20}{21}, \frac{15}{28}$ $\frac{80}{84}, \frac{45}{84}$

Today they're finding the least common denominator, which is the least common multiple of the two denominators. They can look back at Day 68's lesson on finding the least common multiple for a reminder of how to do that.

The trick here is that the fractions must keep their value. The numerator must change along with the denominator to make sure the fractions are equivalent, equal. One half equals three sixths equals five tenths. Each is one half.

To keep the fractions equal, equivalent, you multiply them by 1. Anything times 1 is itself. It doesn't change in value. Any number over itself equals 1. Those "laws" of math are what enable us to multiply ½ by ³/₃ and get three sixths, which is also one half. (Three is half of six.)

Fractions with common denominators enable us to compare the fractions and to add and subtract the fractions.

Lesson 70

LESSON 70 Adding fractions with unlike denominators

A. To add fractions with unlike denominators, rewrite the fractions as equivalent fractions with common denominators and add their numerators. Then simplify the result and convert it to a mixed number, if possible. Here is an example of rewriting fractions with the least common denominator (LCD) before adding. Complete the example.

$$\frac{5}{9}+\frac{7}{15} \Rightarrow \begin{array}{l}9=3\times3\\15=3\times5\\ \text{LCM}=3\times3\times5=45\end{array} \Rightarrow \frac{25}{45}+\frac{21}{45}=\frac{46}{45}=1\frac{1}{45}$$

B. Often simplifying fractions before adding makes the process easier since you'll be dealing with smaller numbers. Complete the example below.

$$\frac{6}{9}+\frac{12}{15}=\frac{2}{3}+\frac{4}{5}=\frac{10}{15}+\frac{12}{15}=\frac{22}{15}=1\frac{7}{15}$$

C. Add the fractions. Simplify and convert your answers to mixed numbers, if possible.

$$\frac{2}{3}+\frac{5}{9}=1\frac{2}{9}$$
$$\frac{20}{24}+\frac{15}{18}=1\frac{2}{3}$$

$$\frac{4}{8}+\frac{6}{7}=1\frac{5}{14}$$
$$\frac{18}{27}+\frac{10}{12}=1\frac{1}{2}$$

$$\frac{6}{9}+\frac{3}{4}=1\frac{5}{12}$$
$$\frac{12}{20}+\frac{11}{15}=1\frac{1}{3}$$

$$\frac{1}{2}+\frac{7}{8}=1\frac{3}{8}$$
$$\frac{21}{24}+\frac{14}{16}=1\frac{3}{4}$$

LESSON 70 Practice

Add the fractions. Simplify and convert your answers to mixed numbers, if possible.

$$\frac{1}{3}+\frac{1}{2}=\frac{5}{6}$$
$$\frac{2}{4}+\frac{9}{20}=\frac{19}{20}$$

$$\frac{5}{8}+\frac{3}{4}=1\frac{3}{8}$$
$$\frac{4}{5}+\frac{8}{12}=1\frac{7}{15}$$

$$\frac{4}{6}+\frac{1}{4}=\frac{11}{12}$$
$$\frac{2}{7}+\frac{10}{25}=\frac{24}{35}$$

$$\frac{8}{9}+\frac{2}{6}=1\frac{2}{9}$$
$$\frac{4}{18}+\frac{22}{36}=\frac{5}{6}$$

$$\frac{3}{9}+\frac{4}{7}=\frac{19}{21}$$
$$\frac{20}{45}+\frac{15}{30}=\frac{17}{18}$$

$$\frac{4}{6}+\frac{5}{8}=1\frac{7}{24}$$
$$\frac{12}{21}+\frac{14}{28}=1\frac{1}{14}$$

They will be adding fractions with unlike denominators today. They should understand why the first step is to find a common denominator. While they can find any common denominator, finding the least common denominator will make adding and reducing the fractions easier. For example, to find a common denominator between 16 and 24, it's easier to multiply 24 by 2 than 24 by 16 to find a common denominator.

After finding a common denominator and adding, they need to remember to check to see if the answer could be reduced. They should always first check to see if the numerator and denominator are both even. If the answer is an improper fraction, it must be simplified into a mixed number.

Lesson 71

LESSON 71 Subtracting fractions with unlike denominators

A. To subtract fractions with unlike denominators, rewrite the fractions as equivalent fractions with common denominators and subtract their numerators. Then simplify the result, if possible. Here is an example of rewriting fractions with the least common denominator (LCD) before subtracting. Complete the example.

$$\frac{7}{10} - \frac{7}{14} \implies \begin{matrix} 10 = 2 \times 5 \\ 14 = 2 \times 7 \\ LCM = 2 \times 5 \times 7 = 70 \end{matrix} \implies \frac{49}{70} - \frac{35}{70} = \frac{14}{70} = \frac{1}{5}$$

B. Often simplifying fractions before subtracting makes the process easier since you'll be dealing with smaller numbers. Complete the example below.

$$\frac{8}{10} - \frac{6}{14} = \frac{4}{5} - \frac{3}{7} = \frac{28}{35} - \frac{15}{35} = \frac{13}{35}$$

C. Subtract the fractions. Simplify your answers to the lowest terms.

$$\frac{2}{3} - \frac{1}{5} = \frac{7}{15} \qquad \frac{11}{15} - \frac{8}{12} = \frac{1}{15}$$

$$\frac{4}{7} - \frac{1}{2} = \frac{1}{14} \qquad \frac{9}{16} - \frac{8}{24} = \frac{11}{48}$$

$$\frac{6}{8} - \frac{2}{4} = \frac{1}{4} \qquad \frac{24}{28} - \frac{16}{48} = \frac{11}{21}$$

$$\frac{5}{6} - \frac{2}{5} = \frac{13}{30} \qquad \frac{16}{20} - \frac{14}{35} = \frac{2}{5}$$

LESSON 71 Practice

Subtract the fractions. Simplify your answers to the lowest terms.

$$\frac{1}{2} - \frac{1}{3} = \frac{1}{6} \qquad \frac{9}{10} - \frac{5}{15} = \frac{17}{30}$$

$$\frac{4}{6} - \frac{3}{9} = \frac{1}{3} \qquad \frac{7}{12} - \frac{3}{16} = \frac{19}{48}$$

$$\frac{4}{5} - \frac{1}{2} = \frac{3}{10} \qquad \frac{17}{18} - \frac{15}{45} = \frac{11}{18}$$

$$\frac{5}{8} - \frac{1}{3} = \frac{7}{24} \qquad \frac{16}{20} - \frac{18}{24} = \frac{1}{20}$$

$$\frac{3}{4} - \frac{1}{5} = \frac{11}{20} \qquad \frac{32}{49} - \frac{20}{35} = \frac{4}{49}$$

$$\frac{5}{9} - \frac{2}{4} = \frac{1}{18} \qquad \frac{54}{60} - \frac{40}{50} = \frac{1}{10}$$

Today's lesson is the same as Lesson 70, except they will be subtracting. They need to find a common denominator, and really should find the least common denominator, then subtract, then simplify their answer.

Make sure they understand why you can subtract fourteen thirty-fifths from sixteen twentieths (the last question in the lesson). Why can they subtract a larger number from a smaller number, 35 from 20? It's because the larger fraction is the one with the smaller denominator.

Lesson 72

LESSON 72 Adding and subtracting negative fractions

A. Just like integers, fractions can be negative. A negative sign can be in the numerator, in the denominator, or in front of the entire fraction. The following examples show three ways to write a negative fraction. Complete the second example.

$$-\frac{3}{4} = \frac{-3}{4} = \frac{3}{-4} \qquad -\frac{11}{15} = \frac{-11}{15} = \frac{11}{-15}$$

B. To add or subtract negative fractions, rewrite negative fractions to have the negative sign in the numerator and then add or subtract as usual. Here are some examples of using this method. Complete the examples.

$$\frac{3}{4} + \left(-\frac{5}{6}\right) = \frac{3}{4} + \frac{-5}{6} = \frac{9}{12} + \frac{-10}{12} = \frac{-1}{12} = -\frac{1}{12}$$

$$\frac{2}{3} - \left(-\frac{3}{5}\right) = \frac{2}{3} - \frac{-3}{5} = \frac{10}{15} - \frac{-9}{15} = \frac{19}{15} = 1\frac{4}{15}$$

$$-\frac{4}{15} - \frac{1}{12} = \frac{-4}{15} - \frac{1}{12} = \frac{-16}{60} - \frac{5}{60} = \frac{-21}{60} = \frac{-7}{20} = -\frac{7}{20}$$

C. Add or subtract the fractions. Simplify and convert your answers to mixed numbers.

$$-\frac{1}{3} - \frac{1}{4} = -\frac{7}{12} \qquad \frac{1}{5} - \left(-\frac{3}{6}\right) = \frac{7}{10}$$

$$-\frac{4}{8} + \frac{7}{6} = \frac{2}{3} \qquad -\frac{7}{9} - \left(-\frac{1}{3}\right) = -\frac{4}{9}$$

$$\frac{3}{4} + \left(-\frac{3}{9}\right) = \frac{5}{12} \qquad -\frac{4}{5} + \left(-\frac{3}{4}\right) = -1\frac{11}{20}$$

LESSON 72 Practice

Add or subtract the fractions. Simplify and convert your answers to mixed numbers.

$$-\frac{1}{2} - \frac{3}{8} = -\frac{7}{8} \qquad \frac{3}{4} - \left(-\frac{1}{2}\right) = 1\frac{1}{4}$$

$$-\frac{3}{4} + \frac{2}{6} = -\frac{5}{12} \qquad -\frac{2}{5} - \left(-\frac{4}{6}\right) = \frac{4}{15}$$

$$-\frac{2}{5} + \frac{1}{4} = -\frac{3}{20} \qquad -\frac{2}{7} + \left(-\frac{5}{6}\right) = -1\frac{5}{42}$$

$$-\frac{4}{7} - \frac{4}{6} = -1\frac{5}{21} \qquad \frac{2}{3} + \left(-\frac{5}{7}\right) = -\frac{1}{21}$$

$$\frac{8}{9} - \left(-\frac{5}{6}\right) = 1\frac{13}{18} \qquad -\frac{1}{3} + \left(-\frac{1}{9}\right) = -\frac{4}{9}$$

$$\frac{1}{4} + \left(-\frac{1}{2}\right) = -\frac{1}{4} \qquad -\frac{2}{5} - \left(-\frac{1}{3}\right) = -\frac{1}{15}$$

Ask your child what is one quarter minus three fourths. Fractions work just like any other number. The answer is negative two fourths, or negative one half.

They will be working with negative numbers today. They need to remember that adding a negative is just the same as subtracting.

On the other hand, subtracting a negative means adding the fraction, they take those two subtraction signs and put them together into an addition sign. A negative number is the opposite of the number. Subtraction is the opposite of addition. Subtracting a negative is the opposite of the opposite, turning it right back around.

Lesson 73

LESSON 73 Word problems: fractions

Solve the word problems.

Yesterday Emily ran one half of a 5-mile trail. Today she ran two fifths of the trail. On which day did she run farther?	Yesterday
Sarah picked three and two-thirds baskets of apples. Chris picked four and a quarter baskets of apples. Who picked more apples?	Chris
On Monday Percy read three eighths of his reading assignment. On Tuesday he read the rest. On which day did he read more?	Tuesday
Alan and Betty had a pizza for dinner. Alan ate $1/3$ of the pizza. Betty ate $2/5$ of the pizza. What fraction of the pizza was eaten?	11/15
There was $7/9$ of a bottle of milk. Danny drank some and $1/3$ of the bottle was left. What fraction of the bottle did Danny drink?	4/9
Carol read $2/6$ of a book yesterday and $5/12$ of the book today. What fraction of the book did she read in all?	3/4
Sarah spent $2/5$ of her allowance on books and $3/8$ on snacks. What fraction of the allowance did she have left?	9/40
Holly finished $3/4$ of the homework. Sam finished $8/9$ of the homework. How much more of the homework did Sam finish?	5/36
Noah had a box of chocolates. He ate $2/8$ of the box and gave $2/3$ to his sister. What fraction of the box was left over?	1/12
Emily had $5/6$ of a carton of eggs. She used $1/3$ of the carton to bake cookies. What fraction of the carton was left over?	1/2
Jessica painted $7/10$ of her room. Her brother painted $1/5$ of the room. What fraction of the room was not painted yet?	1/10
A recipe calls for $3/4$ cup of flour to bake a pie. Dana has only $1/2$ cup of flour. How much more flour does Dana need?	1/4 cup

LESSON 73 Practice

Solve the word problems.

Laura walked two and three-fifths miles. Justin walked two and one-half miles. Who walked the farther distance?	Laura
Ron solved three fourths of the problems on the worksheet. Angie solved five sevenths of the problems. Who solved more?	Ron
Noah sleeps seven and one-half hours on average. Matt sleeps eight hours on average. Who sleeps more hours on average?	Matt
In a library, $2/5$ of the books are fiction and the rest are non-fiction. What fraction of the books are non-fiction?	3/5
Matt drank $1/6$ of a bottle of milk. Now the bottle is $1/4$ full. What fraction of the whole bottle was there at first?	5/12
Jasmine used $2/3$ cup of flour and $1/2$ cup of sugar to bake cookies. How much more flour than sugar was used?	1/6 cup
Jake and Sam had a pizza for dinner. Jake ate $2/5$ of the pizza. Sam ate $3/10$ of the pizza. What fraction of the pizza was left?	3/10
A farmer planted corn on $4/10$ of his field and beans on $4/12$ of the field. What fraction of the field was planted in total?	11/15
Olivia painted $1/5$ of her room yellow and $1/4$ of the room ivory. What fraction of the room was not painted yet?	11/20
Kyle filled $5/9$ of a bucket with water. Amy filled $2/6$ of the bucket. What fraction of the bucket was filled with water?	8/9
Tylor read $4/12$ of a book yesterday. He read $3/8$ of the book today. How much more of the book did he read today?	1/24
Maria spent $1/3$ of her money on a book and $2/9$ on a video game. What fraction of her money did she spend in total?	5/9

They are going to be solving word problems using fractions. They can use any of the regular word problem techniques to help them. Instead of using smaller numbers to help them figure out how to answer the question, they can use whole numbers instead of fractions to simplify the question to help them think through what they need to do.

Here's the set up for some of the word problems on the lesson page.

Which is greater: one half or two fifths? That's five tenths (multiply by 5) and four tenths (multiply by 2). Five is greater than four, so one half is greater, and she ran farther on the first day. They could also notice that 2.5 would be half of 5, and 2 is less than 2.5, so two fifths is less than one half.

The next two are similar comparisons (apples and reading).

The next is one third plus two fifths. Five fifteenths (multiply by five) and six fifteenths (multiply by three) added together is 11/15.

The next one, about milk, is a subtraction problem. It can seem confusing, but if you take out the fractions it's easy to understand what you need to do. If there were 7 cups of milk (instead of seven ninths) and after he drank there was 1 cup left (instead of one third), how much did he drink? Then it's easy to see that he drank six cups and that's 7 − 1 = 6. They will subtract seven ninths and three ninths (multiply by three) to get the answer.

Lesson 74

LESSON 74 Adding and subtracting mixed numbers

A. One way to add mixed numbers is to convert them to improper fractions and add the improper fractions. Then simplify the result and convert it back to a mixed number, if possible. Here is an example of using this method. Complete the example.

$$2\frac{1}{4} + 1\frac{2}{6} = \frac{9}{4} + \frac{8}{6} = \frac{27}{12} + \frac{16}{12} = \frac{43}{12} = 3\frac{7}{12}$$

B. You can subtract mixed numbers in the same way: convert them to improper fractions before subtracting. Complete the example below.

$$5\frac{4}{9} - 1\frac{2}{3} = \frac{49}{9} - \frac{5}{3} = \frac{49}{9} - \frac{15}{9} = \frac{34}{9} = 3\frac{7}{9}$$

C. Add or subtract the fractions. Simplify and convert your answers to mixed numbers.

$$2\frac{2}{3} + 1\frac{3}{4} = 4\frac{5}{12} \qquad 5\frac{4}{7} - 3\frac{1}{2} = 2\frac{1}{14}$$

$$1\frac{2}{5} + 2\frac{1}{6} = 3\frac{17}{30} \qquad 4\frac{1}{6} - 1\frac{4}{5} = 2\frac{11}{30}$$

$$3\frac{1}{2} + 2\frac{5}{6} = 6\frac{1}{3} \qquad 3\frac{8}{9} - 3\frac{1}{6} = \frac{13}{18}$$

$$3\frac{1}{8} + 1\frac{5}{12} = 4\frac{13}{24} \qquad 2\frac{3}{5} - 1\frac{2}{10} = 1\frac{2}{5}$$

LESSON 74 Practice

Add or subtract the fractions. Simplify and convert your answers to mixed numbers.

$$2\frac{3}{5} + 3\frac{4}{5} = 6\frac{2}{5} \qquad 4\frac{5}{6} - 1\frac{3}{6} = 3\frac{1}{3}$$

$$1\frac{2}{3} + 2\frac{4}{9} = 4\frac{1}{9} \qquad 3\frac{1}{4} - 2\frac{1}{6} = 1\frac{1}{12}$$

$$2\frac{3}{4} + 7\frac{1}{2} = 10\frac{1}{4} \qquad 8\frac{7}{9} - 5\frac{2}{3} = 3\frac{1}{9}$$

$$4\frac{1}{2} + 2\frac{3}{5} = 7\frac{1}{10} \qquad 4\frac{1}{3} - 2\frac{5}{6} = 1\frac{1}{2}$$

$$2\frac{6}{9} + 3\frac{2}{6} = 6 \qquad 3\frac{3}{4} - 2\frac{7}{8} = \frac{7}{8}$$

$$3\frac{1}{3} + 1\frac{11}{15} = 5\frac{1}{15} \qquad 5\frac{1}{10} - 1\frac{2}{5} = 3\frac{7}{10}$$

They will be adding and subtracting mixed numbers. The directions on the page have them change the mixed numbers into improper fractions. That way will always work, but they don't have to do it that way.

Fractions are just a way of writing decimals. $1.25 is a dollar and a quarter; a quarter is one fourth. If you were adding $1.25 and $3.85 could you add the dollars and the cents and then combine them together? Of course. That would be $4 and $1.10. The answer would be $5.10. As fractions that's 1 ¼ and 3 $^{17}/_{20}$. They could add 1 + 3 and $^5/_{20}$ + $^{17}/_{20}$ to get 4 and $^{22}/_{20}$ = 5 $^2/_{20}$ = 5 $^1/_{10}$. They could also add $^5/_4$ and $^{77}/_{20}$ to get $^{25}/_{20}$ + $^{77}/_{20}$ = $^{102}/_{20}$ = 5 $^2/_{20}$ = 5 $^1/_{10}$.

They both work out to the same. The improper fractions can just leave you working with much bigger numbers.

Breaking the whole numbers and fractions apart may lead to a negative number when you subtract. Your child may or may not find that easier. For instance, for the subtraction example on the page, they would end up with 4 and $^4/_9$ – $^6/_9$ = 4 - $^2/_9$ = 3 $^7/_9$ (by borrowing one whole from the 4 to get 3 and $^9/_9$).

Again, this is a matter of preference. For a child breezing through, have them try both ways. For a child struggling with one method, try the other. A future lesson will have them try it the other way. They should try both and choose the one that makes the most sense to them.

Lesson 75

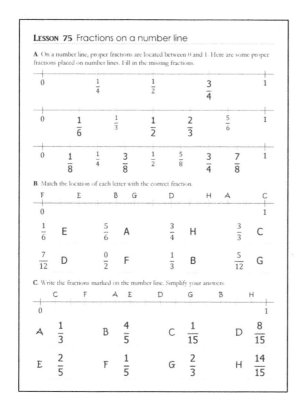

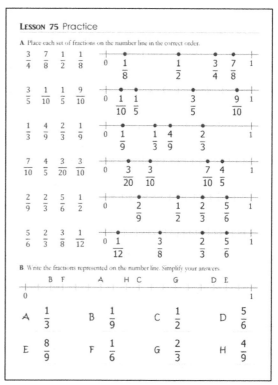

They are going to have to stop and think before completing today's lesson on fractions. You might want to have your child explain to you how they will figure out the missing numbers.

They will need to first figure out how many parts each number line is divided into. That will be their denominator. They also need to realize that the fractions written in are reduced. For example ½ is on a number line that is divided into four parts. It's at two fourths, which has been reduced to one half. All of the fractions in the line have the common denominator of the total number of parts on the number line. They can multiply to give them all that denominator to order them and figure out where on the line each belongs.

They are asked to go about this in three different ways.

Lesson 76

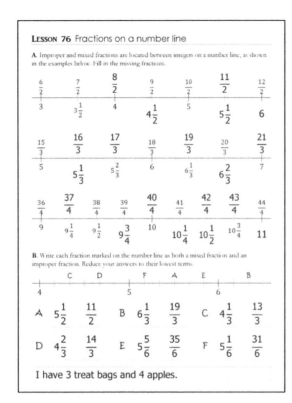

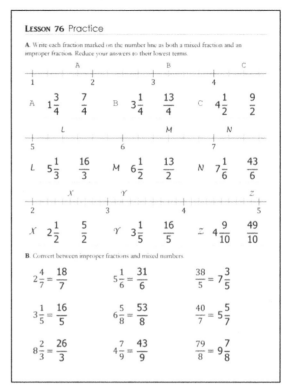

This is a trickier version of Lesson 75. They are going to be ordering mixed numbers and improper fractions, which are one in the same.

At first they are just converting between the two. In the first example, they need to convert four into an improper fraction with two as the denominator. They need to remember that every whole number has a denominator of one. For that example the common denominator is two, so to get from one to two, they will need to multiply the numerator and denominator by two. That gives them eight halves. They can see that equals four because eight divided by two is four. A fraction is a way of writing a division problem. It's all the same thing, just different ways to express it and go about it!

They need to pay attention to three things: how many parts between each whole number, which part they are looking at, and which whole number the fraction comes after.

76 Fractions

Lesson 77

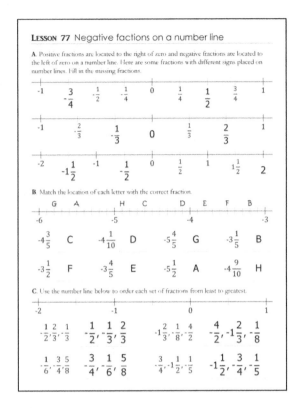

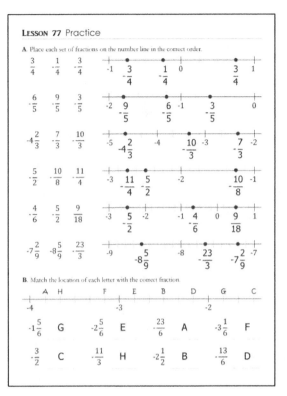

They are going to be working with negative fractions today. They work just like any negative number. A negative number is the opposite of its positive brother. If they are getting stuck, they can realize that the numbers on the number line are just mirror opposites of each other.

They can ignore the negative signs somewhat and think of the numbers getting bigger as they go to the left. (Technically they are smaller as -2 is less than -1, but we tend to think of 2 as being bigger than 1, so it can be helpful to think of the numbers themselves getting bigger as you move to the left.)

Lesson 78

LESSON 78 Adding and subtracting mixed numbers

A. When you add mixed numbers, you can add the whole number parts and the fraction parts separately and then combine the two parts. The example below shows this visually.

Think about how many wholes and how many parts are in the sum.

$$1\frac{3}{8} + 2\frac{7}{8} = (1+2) + \left(\frac{3}{8} + \frac{7}{8}\right) = 3\frac{10}{8} = 4\frac{2}{8} = 4\frac{1}{4}$$

B. You can subtract mixed numbers in the same way: subtract the whole number parts and the fraction parts separately and then combine the two parts. Complete the example below.

$$5\frac{7}{9} - 3\frac{4}{9} = (5-3) + \left(\frac{7}{9} - \frac{4}{9}\right) = 2\frac{3}{9} = 2\frac{1}{3}$$

C. Add or subtract the fractions. Simplify and convert your answers to mixed numbers.

$$3\frac{7}{9} + 4\frac{8}{9} = 8\frac{2}{3} \qquad 3\frac{5}{6} - 2\frac{1}{6} = 1\frac{2}{3}$$

$$2\frac{4}{5} + 6\frac{2}{5} = 9\frac{1}{5} \qquad 8\frac{7}{8} - 2\frac{3}{8} = 6\frac{1}{2}$$

$$4\frac{5}{7} + 3\frac{4}{7} = 8\frac{2}{7} \qquad 5\frac{4}{9} - 2\frac{1}{9} = 3\frac{1}{3}$$

$$2\frac{4}{6} + 7\frac{3}{6} = 10\frac{1}{6} \qquad 6\frac{4}{5} - 4\frac{1}{5} = 2\frac{3}{5}$$

LESSON 78 Practice

Add or subtract the fractions. Simplify and convert your answers to mixed numbers.

$$4\frac{2}{3} + 5\frac{1}{3} = 10 \qquad 3\frac{5}{6} - 1\frac{2}{6} = 2\frac{1}{2}$$

$$1\frac{7}{8} + 3\frac{4}{8} = 5\frac{3}{8} \qquad 5\frac{7}{9} - 2\frac{1}{9} = 3\frac{2}{3}$$

$$2\frac{5}{6} + 5\frac{4}{6} = 8\frac{1}{2} \qquad 8\frac{3}{4} - 2\frac{3}{4} = 6$$

$$1\frac{8}{9} + 5\frac{4}{9} = 7\frac{1}{3} \qquad 4\frac{6}{7} - 3\frac{3}{7} = 1\frac{3}{7}$$

$$3\frac{6}{7} + 1\frac{6}{7} = 5\frac{5}{7} \qquad 6\frac{7}{8} - 4\frac{5}{8} = 2\frac{1}{4}$$

$$2\frac{3}{4} + 5\frac{2}{4} = 8\frac{1}{4} \qquad 7\frac{8}{9} - 5\frac{5}{9} = 2\frac{1}{3}$$

They are adding and subtracting mixed numbers today. The demonstration on this page is to break apart the numbers into whole numbers and fractions. They won't have to borrow to do this.

If you have a child who likes the challenge of solving math equations, they could flip flop the fraction parts of the numbers to have to borrow from the whole number. For example 8 7/8 – 2 3/8 could become 8 3/8 – 2 7/8. That would be 6 and - 4/8. That's 6 – ½ which is 5 ½.

Lesson 79

LESSON 79 Adding and subtracting mixed numbers

A. To add mixed numbers with unlike denominators, rewrite them as equivalent fractions with common denominators and then add the whole number parts and the fraction parts separately. Here is an example of using this method. Complete the example.

$$2\frac{3}{4} + 3\frac{4}{5} = 2\frac{15}{20} + 3\frac{16}{20} = 2 + 3 + \frac{15}{20} + \frac{16}{20} = 5\frac{31}{20} = 6\frac{11}{20}$$

B. You subtract mixed numbers with unlike denominators in the same way: rewrite them using a common denominator before subtracting. Complete the example below.

$$5\frac{2}{3} - 3\frac{1}{4} = 5\frac{8}{12} - 3\frac{3}{12} = (5 - 3) + \left(\frac{8}{12} - \frac{3}{12}\right) = 2\frac{5}{12}$$

C. Add or subtract the fractions. Simplify and convert your answers to mixed numbers.

$$2\frac{5}{6} + 3\frac{5}{9} = 6\frac{7}{18} \qquad 4\frac{2}{3} - 2\frac{1}{5} = 2\frac{7}{15}$$

$$4\frac{2}{3} + 5\frac{1}{6} = 9\frac{5}{6} \qquad 6\frac{5}{9} - 2\frac{1}{3} = 4\frac{2}{9}$$

$$1\frac{6}{9} + 6\frac{3}{4} = 8\frac{5}{12} \qquad 7\frac{5}{9} - 1\frac{2}{4} = 6\frac{1}{18}$$

$$2\frac{1}{2} + 4\frac{7}{8} = 7\frac{3}{8} \qquad 3\frac{5}{6} - 3\frac{1}{8} = \frac{17}{24}$$

LESSON 79 Practice

Add or subtract the fractions. Simplify and convert your answers to mixed numbers.

$$4\frac{2}{3} + 3\frac{1}{2} = 8\frac{1}{6} \qquad 7\frac{1}{2} - 4\frac{1}{3} = 3\frac{1}{6}$$

$$2\frac{5}{8} + 5\frac{3}{4} = 8\frac{3}{8} \qquad 8\frac{3}{6} - 2\frac{1}{9} = 6\frac{7}{18}$$

$$1\frac{5}{6} + 3\frac{3}{4} = 5\frac{7}{12} \qquad 6\frac{4}{5} - 3\frac{1}{2} = 3\frac{3}{10}$$

$$6\frac{7}{9} + 2\frac{1}{6} = 8\frac{17}{18} \qquad 6\frac{5}{8} - 1\frac{1}{3} = 5\frac{7}{24}$$

$$2\frac{3}{4} + 4\frac{2}{3} = 7\frac{5}{12} \qquad 7\frac{3}{4} - 3\frac{1}{2} = 4\frac{1}{4}$$

$$1\frac{4}{6} + 2\frac{5}{8} = 4\frac{7}{24} \qquad 9\frac{8}{9} - 3\frac{2}{3} = 6\frac{2}{9}$$

This is another lesson in adding and subtracting mixed numbers except there is the added step that they have unlike denominators. The directions have them break apart the whole number and the fraction, add the parts, and then put them back together. If your child is more comfortable working with them as improper fractions, they can do that and get the same results. They just need to simplify their answers into mixed numbers.

They won't have to borrow to do these subtraction problems. If they want a challenge, they could again flip one or more of the fraction parts in the subtraction problems to challenge themselves and have to borrow from the whole number.

Lesson 80

LESSON 80 Word problems: mixed numbers

Solve the word problems.

Kate ran $2\frac{1}{2}$ miles yesterday. She ran $3\frac{3}{4}$ miles today. How many miles did she run altogether? **6 1/4 miles**

Olivia had a ribbon 5 feet long. She used $1\frac{1}{2}$ feet of the ribbon to wrap a gift. How many feet of the ribbon are left? **3 1/2 feet**

David used $2\frac{5}{6}$ gallons of red paint and $3\frac{2}{3}$ gallons of white paint to paint his room. How many gallons of paint did he use in all? **6 1/2 gallons**

Sarah weighs $110\frac{3}{5}$ pounds. When she holds her dog Max, she weighs $125\frac{9}{10}$ pounds. How many pounds does Max weigh? **15 3/10 pounds**

Leah spent $1\frac{1}{4}$ hours studying math and 2 hours studying science. What is the total time she spent studying? **3 1/4 hours**

Andrew is $12\frac{5}{6}$ years old. His younger brother Joey is $4\frac{1}{2}$ years younger than Andrew. How old is Joey? **8 1/3 years old**

This morning $2\frac{11}{16}$ inches of snow fell. By afternoon a quarter of an inch melted away. How many inches of snow are left? **2 7/16 inches**

Mia planted $3\frac{3}{8}$ rows of roses, $4\frac{1}{2}$ rows of violets, and $5\frac{3}{4}$ rows of daisies. How many rows of flowers did Mia plant in total? **13 7/8 rows**

Kyle bought $2\frac{7}{10}$ pounds of beef and used $1\frac{1}{2}$ pounds to cook dinner. How many pounds of beef did Kyle have left after that? **1 1/5 pounds**

Ana lives $2\frac{5}{8}$ miles from a park. This afternoon she walked to the park and back home. How many miles did she walk in total? **5 1/4 miles**

A restaurant had $10\frac{5}{6}$ pounds of potatoes. They used $8\frac{1}{3}$ pounds to make fries and brought in another 5 pounds. How many pounds of potatoes did the restaurant have then? **7 1/2 pounds**

LESSON 80 Practice

Solve the word problems.

Matt ran $1\frac{1}{4}$ miles yesterday. He ran $3\frac{1}{2}$ miles today. How many more miles did he run today than yesterday? **2 1/4 miles**

A recipe calls for $2\frac{1}{6}$ cups of sugar for batter and $1\frac{3}{4}$ cups for sprinkling. How many cups of sugar are needed in total? **3 11/12 cups**

A tank had 8 gallons of water. Kyle used $4\frac{2}{5}$ gallons of water from the tank. How many gallons of water was left in the tank? **3 3/5 gallons**

Brandon is $11\frac{2}{3}$ years old. His sister Sarah is $5\frac{1}{6}$ years older than Brandon. How old is Sarah? **16 5/6 years old**

Last night $3\frac{5}{8}$ inches of snow fell. This morning $2\frac{1}{4}$ inches of more snow fell. How many inches of snow are on the ground? **5 7/8 inches**

Mark ordered 6 pizzas for his birthday party. After the party, $1\frac{3}{4}$ pizzas were left. How many pizzas were eaten? **4 1/4 pizzas**

Jennifer used $1\frac{1}{3}$ cups of carrots and $2\frac{1}{2}$ cups of onions to make soup. How many cups of vegetables did Jennifer use in total? **3 5/6 cups**

Josh picked $4\frac{5}{6}$ baskets of apples. Tom picked $5\frac{1}{3}$ baskets of apples. How many baskets of apples did they pick altogether? **10 1/6 baskets**

A restaurant had 12 loaves of bread. They used $5\frac{7}{9}$ loaves to make sandwiches. How many loaves of bread were left? **6 2/9 loaves**

A farmer decided to plant 25 rows of corns. He planted $8\frac{7}{10}$ rows yesterday and $7\frac{3}{5}$ rows today. How many rows are left? **8 7/10 rows**

Sam's cat weighs $6\frac{3}{4}$ pounds. Emily's cat weighs $1\frac{1}{3}$ pounds less than Sam's cat. Laura's cat weighs $2\frac{5}{6}$ pounds more than Emily's cat. How many pounds does Laura's cat weigh? **8 1/4 pounds**

There is a page of word problems for today that will require them to add and subtract mixed numbers. They should use whatever word problem techniques help them.

Here's the set up for the first several problems.

When a question asks "altogether" it's an addition problem. They will add 2 ½ and 3 ¾ to get 5 and $^5/_4$ = 5 and 1 ¼ = 6 ¼

The next question is asking what's left after something has been taken away. Taking away is a clue it's a subtraction problem. 5 – 1 ½ = 4 – ½ = 3 ½

The next question asks how many in all. That's another clue for an addition problem. They will add two and five sixths and three and two thirds. $2\ ^5/_6 + 3\ ^4/_6$ = 5 and $^9/_6$ = 6 and 1 $^3/_6$ = 6 ½ They need to remember to reduce and simplify their answers, as well as label them. This is 6 ½ gallons of paint.

The next one would be good to use simpler numbers for if they are struggling to know how to approach it. If she weighed 100 pounds and then held the dog and weighed 125 pounds, how much did the dog weigh? They subtracted 125 -100 to get their easy answer of 25 pounds. They will subtract the mixed numbers to get their answer.

Lesson 81

LESSON 81 Multiplying fractions

A. To multiply fractions, multiply the numerators to find the new numerator and multiply the denominators to find the new denominator. Then simplify the result, if possible. Here is an example of using this method. Complete the example.

$$\frac{5}{8} \times \frac{4}{9} = \frac{5 \times 4}{8 \times 9} = \frac{20}{72} = \frac{5}{18}$$

B. Another way to multiply fractions is to simplify them using cross reducing before multiplying. Cross reducing means dividing the numerator of one fraction and the denominator of the other fraction by a common factor. This method is easier and faster because it helps you avoid dealing with large numbers. Here are some examples of using cross reducing. Complete the examples.

$$\frac{5}{8} \times \frac{4}{9} \quad \Rightarrow \quad \text{4 and 8 have a common factor 4.} \quad \Rightarrow \quad \frac{5}{8\!\!\!/\,2} \times \frac{4\!\!\!/\,1}{9} = \frac{5}{18}$$

$$\frac{5}{6} \times \frac{4}{15} \quad \Rightarrow \quad \begin{array}{l}\text{5 and 15 have a}\\\text{common factor.}\\\text{So do 4 and 6.}\end{array} \quad \Rightarrow \quad \frac{5\!\!\!/\,1}{6\!\!\!/\,3} \times \frac{4\!\!\!/\,2}{15\!\!\!/\,3} = \frac{2}{9}$$

C. Multiply the fractions. Simplify and convert your answers to mixed numbers.

$$\frac{1}{2} \times \frac{4}{5} = \frac{2}{5} \qquad\qquad \frac{8}{12} \times \frac{9}{10} = \frac{3}{5}$$

$$\frac{3}{8} \times \frac{2}{9} = \frac{1}{12} \qquad\qquad \frac{9}{24} \times \frac{6}{18} = \frac{1}{8}$$

$$\frac{4}{9} \times \frac{6}{8} = \frac{1}{3} \qquad\qquad \frac{10}{21} \times \frac{14}{15} = \frac{4}{9}$$

LESSON 81 Practice

Multiply the fractions. Simplify and convert your answers to mixed numbers.

$$\frac{2}{3} \times \frac{1}{4} = \frac{1}{6} \qquad\qquad \frac{8}{22} \times \frac{2}{16} = \frac{1}{22}$$

$$\frac{3}{5} \times \frac{5}{7} = \frac{3}{7} \qquad\qquad \frac{7}{12} \times \frac{6}{14} = \frac{1}{4}$$

$$\frac{2}{6} \times \frac{3}{4} = \frac{1}{4} \qquad\qquad \frac{6}{13} \times \frac{13}{15} = \frac{2}{5}$$

$$\frac{2}{9} \times \frac{5}{6} = \frac{5}{27} \qquad\qquad \frac{5}{54} \times \frac{18}{40} = \frac{1}{24}$$

$$\frac{3}{8} \times \frac{2}{5} = \frac{3}{20} \qquad\qquad \frac{15}{16} \times \frac{12}{18} = \frac{5}{8}$$

$$\frac{6}{9} \times \frac{3}{4} = \frac{1}{2} \qquad\qquad \frac{27}{50} \times \frac{25}{60} = \frac{9}{40}$$

This lesson features a favorite of mine, crossing off and simplifying before you have to multiply. This makes their work easier, so I suggest they do it!

Why does it work? Remember that fractions are a way to set up a division problem. Four divided by eight is $^4/_8$ is ½. Eight fourths is eight divided by four, or two. Also, numbers are just a combination of multiples (think prime factorization). What's really going on is that they are pulling out 1. In the example on the page, they are pulling out $^4/_4$ and leaving smaller factors behind. Multiplying the number by 1 doesn't change the value of the number and basically makes the $^4/_4$ just disappear. In the second example they are pulling out $^2/_2$ and $^5/_5$.

If the example question was instead five fifteenths and four sixths, could they still do this? (I reversed the denominators.) Yes, they could, instead of working across, they would be basically just reducing the fraction before they multiply.

Reducing the fraction in these ways makes the numbers smaller to work with. That's not only easier for multiplying, it's easier to reduce at the end and is less likely to need reducing at the end.

Lesson 82

LESSON 82 Multiplying mixed numbers

A. To multiply mixed numbers, convert them to improper fractions and multiply the improper fractions. Then simplify the result and convert it back to a mixed number, if possible. Here is an example of using this method. Complete the example.

$$5\frac{1}{4} \times 3\frac{5}{9} = \frac{21}{4} \times \frac{32}{9} \implies \frac{21\,7}{4\,1} \times \frac{32\,8}{9\,3} = \frac{56}{3} = 18\frac{2}{3}$$

B. Multiply the fractions. Simplify and convert your answers to mixed numbers.

$$1\frac{1}{2} \times 1\frac{1}{9} = 1\frac{2}{3} \qquad 2\frac{2}{5} \times 2\frac{1}{12} = 5$$

$$2\frac{1}{4} \times 1\frac{5}{6} = 4\frac{1}{8} \qquad 2\frac{1}{7} \times 1\frac{2}{15} = 2\frac{3}{7}$$

$$2\frac{1}{3} \times 3\frac{3}{7} = 8 \qquad 2\frac{5}{8} \times 1\frac{1}{15} = 2\frac{4}{5}$$

$$5\frac{5}{9} \times 4\frac{4}{5} = 26\frac{2}{3} \qquad 2\frac{2}{3} \times 2\frac{7}{10} = 7\frac{1}{5}$$

$$2\frac{5}{8} \times 5\frac{1}{3} = 14 \qquad 3\frac{3}{7} \times 1\frac{1}{8} = 3\frac{6}{7}$$

LESSON 82 Practice

Multiply the fractions. Simplify and convert your answers to mixed numbers.

$$3\frac{3}{8} \times 1\frac{1}{3} = 4\frac{1}{2} \qquad 3\frac{1}{3} \times 1\frac{7}{10} = 5\frac{2}{3}$$

$$1\frac{3}{5} \times 2\frac{1}{8} = 3\frac{2}{5} \qquad 4\frac{3}{8} \times 1\frac{5}{21} = 5\frac{5}{12}$$

$$5\frac{2}{5} \times 1\frac{1}{3} = 7\frac{1}{5} \qquad 4\frac{1}{6} \times 1\frac{3}{15} = 5$$

$$1\frac{3}{4} \times 2\frac{2}{7} = 4 \qquad 3\frac{1}{7} \times 3\frac{6}{11} = 11\frac{1}{7}$$

$$2\frac{5}{8} \times 1\frac{3}{9} = 3\frac{1}{2} \qquad 1\frac{2}{3} \times 1\frac{7}{20} = 2\frac{1}{4}$$

$$3\frac{1}{7} \times 1\frac{3}{4} = 5\frac{1}{2} \qquad 6\frac{1}{8} \times 1\frac{4}{14} = 7\frac{7}{8}$$

They are multiplying mixed numbers today. It's important that they see they can't break apart the whole numbers and fractions in the same way to solve these. They can be broken apart, but it's not as easy this time. Let me explain.

To multiply 53 by 76 you have to multiply the 50 by the 70 and the 50 by the 6 and the 3 by the 70 and the 3 by the 6. That's what they would have to do to break apart the whole number and the fraction.

To multiply 3 ½ by 5 ¾ They would have to multiply 3 by 5 and 3 by ¾ and ½ by 5 and ½ by ¾. They can do that if they like. It will work. That's $15 + \frac{9}{4} + \frac{5}{2} + \frac{3}{8} = 15 + \frac{18}{8} + \frac{20}{8} + \frac{3}{8} = 15 + 2\frac{2}{8} + 2\frac{4}{8} + \frac{3}{8} = 19 + \frac{9}{8} = 20\frac{1}{8}$ Not so simple.

In their lesson it tells them to convert the mixed numbers into improper fractions and then multiply. That would be (for the same example I just gave) $\frac{7}{2} \times \frac{23}{4} = \frac{161}{8} = 20\frac{1}{8}$ This does involve having to multiply much bigger numbers, but the other involved finding common denominators, so neither way is the easy way. It's more straight forward to use improper fractions as shown on the page.

Fractions

Lesson 83

LESSON 83 Multiplying fractions and whole numbers

A. To multiply fractions with whole numbers, rewrite the whole numbers as fractions and multiply the fractions as usual. To rewrite a whole number as a fraction, simply put the whole number over 1. Here is an example of using this method. Complete the example.

$$2\frac{7}{9} \times 12 = \frac{25}{9} \times \frac{12}{1} \Rightarrow \frac{25}{\cancel{9}3} \times \frac{\cancel{12}4}{1} = \frac{100}{3} = 33\frac{1}{3}$$

B. Multiply the fractions. Simplify and convert your answers to mixed numbers.

$$\frac{3}{8} \times 4 = 1\frac{1}{2} \qquad 14 \times \frac{8}{21} = 5\frac{1}{3}$$

$$7 \times \frac{2}{5} = 2\frac{4}{5} \qquad \frac{5}{24} \times 18 = 3\frac{3}{4}$$

$$\frac{5}{9} \times 6 = 3\frac{1}{3} \qquad 16 \times 2\frac{5}{6} = 45\frac{1}{3}$$

$$8 \times \frac{2}{3} = 5\frac{1}{3} \qquad 20 \times 1\frac{2}{8} = 25$$

$$6 \times \frac{1}{4} = 1\frac{1}{2} \qquad 2\frac{3}{4} \times 10 = 27\frac{1}{2}$$

Did you know? A 'jiffy' is an actual unit of time. One jiffy is 1/100th of a second.

LESSON 83 Practice

Multiply the fractions. Simplify and convert your answers to mixed numbers.

$$\frac{1}{2} \times 4 = 2 \qquad 16 \times \frac{5}{12} = 6\frac{2}{3}$$

$$9 \times \frac{1}{6} = 1\frac{1}{2} \qquad 21 \times \frac{7}{15} = 9\frac{4}{5}$$

$$\frac{3}{4} \times 6 = 4\frac{1}{2} \qquad 10 \times 2\frac{3}{5} = 26$$

$$\frac{5}{6} \times 8 = 6\frac{2}{3} \qquad 1\frac{1}{9} \times 15 = 16\frac{2}{3}$$

$$8 \times \frac{5}{8} = 5 \qquad 8 \times 1\frac{5}{12} = 11\frac{1}{3}$$

$$7 \times \frac{7}{9} = 5\frac{4}{9} \qquad 2\frac{3}{20} \times 6 = 12\frac{9}{10}$$

This lesson in some ways is exactly the same as what they did in Lesson 82. This time they are multiplying fractions and mixed numbers by whole numbers.

They need to remember that a whole number has a denominator of one.

They can also consider using the break apart method this time if they choose. For instance, in the lesson there is the problem 20 x 1 $\frac{2}{8}$. They could do 20 x $\frac{10}{8}$ and end up with $\frac{200}{8}$ to reduce, or they could do 20 x 1 and 20 x $\frac{2}{8}$ which equals 20 and $\frac{40}{8}$ which is easier to see that the answer will be 25.

They should also use the cross-off method to reduce the fractions as much as possible before they multiply. One problem is $\frac{5}{9}$ times 6. They can pull out 3 from the numerator and denominator and end up with $\frac{5}{3}$ x 2.

Lesson 84

This is another word problem lesson. It's named multiplying fractions, so that's a big clue as to what they will need to do, but I want to point out the clue word in the word problems. It's "of." The word "of" is the clue that you need to multiply. If you say, "We need half of those," and there are ten, then you multiply 10 by ½ and get 5. You may be thinking that you would divide by two, but that's all you are doing by multiplying by ½. 10 x ½ = $^{10}/_2$ which is just another way to write the division problem 10 ÷ 2.

Here's the setup of the first word problems.

candies: 9 x 1/3 < or > 8 x 1/4

studying: 2 5/6 x 3/5

pets: 2/3 x 3/5 Two thirds of the three fifths that have pets, have dogs.

pizza: 2/3 x 2 ¾ Two thirds of the two and three-fourths pizzas

money: There are two ways to think about this.
        18 – (18 x 5/9) < or > 25 – (25 x 3/5)
        How much they have – how much they spent
                        OR
        18 x 4/9 < or > 25 x 2/5 (If they spent 5/9, they didn't spend 4/9.)
        Multiplying how much they have by how much they didn't spend

Lesson 85

A. To divide fractions, rewrite division as multiplication by multiplying by the reciprocal of the divisor and then multiply the fractions as usual. Simplify the result and convert it to a mixed number, if possible. The reciprocal of a fraction is the fraction turned upside down. Here is an example of using this method. Complete the example.

$$\frac{8}{15} \div \frac{4}{25} = \frac{\cancel{8}2}{\cancel{15}3} \times \frac{\cancel{25}5}{\cancel{4}1} = \frac{10}{3} = 3\frac{1}{3}$$

B. A whole number can be expressed as a fraction by placing the whole number over 1. The reciprocal of a whole number (except 0) is 1 over the number. Here are some examples of rewriting whole numbers as fractions before dividing. Complete the examples.

$$\frac{7}{12} \div 21 = \frac{7}{12} \div \frac{21}{1} = \frac{\cancel{7}1}{12} \times \frac{1}{\cancel{21}3} = \frac{1}{36}$$

$$27 \div \frac{6}{11} = \frac{27}{1} \div \frac{6}{11} = \frac{\cancel{27}9}{1} \times \frac{11}{\cancel{6}2} = \frac{99}{2} = 49\frac{1}{2}$$

C. Divide the fractions. Simplify and convert your answers to mixed numbers.

$$\frac{5}{6} \div \frac{3}{4} = 1\frac{1}{9}$$
$$\frac{11}{12} \div \frac{33}{45} = 1\frac{1}{4}$$

$$8 \div \frac{6}{7} = 9\frac{1}{3}$$
$$16 \div \frac{48}{49} = 16\frac{1}{3}$$

$$\frac{3}{5} \div 9 = \frac{1}{15}$$
$$\frac{10}{14} \div 35 = \frac{1}{49}$$

Divide the fractions. Simplify and convert your answers to mixed numbers.

$$\frac{2}{3} \div \frac{1}{4} = 2\frac{2}{3}$$
$$\frac{9}{14} \div \frac{18}{32} = 1\frac{1}{7}$$

$$\frac{1}{2} \div \frac{5}{6} = \frac{3}{5}$$
$$\frac{12}{13} \div \frac{20}{39} = 1\frac{4}{5}$$

$$4 \div \frac{8}{9} = 4\frac{1}{2}$$
$$10 \div \frac{15}{18} = 12$$

$$6 \div \frac{6}{7} = 7$$
$$25 \div \frac{12}{15} = 31\frac{1}{4}$$

$$\frac{3}{5} \div 9 = \frac{1}{15}$$
$$\frac{16}{40} \div 24 = \frac{1}{60}$$

$$\frac{4}{7} \div 2 = \frac{2}{7}$$
$$\frac{12}{27} \div 36 = \frac{1}{81}$$

Today they are dividing fractions. There's a simple process for this. To divide by a fraction, you multiply by its reciprocal. The reciprocal of a fraction is the fraction turned upside down. With a whole number, they need to remember that it has a denominator of one. That means that when dividing by a whole number, they multiply by a fraction that has one as the numerator and the whole number as the denominator.

Now why…why does multiplying by the reciprocal equal dividing by the fraction. I showed you that in the last lesson, how multiplying by one half was the same as dividing by two. The reciprocal of two is ½.

> If you say, "We need half of those," and there are ten, then you multiply 10 by ½ and get 5. You may be thinking that you would divide by two, but that's all you are doing by multiplying by ½. 10 x ½ = $^{10}/_2$ which is just another way to write the division problem 10 ÷ 2.

Lesson 86

LESSON 86 Word problems: dividing fractions

A. Division is the inverse of multiplication. Dividing by a number is the same as multiplying by its reciprocal or multiplicative inverse. Consider the example below.

Divide 12 candies equally into 4 boxes. $= 12 \div 4 = 12 \times \frac{1}{4} =$ Put $\frac{1}{4}$ of 12 candies into each box.

B. Dividing by a fraction means finding how many of the fractional parts are in a whole. Follow the examples below to understand what it means in real life.

How many half hours are in 4 hours? $= 4 \div \frac{1}{2} = \frac{4}{1} \times \frac{2}{1} = 8 =$ There are 8 half hours in 4 hours.

How many quarter inches are in 1 ½ inches? $= 1\frac{1}{2} \div \frac{1}{4} = \frac{3}{2} \times \frac{4}{1} = 6 =$ There are 6 quarter inches in 1 ½ inches.

C. Solve the word problems.

Sam did a total of 4 hours of fitness training, which consisted of half hour sessions. How many sessions did he do? — **8 sessions**

Mia had a 7½-inch ribbon. For her craft project, she cut it into quarter-inch pieces. How many pieces did she have in total? — **30 pieces**

Mark had 6½ gallons of milk. He divided the milk evenly into 4 bottles. How much milk did he put in each bottle? — **1 5/8 gallons**

Brian took a walk for 1½ hours. It usually takes him ⅓ hour to walk a mile. How many miles did he walk? — **4 1/2 miles**

Charlie takes 1⅕ minutes to solve one fraction problem. How many problems can he solve in 30 minutes? — **25 problems**

Brian used $4\frac{3}{10}$ gallons of red paint and $3\frac{2}{5}$ gallons of blue paint to paint 7 bookshelves. How many gallons of paint did he use for each bookshelf? — **1 1/10 gallons**

2,520

LESSON 86 Practice

Solve the word problems.

Paul takes $3\frac{1}{3}$ minutes to read a page of his reading assignment. How many pages can he read in an hour? — **18 pages**

A cook used $4\frac{1}{2}$ cups of flour to bake 5 pies. How many cups of flour did the cook use to make one pie? — **9/10 cups**

Sara has $\frac{3}{4}$ of a cake. She shares it equally among herself and 2 friends. What fraction of the cake will each get? — **1/4**

Amy has $7\frac{2}{5}$ gallons of gas in her car. Her car uses $\frac{1}{25}$ of a gallon per mile. How far can Amy drive before the tank is empty? — **185 miles**

A recipe calls for $1\frac{3}{4}$ cups of flour to make a pie. Ron has $10\frac{1}{2}$ cups of flour. How many pies will he be able to make? — **6 pies**

Mason used $2\frac{3}{4}$ cans of paint to paint 4 chairs of the same shape and size. How many cans of paint did he use for each chair? — **11/16 cans**

Glen runs a lap of the track in $3\frac{3}{4}$ minutes. How many laps will he run in 45 minutes? — **12 laps**

Debora made $2\frac{5}{6}$ gallons of lemonade. Each cup holds $\frac{1}{12}$ of a gallon. How many cups will Debora be able to fill? — **34 cups**

A farmer plans to plant four different vegetables in $\frac{6}{7}$ of his field. What fraction of the field will be occupied by each vegetable? — **3/14**

Mike is making a $7\frac{7}{8}$ inch square game board. If he uses $1\frac{5}{16}$ inch square tiles, how many tiles will he use? — **36 tiles**

A recipe calls for $2\frac{3}{4}$ cups of diced vegetables to make 4 servings of soup. Sally wants to make 10 servings. How many cups of vegetables does she need? — **6 7/8 cups**

This lesson is a continuation of the same concept. Dividing is multiplying by a number's inverse, its opposite, its reciprocal.

Here's the setup of the first word problems.

sessions: 4 ÷ ½ = 4 x 2

ribbon: 7 ½ ÷ ¼ = 7 ½ x 4 = 28 + 2 = 30
In that case it was easier to break apart the 7 ½ into 7 + ½ and multiply 4 by each separately than to multiply 4 by $^{15}/_2$ and then simplify.

gallons: 6 ½ ÷ 4 = 6 ½ x ¼ They could multiply $^{13}/_2$ x ¼ = $^{13}/_8$ or they could multiply 6 x ¼ and add that to ¼ x ½ , which would be $^{12}/_8$ + $^1/_8$ = $^{13}/_8$. In the ribbon one, it was easier to break them apart. In this one, it's probably easier to use the improper fraction. In order to add the fractions at the end, you have to first find a common denominator which adds an extra step.

walk: 1 ½ ÷ $^1/_3$ = $^3/_2$ x 3 = $^9/_2$ = 4 ½

Lesson 87

LESSON 87 Reciprocal of a mixed number

A. To find the reciprocal of a fraction, just turn the fraction upside down. The reciprocal of a whole number (except 0) is 1 over the number. The reciprocal of a unit fraction, a fraction whose numerator is 1, is a whole number. Write the reciprocal of each fraction.

$\frac{7}{12}$ $\frac{12}{7}$ 18 $\frac{1}{18}$ $\frac{20}{9}$ $\frac{9}{20}$ $\frac{1}{45}$ 45

B. To find the reciprocal of a mixed number, convert it to an improper fraction and turn the improper fraction upside down. Write the reciprocal of each mixed number.

$3\frac{1}{2}$ $\frac{2}{7}$ $4\frac{1}{5}$ $\frac{5}{21}$ $3\frac{3}{5}$ $\frac{5}{18}$ $1\frac{7}{10}$ $\frac{10}{17}$

$6\frac{2}{7}$ $\frac{7}{44}$ $1\frac{4}{9}$ $\frac{9}{13}$ $2\frac{5}{6}$ $\frac{6}{17}$ $3\frac{4}{15}$ $\frac{15}{49}$

C. Find the reciprocal of each fraction. Write your answers as mixed numbers, if possible.

$\frac{17}{6}$ $\frac{6}{17}$ $\frac{1}{18}$ 18 $\frac{13}{35}$ $2\frac{9}{13}$ 16 $\frac{1}{16}$

20 $\frac{1}{20}$ $\frac{21}{4}$ $\frac{4}{21}$ $\frac{1}{30}$ 30 $\frac{11}{25}$ $2\frac{3}{11}$

D. What fraction am I? Use the clues to find the correct fractions.

My numerator is a factor of all numbers. The sum of myself and my reciprocal is five and one fifth. What fraction am I? 1/5

My denominator is 6 more than my numerator. The simplest form of my reciprocal is two and one half. What fraction am I? 4/10

The denominator of my reciprocal is the smallest even prime number. My denominator is 5 more than my numerator. What fraction am I? 2/7

My numerator is the largest prime factor of 455. My denominator is the sum of all prime factors of 455. What fraction am I? 13/25

LESSON 87 Practice

A. Find the reciprocal of each fraction. Write your answers as mixed numbers, if possible.

$\frac{1}{25}$ 25 $2\frac{7}{10}$ $\frac{10}{27}$ 40 $\frac{1}{40}$ $\frac{12}{25}$ $2\frac{1}{12}$

26 $\frac{1}{26}$ $3\frac{6}{13}$ $\frac{13}{45}$ $\frac{1}{23}$ 23 $5\frac{2}{7}$ $\frac{7}{37}$

$3\frac{2}{3}$ $\frac{3}{11}$ $\frac{1}{48}$ 48 $\frac{21}{32}$ $1\frac{11}{21}$ 52 $\frac{1}{52}$

$\frac{15}{49}$ $3\frac{4}{15}$ 35 $\frac{1}{35}$ $3\frac{7}{8}$ $\frac{8}{31}$ $\frac{1}{19}$ 19

B. What fraction am I? Use the clues to find the correct fractions.

I am the sum of $1\frac{1}{2}$ and its reciprocal. What fraction am I? 2 1/6

I am the difference of $1\frac{1}{5}$ and its reciprocal. What fraction am I? 11/30

I am equivalent to $2\frac{1}{2}$ and my numerator is 5^2. What fraction am I? 25/10

My denominator is 2 more than my numerator. The simplest form of my reciprocal is one and one third. What fraction am I? 6/8

My denominator is 3 less than my numerator. My reciprocal is equivalent to three fourths. What fraction am I? 12/9

My numerator is 3 less than my denominator. If both my numerator and my denominators are increased by 2, I become equivalent to four fifths. What fraction am I? 10/13

I am a proper fraction. My numerator and my denominator are prime numbers. The least common denominator of myself and my reciprocal is 6. What fraction am I? 2/3

They are just finding reciprocals today. The new thing is that they are finding the reciprocal of mixed numbers.

What's the reciprocal of 6 ¼? To find it they need to first create a fraction. They will convert it to an improper fraction and then turn it upside down to make the reciprocal.

There are some riddles for them to solve at the bottom of the page. Encourage them to have fun challenging themselves to figure it out. Don't let them give up.

Lesson 88

LESSON 88 Dividing mixed numbers

A. To divide mixed numbers, convert them to improper fractions and divide the improper fractions. Then simplify the result and convert it back to a mixed number, if possible. Here is an example of using this method. Complete the example.

$$5\frac{1}{4} \div 3\frac{1}{9} = \frac{21}{4} \div \frac{28}{9} = \frac{21}{4} \times \frac{9}{28} = \frac{27}{16} = 1\frac{11}{16}$$

B. The rules for multiplying and dividing negative fractions are the same as those for multiplying and dividing negative integers: two like signs become a positive sign, and two unlike signs become a negative sign. Here are some examples of applying these rules.

$$2\frac{1}{4} \times -1\frac{3}{5} = \frac{9}{4} \times -\frac{8}{5} = \frac{9}{4} \times -\frac{8}{5} = -\frac{18}{5} = -3\frac{3}{5}$$

$$-1\frac{3}{5} \div \frac{9}{10} = -1\frac{3}{5} \div \frac{9}{10} = -\frac{8}{5} \times \frac{10}{9} = -\frac{16}{9} = -1\frac{7}{9}$$

C. Divide the fractions. Simplify and convert your answers to mixed numbers.

$$2\frac{4}{5} \div 3\frac{1}{2} = \frac{4}{5}$$

$$-4\frac{3}{8} \div 1\frac{1}{6} = -3\frac{3}{4}$$

$$4\frac{2}{7} \div 3\frac{3}{4} = 1\frac{1}{7}$$

$$1\frac{4}{9} \div -3\frac{1}{4} = -\frac{4}{9}$$

$$4\frac{1}{6} \div 3\frac{4}{7} = 1\frac{1}{6}$$

$$-5\frac{3}{5} \div -1\frac{3}{4} = 3\frac{1}{5}$$

LESSON 88 Practice

Divide the fractions. Simplify and convert your answers to mixed numbers.

$$3\frac{1}{5} \div 6\frac{2}{3} = \frac{12}{25}$$

$$3\frac{1}{9} \div 5\frac{1}{4} = \frac{16}{27}$$

$$2\frac{4}{7} \div 3\frac{1}{3} = \frac{27}{35}$$

$$9\frac{1}{3} \div 2\frac{4}{5} = 3\frac{1}{3}$$

$$4\frac{3}{8} \div 1\frac{2}{5} = 3\frac{1}{8}$$

$$8\frac{3}{4} \div 2\frac{1}{7} = 4\frac{1}{12}$$

$$-9\frac{1}{6} \div 3\frac{4}{7} = -2\frac{17}{30}$$

$$-5\frac{5}{8} \div -3\frac{3}{4} = 1\frac{1}{2}$$

$$4\frac{1}{2} \div -3\frac{3}{8} = -1\frac{1}{3}$$

$$-7\frac{1}{3} \div 1\frac{1}{2} = -4\frac{8}{9}$$

$$-2\frac{3}{4} \div 1\frac{1}{2} = -1\frac{5}{6}$$

$$-3\frac{3}{7} \div -5\frac{1}{3} = \frac{9}{14}$$

The natural next step is dividing by mixed numbers. They will multiply by the reciprocal, and to find the reciprocal they will first convert the mixed number into an improper fraction.

There's another twist on this page, dividing and multiplying by a negative number. This is just the same as when they are using whole numbers. A negative times a positive is a negative. A negative times a negative is a positive.

As I've said before, that's just like subtracting a negative and those two minus signs come together to make a plus sign. Multiplying a negative by a negative is saying you want the opposite of the opposite, which is how you end up with a positive number.

Lesson 89

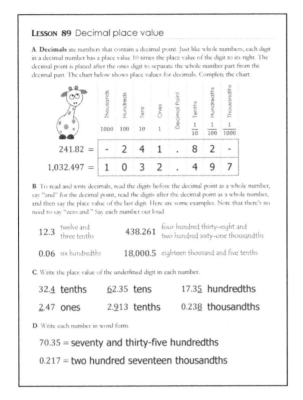

LESSON 89 Decimal place value

A. Decimals are numbers that contain a decimal point. Just like whole numbers, each digit in a decimal number has a place value 10 times the place value of the digit to its right. The decimal point is placed after the ones digit to separate the whole number part from the decimal part. The chart below shows place values for decimals. Complete the chart.

	Thousands	Hundreds	Tens	Ones	Decimal Point	Tenths	Hundredths	Thousandths
	1000	100	10	1		$\frac{1}{10}$	$\frac{1}{100}$	$\frac{1}{1000}$
241.82 =	-	2	4	1	.	8	2	-
1,032.497 =	1	0	3	2	.	4	9	7

B. To read and write decimals, read the digits before the decimal point as a whole number, say "and" for the decimal point, read the digits after the decimal point as a whole number, and then say the place value of the last digit. Here are some examples. Note that there's no need to say "zero and." Say each number out loud.

12.3 twelve and three tenths   438.261 four hundred thirty-eight and two hundred sixty-one thousandths

0.06 six hundredths   18,000.5 eighteen thousand and five tenths

C. Write the place value of the underlined digit in each number.

32.4 tenths   62.35 tens   17.35 hundredths

2.47 ones   2.913 tenths   0.238 thousandths

D. Write each number in word form.

70.35 = seventy and thirty-five hundredths

0.217 = two hundred seventeen thousandths

LESSON 89 Practice

A. Make a number using each set of place values.

7 tens	5 hundreds	6 thousands	3 tenths
1 one	2 tens	3 hundreds	4 tens
4 tenths	0 ones	4 tens	8 thousandths
3 hundredths	8 tenths	9 ones	2 hundredths
5 thousandths	4 hundredths	2 tenths	6 ones
71.435	**520.84**	**6,349.2**	**46.328**

B. Write the place value of the underlined digit in each number.

17.3 tens   23.15 tenths   0.527 thousandths

2.61 tenths   5.434 ones   12.35 hundredths

C. Write each number in word form.

215.4 = two hundred fifteen and four tenths

0.639 = six hundred thirty-nine thousandths

9,015.02 = nine thousand, fifteen and two hundredths

D. What number am I? Use the clues to find the decimal.

I have 2 digits in total. If you multiply any number by my tenths digit, you get the number itself. My ones digit is the square of my tenths digit. What number am I?	1.1
I have 3 digits in total. If you multiply any number by my ones digit, you get zero. My tens digit is the largest single digit. The sum of my digits is 18. What number am I?	90.9
I have 3 digits in total. All of my digits are even. My ones digit is twice my tenths digit. My tenths digit is twice my hundredths digit. What number am I?	8.42

We're onto a new, though related, topic. Fractions, decimals, and percentages are all the same thing written different ways, but we'll get to that another day. Today is about reading decimals.

There is a chart on their page to show the decimal place value. They should notice why hundredths are called hundredths and thousandths, thousandths.

one hundredth = $^1/_{100}$ = 0.01

One way to think about it is that the number of decimal places equals the number of zeros. There are two decimal places in 0.01 and two zeros in 100. 0.01 is one hundredth.

Lesson 90

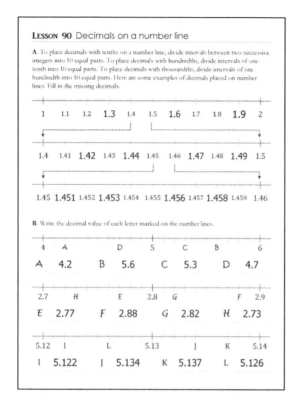

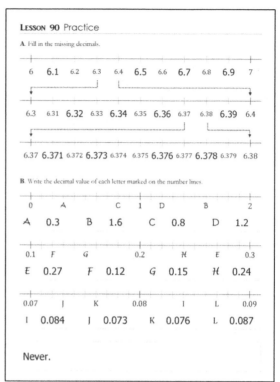

Today they will be figuring out tenths, hundredths, and thousandths on number lines. They need to notice what's different about the different number lines. Some run between whole numbers, some between tenths, some between hundredths. The lines are divided into ten parts, so between each line segment is one tenth of what's on the number line. Between the whole numbers, that's tenths, but between tenths (for example between 1.1 and 1.2 each line is one hundredth (1.11, 1.12,...). Between hundredths each tenth of the line is one thousandth. Dividing into tens changes the place value.

If they are aware of what numbers they are counting between and what place value they are working with, the rest is pretty simple. They just need to count the lines from there.

Lesson 91

LESSON 91 Rounding decimals

A. Rounding decimals is similar to rounding whole numbers except for one thing: you drop the digits to the right of the given place value instead of replacing them with zeros. Here is an example of rounding a decimal to various place values. Complete the example.

	Nearest whole number	Nearest tenth	Nearest hundredth
8.547	9	8.5	8.55
	The tenths place is 5. Round up and drop 547.	The hundredths place is 4. Round down and drop 47.	The thousandths place is 7. Round up and drop 7.

B. Rounding is finding the closest number on a number line. Consider the questions below and compare your answers with Part A. Use the number line provided if it helps you.

8.547	9	8.5	8.55
	Is 8.547 closer to 8 or 9?	Is 8.547 closer to 8.5 or 8.6?	Is 8.547 closer to 8.54 or 8.55?

C. Round each number to the nearest whole number, tenth, and thousandth.

	Nearest whole number	Nearest tenth	Nearest hundredth
6.765	7	6.8	6.77
2.203	2	2.2	2.2
18.397	18	18.4	18.4
64.055	64	64.1	64.06
819.542	820	819.5	819.54
230.609	231	230.6	230.61
1,378.003	1,378	1,378	1,378

LESSON 91 Practice

A. Round each number to the nearest whole number.

0.2	0	1.57	2	1.939	2
19.8	20	43.26	43	25.088	25
353.7	354	179.92	180	960.507	961

B. Round each number to the nearest tenth.

0.07	0.1	5.02	5	1.769	1.8
24.39	24.4	13.25	13.3	80.204	80.2
569.72	569.7	294.99	295	343.556	343.6

C. Round each number to the nearest hundredth.

0.008	0.01	2.135	2.14	5.705	5.71
0.051	0.05	36.759	36.76	23.091	23.09
0.967	0.97	120.022	120.02	458.399	458.4

D. Use the clues to find the correct decimal from the six possibilities.

7.09	4.64	5.18	6.23	4.94	5.02

To the nearest whole number, I round to 5. My tenths digit is odd. I round down to the nearest tenth. What number am I?	4.94
To the nearest ten, I round to 10. My tenths digit is neither positive nor negative. I round up to the nearest tenth. What number am I?	7.09
I round down to the nearest whole number. I round down to the nearest tenth. On a number line, I am left of 6. What number am I?	5.02

Today's lesson is on rounding. They are going to round decimals just like any other number. You use the digit to the right of the place value you are rounding to. If it's five or greater, you change the number to one more, otherwise it stays the same. All the digits to the right of the place value you are rounding to become zeros. In the case of decimals, that means they just disappear. We don't round .9 to 1.0, just to 1.

1.09 rounds to 1 if you are rounding to the nearest whole number because 0 is less than five, but it rounds to 1.1 if you are rounding to the nearest tenth because 9 is greater than five.

Lesson 92

LESSON 92 Estimation with decimals

A. Rounding is used when we don't need an exact value and an estimate is good enough. In real life, we often round decimals to the nearest whole number to estimate sums and differences. The following example shows one such situation. Complete the example.

Mia saved $26.75 last month and $38.16 this month. About how much money did she save in total?   **$65**

Estimate each amount to the nearest dollar:
Last month: $26.75 is about $27.
This month: $38.16 is about $38.

Find the estimated sum:
$27 + $38 = **$65**

B. Estimate the answers by rounding each decimal to the nearest whole number.

$8.2 + 6.7 = $ **15** $9.3 - 2.7 = $ **6**

$8.54 + 9.10 = $ **18** $6.45 - 3.52 = $ **2**

$92.48 + 63.05 = $ **155** $84.27 - 26.61 = $ **57**

$25.12 + 39.76 = $ **65** $43.35 - 19.88 = $ **23**

C. Solve the word problems.

A video game costs $27.99. It's on sale for $19.99. About how much less is the sale price than the original price?   **$8**

At a book store, Max bought three books at $9.20, $11.65, and $14.80 each. About how much money did Max spend in all?   **$36**

Last night 3.7 inches of snow fell. This morning 2.25 inches of more snow fell. About how much snow is on the ground?   **6 inches**

Dallas, Texas, receives 2.1 inches of rainfall on average in January. In February, it receives 2.6 inches on average. About how much rainfall does Dallas receive during these two months?   **5 inches**

A lion can run up to 80.5 kilometers per hour. A cheetah can run 120.7 kilometers per hour. About how much faster can the cheetah run than the lion?   **40 km/h**

LESSON 92 Practice

A. Estimate the sums by rounding each decimal to the nearest whole number.

$9.2 + 4.5 = $ **14** $6.9 + 3.2 = $ **10**

$18.7 + 25.4 = $ **44** $45.4 + 20.9 = $ **66**

$56.26 + 20.13 = $ **76** $67.68 + 11.55 = $ **80**

B. Estimate the differences by rounding each decimal to the nearest whole number.

$9.1 - 4.5 = $ **4** $8.9 - 5.3 = $ **4**

$50.2 - 25.5 = $ **24** $68.6 - 49.7 = $ **19**

$37.53 - 12.76 = $ **25** $79.09 - 30.82 = $ **48**

C. Solve the word problems.

Adam is buying a math puzzle book for $8.50. If he pays with a $20 bill, about how much change will he get back?   **$11**

Lisa wants to buy a hat for $12.44 and a shirt for $23.60. About how much money will she need to buy both?   **$36**

This morning 2.3 inches of snow fell. By afternoon 0.9 inch of snow melted away. About how much snow is left?   **1 inch**

Ana used 4.8 gallons of red paint and 3.6 gallons of white paint to paint her room. About how much paint did she use in all?   **9 gallons**

David went for a run on a 5.2-mile trail. He ran 3.8 miles and walked the rest. About how many miles did he walk?   **1 mile**

At a bookstore, Jamie bought three books at $11.99, $7.45, and $12.55 each. About how much money did Jamie spend in all?   **$32**

Mercury travels around the sun at 47.87 kilometers per second. Earth travels at 29.78 kilometers per second. About how much faster does Mercury travel than Earth?   **18 km/s**

Like with any lesson on rounding, the next step is using the rounded numbers. We call that estimation. They are just being asked to round to the nearest whole number and then use those numbers. There are addition and subtraction problems on the page but also some word problems.

Here's the setup for the word problems.

sale: $27.99 - $19.99 = $28 – $20

book store: $9.20 + $11.65 + $14.80 = $9 + $12 + $15

snow: 3.7 + 2.25 = 4 + 2   inches

rainfall: 2.1 + 2.6 = 2 + 3   inches

lion: 120.7 – 80.5 = 121 – 81   km/hr

Lesson 93

LESSON 93 Comparing decimals

A. Adding zeros to the end of a decimal number does not change its value. Note that the following decimals all have the same value.

0.3 = 0.30 = 0.300   3 tenths = 30 hundredths = 300 thousandths

B. Here are the steps for comparing decimals. Complete the example.

(1) **57.36**   57.3

To compare 57.36 to 57.3:
1. Compare the whole number parts. Both are 57.
2. Compare the decimal parts. If the decimal parts have different lengths (different numbers of digits), add zeros to the end of the shorter decimal so they have the same length. Add one zero to the end of 57.3 and compare 36 to 30.

(2) 57.36 > 57.30

C. Compare the decimals.

9.2 > 8.8   2.19 > 2.109   5.3 > 4.317

3.5 < 3.7   4.33 < 4.37   3.07 = 3.070

4.60 = 4.6   8.15 > 8.1   5.291 < 5.298

D. Order the decimals from least to greatest.

6.2, 9.3, 2.9, 5.8   1.2, 4.78, 3.9, 4.75
2.9, 5.8, 6.2, 9.3   1.2, 3.9, 4.75, 4.78

3.2, 0.02, 0.576, 1.576   2.67, 47.12, 80.3, 2.495
0.02, 0.576, 1.576, 3.2   2.495, 2.67, 47.12, 80.3

0.823, 1.845, 1.8, 0.85   5.02, 2.37, 5.109, 0.506
0.823, 0.85, 1.8, 1.845   0.506, 2.37, 5.02, 5.109

LESSON 93 Practice

A. Compare the decimals.

4.3 < 4.7   1.36 < 1.362   9.2 > 8.253

2.5 > 0.7   8.02 < 8.05   2.50 = 2.500

5.25 > 5.2   4.10 = 4.1   6.426 < 6.476

B. Order the decimals from least to greatest.

7.5, 8.12, 5.82, 8.13   0.73, 0.03, 0.3, 0.37
5.82, 7.5, 8.12, 8.13   0.03, 0.3, 0.37, 0.73

6.25, 12.01, 8.4, 0.113   9.2, 10.2, 5.279, 5.273
0.113, 6.25, 8.4, 12.01   5.273, 5.279, 9.2, 10.2

C. Order the decimals from greatest to least.

2.2, 2.15, 2.58, 2.5   4.87, 4.75, 4.25, 4.82
2.58, 2.5, 2.2, 2.15   4.87, 4.82, 4.75, 4.25

3.146, 4.8, 3.72, 4.827   2.37, 5.203, 2.1, 5.84
4.827, 4.8, 3.72, 3.146   5.84, 5.203, 2.37, 2.1

D. Make the smallest possible number using each set of digits. Use each digit only once. You can include a decimal point.

7, 0, 5, 1   0, 4, 0, 9   6, 0, 0, 0
0.157   0.049   0.006

The lesson today is on comparing decimals. They need to think about how they compare any numbers. 10 is greater than 9 even though 9 is greater than 1 or 0. It's the place value that matters.

On their lesson page it gives the instruction to add on zeros to the end of a decimal until the two sides have the same number of decimal places to compare the numbers. For instance 3.76 is less than 3.80 because 76 is less than 80. If that helps them to think about it, then they can do that.

Another way to think about it is like how you put words in alphabetical order. You start on the left and work your way over. When comparing 3.76 and 3.8, you would see that the 3s are the same and move onto the next digits, the 7 and 8. Eight is greater so that number is greater.

Lesson 94

LESSON 94 Adding decimals	LESSON 94 Practice

LESSON 94 Adding decimals

A. Here are the steps for adding decimals.

```
  1 2 . 5 0 0
      4 . 0 6 3
 +   9 . 7 8 0
  2 6 . 3 4 3
```

To solve 12.5 + 4.063 + 9.78:
1. Line up the decimal points vertically.
2. Add zeros so the decimal parts have the same length. Add two zeros to 12.5 and one zero to 9.78.
3. Add the numbers as you would whole numbers.
4. Carry the decimal point directly down into the answer.

B. Add the decimals with tenths.

0.6 + 0.8 = **1.4**   2.7 + 0.5 = **3.2**

8.5 + 3.4 = **11.9**   7.4 + 3.9 = **11.3**

9.2 + 5.6 = **14.8**   0.6 + 4.5 = **5.1**

5.8 + 9.8 = **15.6**   0.3 + 0.7 = **1**

C. Add the decimals.

1.4	5.25	6.7	0.02	0.75
+ 2.38	+ 2.7	+ 4.85	+ 4.3	+ 0.95
3.78	7.95	11.55	4.32	1.7

2.718	0.7	4.253	5.76	2.478
+ 3.5	+ 2.459	+ 7.86	+ 8.421	+ 9.522
6.218	3.159	12.113	14.181	12

LESSON 94 Practice

A. Add the decimals with tenths.

3.8 + 5.8 = **9.6**   8.7 + 0.8 = **9.5**

2.7 + 1.5 = **4.2**   2.1 + 7.9 = **10**

4.6 + 9.6 = **14.2**   0.9 + 0.5 = **1.4**

0.6 + 9.7 = **10.3**   3.5 + 7.4 = **10.9**

B. Add the decimals.

2.1	3.62	5.3	6.85	1.46
+ 4.93	+ 7.7	+ 2.09	+ 4.9	+ 3.85
7.03	11.32	7.39	11.75	5.31

3.807	0.5	2.598	9.57	0.798
+ 7.6	+ 2.509	+ 7.15	+ 8.643	+ 0.004
11.407	3.009	9.748	18.213	0.802

7.3	6.215	4.38	0.023	8.524
+ 9.482	+ 5.9	+ 5.659	+ 3.48	+ 1.476
16.782	12.115	10.039	3.503	10

To add decimals the most important thing to remember is place value. The decimal points must line up. Again in this lesson, the example shows adding zeros to the end of the decimal so that each number has the same amount of decimal places.

It's not necessary to add zeros, but they can do that if it helps them. But, they can also think about adding 100 and 78. They have a different number of place values, but they don't need to add a 0 before the 7 in order to add them as long as they line up the decimal places. The 1 in one hundred is just added to nothing.

They will borrow or carry just like normal and add one to the next place value, even if it's across the decimal point.

```
      1
    2.76
 +  8.421
   11.181
```

Lesson 95

LESSON 95 Adding decimals

A. A whole number has no decimal part, so all decimal places after the decimal point are equal to zero. Note that all of the following numbers are equal.

$43 = 43.0 = 43.00 = 43.000 = \dots = 43.0000000$

B. Here are the steps for adding decimals and whole numbers.

```
  1 2 . 0 0 0
+   4 . 1 6 3
  2 6 . 1 6 3
```

To solve 12 + 4.163:
1. Express whole numbers as decimals by adding a decimal point and zeros. 12 is expressed as 12.000.
2. Add the decimals as usual.

C. Add the decimals.

$42 + 17.3 = 59.3$ $80.527 + 14.5 = 95.027$

$56.8 + 29 = 85.8$ $29.5 + 52.853 = 82.353$

$37 + 18.54 = 55.54$ $23.11 + 36.89 = 60$

$72.49 + 16 = 88.49$ $86.53 + 6.034 = 92.564$

$25 + 8.203 = 33.203$ $39.258 + 5.27 = 44.528$

LESSON 95 Practice

Add the decimals.

$55 + 7.99 = 62.99$ $50.084 + 20.8 = 70.884$

$12.9 + 72 = 84.9$ $69.8 + 84.304 = 154.104$

$73 + 61.89 = 134.89$ $40.65 + 96.78 = 137.43$

$14.94 + 67 = 81.94$ $39.49 + 2.853 = 42.343$

$39 + 2.905 = 41.905$ $27.475 + 3.83 = 31.305$

$8.052 + 78 = 86.052$ $4.305 + 82.07 = 86.375$

$6.75 + 8.27 = 15.02$ $99.99 + 9.999 = 109.989$

They will continue to add decimals today. The only difference is that they will be adding some thousandths as well as adding decimals to whole numbers. The only trick here is to remember that the decimal is after the whole number, that 12 equals 12.000.

The same most important rule applies, to make sure the place values are lined up.

```
   12          12.00
+  5.67       +5.67
  17.67        17.67
```

When they come to subtracting decimals, adding in the zeros will become more useful.

Lesson 96

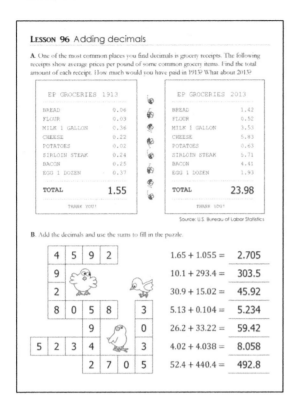

LESSON 96 Adding decimals

A. One of the most common places you find decimals is grocery receipts. The following receipts show average prices per pound of some common grocery items. Find the total amount of each receipt. How much would you have paid in 1913? What about 2013?

```
EP GROCERIES 1913              EP GROCERIES 2013

BREAD              0.06        BREAD              1.42
FLOUR              0.03        FLOUR              0.52
MILK 1 GALLON      0.36        MILK 1 GALLON      3.53
CHEESE             0.22        CHEESE             5.83
POTATOES           0.02        POTATOES           0.63
SIRLOIN STEAK      0.24        SIRLOIN STEAK      5.71
BACON              0.25        BACON              4.41
EGG 1 DOZEN        0.37        EGG 1 DOZEN        1.93

TOTAL             1.55        TOTAL             23.98

    THANK YOU!                    THANK YOU!
```
Source: U.S. Bureau of Labor Statistics

B. Add the decimals and use the sums to fill in the puzzle.

4	5	9	2	
9				
2				
8	0	5	8	3
	9			0
5	2	3	4		3
	2	7	0	5

$1.65 + 1.055 =$ 2.705

$10.1 + 293.4 =$ 303.5

$30.9 + 15.02 =$ 45.92

$5.13 + 0.104 =$ 5.234

$26.2 + 33.22 =$ 59.42

$4.02 + 4.038 =$ 8.058

$52.4 + 440.4 =$ 492.8

LESSON 96 Practice

A. Add the money amounts. Don't forget to put the currency symbol in your answer.

$2.00	$5.54	$8.02	$4.65
+ $3.47	+ $0.32	+ $0.16	+ $3.02
$5.47	$5.86	$8.18	$7.67

Pound	Euro	Chinese Yuan	Russian Ruble
£9.58	€5.64	¥2.47	₽7.63
+ £3.14	+ €8.42	+ ¥9.17	+ ₽2.20
£12.72	€14.06	¥11.64	₽9.83

B. Add the decimals.

$64 + 5.38 = 69.38$ $21.613 + 78.6 = 100.213$

$52.5 + 74 = 126.5$ $15.4 + 71.874 = 87.274$

$84 + 69.13 = 153.13$ $32.47 + 73.98 = 106.45$

$22.93 + 58 = 80.93$ $26.68 + 5.629 = 32.309$

They are adding decimals again today. First they are going to be adding multiple decimals by adding a list of decimal prices.

For the second half of the page, they will add the decimals and then fill the answers into the puzzle.

Fractions, Decimals, and Percents

Lesson 97

LESSON 97 Subtracting decimals

A. Here are the steps for subtracting decimals.

```
  1 2 . 5 0 0      To solve 12.5 - 4.063:
-   4 . 0 6 3      1.  Line up the decimal points vertically.
  ───────────      2.  Add zeros so the decimal parts have the same length.
      8 . 4 3 7    3.  Subtract the numbers as you would whole numbers.
                   4.  Carry the decimal point directly down into the answer.
```

B. Subtract the decimals with tenths.

0.9 − 0.2 = 0.7   20.8 − 10.5 = 10.3

7.5 − 5.4 = 2.1   48.4 − 23.9 = 24.5

9.2 − 5.6 = 3.6   90.6 − 18.6 = 72

C. Subtract the decimals.

5.3	6.26	4.3	9.22	0.92
− 2.38	− 4.7	− 0.82	− 3.8	− 0.06
2.92	1.56	3.48	5.42	0.86

4.061	7.7	8.103	0.92	6.002
− 1.5	− 5.809	− 3.86	− 0.183	− 2.586
2.561	1.891	4.243	0.737	3.416

A decimal point.

LESSON 97 Practice

A. Subtract the decimals with tenths.

5.6 − 3.6 = 2   50.7 − 20.3 = 30.4

2.4 − 0.7 = 1.7   26.5 − 11.9 = 14.6

9.2 − 7.6 = 1.6   93.4 − 36.4 = 57

6.3 − 2.5 = 3.8   74.5 − 17.9 = 56.6

B. Subtract the decimals.

4.1	7.72	5.2	6.38	8.42
− 3.93	− 5.8	− 1.64	− 4.9	− 0.79
0.17	1.92	3.56	1.48	7.63

7.807	9.5	7.903	9.52	0.415
− 2.4	− 8.829	− 4.39	− 8.043	− 0.018
5.407	0.671	3.513	1.477	0.397

4.3	9.005	6.23	8.023	5.532
− 2.074	− 3.5	− 5.548	− 2.49	− 5.478
2.226	5.505	0.682	5.533	0.054

They are subtracting the decimals today. The example shows adding in the zeros to make the numbers have an equal amount of decimal places.

They can subtract just like any normal number. They just need to make sure to line up the decimal points and drop the decimal straight down into the answer.

```
  4 2₁
  5.30
- 2.38
──────
  2.92
```

Lesson 98

LESSON 98 Subtracting decimals

A. In real life, we commonly subtract decimals from whole numbers to make change. Determine how much change you would receive in each situation below.

You buy an item at $2.53 and pay with a $5 bill.	$2.47
You buy an item at $11.99 and pay with a $20 bill.	$8.01
You pay a check of $22.87 with three $10 bills.	$7.13
You pay a check of $65.40 with four $20 bills.	$14.60

B. Subtract the decimals.

$42 - 15.3 = 26.7$ $50.327 - 14.5 = 35.827$

$56.8 - 29 = 27.8$ $52.5 - 29.853 = 22.647$

$37 - 18.54 = 18.46$ $36.11 - 23.89 = 12.22$

$70.49 - 28 = 42.49$ $82.03 - 6.534 = 75.496$

$35 - 9.103 = 25.897$ $39.255 - 5.27 = 33.985$

LESSON 98 Practice

A. Determine how much change you would receive in each situation.

You buy an item at $3.99 and pay with a $10 bill.	$6.01
You buy an item at $9.25 and pay with a $20 bill.	$10.75
You pay a check of $12.43 with three $5 bills.	$2.57
You pay a check of $35.90 with two $20 bills.	$4.10

B. Subtract the decimals.

$54 - 7.99 = 46.01$ $50.084 - 20.8 = 29.284$

$72.9 - 18 = 54.9$ $84.3 - 48.704 = 35.596$

$73 - 26.89 = 46.11$ $96.25 - 30.78 = 65.47$

$64.94 - 37 = 27.94$ $39.49 - 2.853 = 36.637$

$59 - 2.905 = 56.095$ $46.202 - 3.84 = 42.362$

They will be subtracting decimals again today. The same rules apply. They will also be subtracting money. They can just add on zeros as they would with any other problem. $20 becomes $20.00. When subtracting across lots of zeros, they can use the "box method" from Lesson 9 in Adding and Subtracting.

Otherwise, this is the same type of activity. Here's one example.

$$\begin{array}{r} {}^{3}\cancel{4}^{1}\cancel{2}.^{1}0 \\ -\ 15.3 \\ \hline 26.7 \end{array}$$

Lesson 99

LESSON 99 Word problems: adding/subtracting decimals

Solve the word problems.

Ana used 2.4 gallons of red paint and 3.9 gallons of white paint to paint her room. How much paint did she use in all?	6.3 gallons
Dana bought $43.12 in groceries at a store and paid with a $50 bill. How much change did she receive?	$6.88
Mia saved $36.25 last month and $28.59 this month. How much money did she save in total?	$64.84
David went for a run on a 4-mile trail. He ran 2.7 miles and walked the rest. How many miles did he walk?	1.3 miles
A video game costs $37.10. It's on sale for $24.99. How much less is the sale price than the original price?	$12.11
Ron has $24.35. Matt has $19.46 more than Ron. Naomi has $12.58 less than Matt. How much money does Naomi have?	$31.23
This morning 1.7 inches of snow fell. By afternoon 0.8 inch of snow melted away. How much snow is left?	0.9 inch
The international standard A4 paper is 8.27 inches wide and 11.69 inches long. What is the perimeter of A4 paper?	39.92 inches
Fresh water freezes at 32° F, but seawater freezes at about 28.4° F. At how much lower of a temperature does sea water freeze?	3.6° F
Sam weighs 32.5 kg, Max weighs 37.9 kg, and Ron weighs 29.8 kg. What is the difference between the lightest and heaviest?	8.1 kg
Kate rode her bike 6.25 miles to the library and 8.5 miles to the park. Later she came home the same way. How many miles did Kate ride altogether?	29.5 miles
The tallest building in the world is Burj Khalifa, which is 0.828 km tall. The second tallest building is Shanghai Tower, which is 0.632 km tall. What is the difference of their heights?	0.196 km

LESSON 99 Practice

Solve the word problems.

Tom wants to buy a hat for $11.32 and a shirt for $18.79. How much money will he need to buy both?	$30.11
Adam is buying a math puzzle book for $8.37. If he pays with a $10 bill, how much change will he get back?	$1.63
Last night 3.4 inches of snow fell. This morning 1.8 inches of more snow fell. How much snow is on the ground?	5.2 inches
A tank had 8 gallons of water. Kyle used 2.6 gallons of water from the tank. How much water was left in the tank?	5.4 gallons
Kate ran 2.6 miles yesterday. She ran 3.75 miles today. How many miles did she run altogether?	6.35 miles
At a store, Jessica paid her groceries with two $20 bills and received $1.46 as change. What was the cost of her groceries?	$38.54
Max bought three books at $12.65, $13.78, and $10.89 each. How much money did Max spend in all?	$37.32
Max's room is 120.85 square feet. Mia's room is 140.18 square feet. How much bigger is Mia's room than Max's?	19.33 sq ft
This morning the temperature was 62.34° F. In the evening, it was 55.90° F. How far did the temperature drop during the day?	6.44° F
US Letter paper is 21.59 centimeters wide and 27.94 centimeters long. What is the perimeter of US Letter paper?	99.06 cm
An ostrich can run up to 96.6 kilometers per hour. A horse can run 70.76 kilometers per hour. How much faster can the ostrich run than the horse?	25.84 km/h
Light from the sun reaches Earth in 8.3 minutes. It reaches Saturn in 79.3 minutes. How many more minutes does it take to reach Saturn than Earth?	71 minutes

They are solving word problems today. The title says they are adding and subtracting decimals, so they shouldn't have a problem figuring out what operation to use. If they get one wrong, have them try to find their mistake. If they can't find a mistake in their math, maybe they made a mistake in understanding the question and just need to read it again more carefully.

Here's the set up for the first several.

paint: 2.4 + 3.9
groceries: 50.00 − 43.12   (They can quickly turn 50 into 49.9^10 to subtract.)
save: 36.25 + 28.59
walk: 4.0 − 2.7
game: 37.10 − 24.99
money: 24.35 + 19.46 − 12.58
snow: 1.7 − 0.8
perimeter: (2 x 8.27) + (2 x 11.69) They can just add to double each length.
freeze: 32.0 − 28.4
weigh: 37.9 − 29.8
bike: 2 x (6.25 + 8.5)
building: 0.828 − 0.632

Lesson 100

<table>
<tr><td>

LESSON 100 Multiplying decimals by powers of 10

A. A power of 10 is 10 multiplied by itself a certain number of times, as shown below.

$10^2 = 10 \times 10 = 100$

$10^5 = 100,000$ (5 zeros)

$10^3 = 10 \times 10 \times 10 = 1,000$

$10^7 = 10,000,000$ (7 zeros)

B. To multiply decimals by a power of 10, move the decimal point to the right as many places as the number of zeros in the power of 10. The following table shows the place value pattern when decimals are multiplied by powers of 10. Complete the table.

	42.5	3.27	0.069	0.0083
× 10	425	32.7	0.69	0.083
× 100	4,250	327	6.9	0.83
× 1000	42,500	3,270	69	8.3

C. Multiply the decimals by a power of 10.

$0.214 \times 10^2 = 21.4$

$0.002 \times 10^2 = 0.2$

$0.508 \times 10^4 = 5,080$

$3.404 \times 10^3 = 3,404$

$0.2746 \times 10^2 = 27.46$

$0.6712 \times 10^5 = 67,120$

$0.0628 \times 10^5 = 6,280$

$5.4203 \times 10^3 = 5,420.3$

D. Fill in the blank to make each statement true.

$0.15 \times \underline{10^2} = 15$

$0.038 \quad \underline{\times 10^2} = 3.8$

$0.002 \times \underline{10} = 0.02$

$0.973 \quad \underline{\times 10^3} = 973$

$72.50 \times \underline{10^2} = 7,250$

$0.092 \quad \underline{\times 10^5} = 9,200$

</td><td>

LESSON 100 Practice

A. Evaluate each expression.

$10^1 = 10$

$10^6 = 1,000,000$

$10^4 = 10,000$

$10^9 = 1,000,000,000$

B. Multiply the decimals by a power of 10.

$0.0762 \times 10 = 0.762$

$49.9 \times 10^2 = 4,990$

$0.0762 \times 10^2 = 7.62$

$5.816 \times 10^3 = 5,816$

$0.0762 \times 10^3 = 76.2$

$0.329 \times 10^4 = 3,290$

$0.0762 \times 10^4 = 762$

$0.0573 \times 10^2 = 5.73$

$0.0762 \times 10^5 = 7,620$

$0.0004 \times 10^7 = 4,000$

C. Fill in the blank to make each statement true.

$0.327 \times \underline{10} = 3.27$

$0.638 \quad \underline{} \times 10^2 = 63.8$

$0.002 \times \underline{10^6} = 2,000$

$0.42 \quad \underline{} \times 10^4 = 4,200$

$3.008 \times \underline{10^2} = 300.8$

$0.974 \quad \underline{} \times 10^5 = 97,400$

D. Scientists write numbers in a special way called **scientific notation** to make them easy to work with. A number is written as the product of a number between 1 and 10 and a power of 10. Using this notation, you can shorten very large numbers in a consistent form. Let's try writing some numbers in scientific notation.

Distance from the earth to the moon: 240,000 miles = 2.4×10^5

Population of the world: 7,000,000,000 = 7×10^9

The sun's core temperature: 27,000,000° F = 2.7×10^7

</td></tr>
</table>

This lesson is on multiplying by powers of ten. That means multiplying by numbers like 10, 100, 1000, etc. One hundred is ten to the power of two, 10^2. That's what is meant by powers of ten. That exponent will tell you the number of zeros in the answer. 10^3 has three zeros, 1000.

We're talking about decimals, though, so let me rephrase that. The exponent not only tells you the number of zeros, it tells you the number of places the decimal point will move. Why? When you add a zero to a number, say 1, it changes its place value. One becomes ten. The digit is the same, but it moved to the next place value. What also happened invisibly is that the decimal point moved.

1.0 x 10 = 10   1.00 x 100 = 100   1.000 x 1000 = 1000.00000000...

They need to remember those invisible zeros. There are an infinite amount of them.

They really only need to be able to count to do today's lesson. It's more about understanding the concept of the changing place value and how the placement of the decimal point shows the change.

Here's an example from the lesson. $0.0628 \times 10^5 = 6,280$ The decimal point moves 5 places.

For part D they just need to remember that the exponent tells you how many decimal places to move.

Fractions, Decimals, and Percents

Lesson 101

LESSON 101 Multiplying decimals

A. Here are the steps for multiplying decimals.

```
    1 2 . 5
  × 0 . 5 3
    3 7 5
  6 2 5
  6 . 6 2 5
```

To solve 12.5 × 0.53:
1. Ignore the decimal point and multiply as usual.
2. Count the total number of decimal places in the factors. 12.5 and 0.53 have a total of 3 decimal places.
3. Place a decimal point in the answer so that the answer has the same number of decimal places as you counted. Place a decimal point in 6625 so that it has 3 decimal places.

B. Multiply the decimals.

31.7	0.075	0.65	47.6
× 0.92	× 4.28	× 0.48	× 26.4
29.164	0.321	0.312	1,256.64

7.368	5.42	0.78	0.095
× 42.8	× 1.225	× 796.3	× 25.17
315.3504	6.6395	621.114	2.39115

LESSON 101 Practice

Multiply the decimals.

0.08	9.6	0.62	1.79	20.9
× 0.9	× 0.7	× 8.4	× 2.3	× 0.42
0.072	6.72	5.208	4.117	8.778

3.82	50.6	3.29	0.672
× 47.6	× 0.114	× 4.15	× 3.07
181.832	5.7684	13.6535	2.06304

0.3645	605.2	0.047	0.38
× 12.8	× 73.4	× 27.16	× 440.5
4.6656	44,421.68	1.27652	167.39

The lesson today is on multiplying decimals. There is only one important thing here, to keep track of the number of decimal places. Again, the important part will be counting decimal places.

They just need to multiply normally. Then they count the number of decimal places. That's how many decimal places are in the answer. This isn't like adding and subtracting where the decimal point doesn't move. When you add two decimal places to two decimal places, you end up with two decimal places. When you multiply two decimal places by two decimal places, you end up with four decimal places.

Here's an example from the lesson. 0.075 x 4.28. That's just 428 x 75. The answer to that is 32,100. Then you count up the decimal places. 3 + 2 = 5 decimal places. The decimal point now is at the end after the last zero. Counting over five, we end up with 0.321 as the answer. The final zeros are redundant and don't need to be there.

Lesson 102

LESSON 102 Dividing decimals by powers of 10

A. To divide decimals by a power of 10, move the decimal point to the left as many places as the number of zeros in the power of 10. The following table shows the place value pattern when decimals are divided by powers of 10. Complete the table.

	8,500	463	10.3	2.6
÷ 10	850	46.3	1.03	0.26
÷ 100	85	4.63	0.103	0.026
÷ 1000	8.5	0.463	0.0103	0.0026

B. Divide the decimals by a power of 10.

$703 \div 10^2 = 7.03$ $2.5 \div 10^2 = 0.025$

$22.6 \div 10^3 = 0.0226$ $340 \div 10^4 = 0.034$

$574.5 \div 10^2 = 5.745$ $6,710 \div 10^5 = 0.0671$

$12,800 \div 10^5 = 0.128$ $14,203 \div 10^3 = 14.203$

C. Fill in the blank to make each statement true.

$0.42 \div$ __10__ $= 0.042$ 247 __$\div 10^2 = 2.47$__

$25.6 \div$ __10^2__ $= 0.256$ 98.8 __$\div 10^2 = 0.988$__

$7,250 \div$ __10^4__ $= 0.725$ $3,060$ __$\div 10^5 = 0.0306$__

D. Solve the word problems.

| A roll of 100 stamps costs $49. What's the price of one stamp? | $0.49 |
| Randy bought 10 stamps with $20. What was his change? | $15.10 |

LESSON 102 Practice

A. Divide the decimals by a power of 10.

$8,6200 \div 10 = 8,620$ $16 \div 10^4 = 0.0016$

$8,6200 \div 10^2 = 862$ $4.2 \div 10^2 = 0.042$

$8,6200 \div 10^3 = 86.2$ $273 \div 10^3 = 0.273$

$8,6200 \div 10^4 = 8.62$ $5,800 \div 10^5 = 0.058$

$8,6200 \div 10^5 = 0.862$ $78,253 \div 10^3 = 78.253$

B. Fill in the blank to make each statement true.

$0.64 \div$ __10__ $= 0.064$ __307__ $\div 10^2 = 3.07$

$50.2 \div$ __10^2__ $= 0.502$ __15.8__ $\div 10^2 = 0.158$

$62.8 \div$ __10^3__ $= 0.0628$ __425__ $\div 10^3 = 0.425$

$4,300 \div$ __10^6__ $= 0.0043$ __12.03__ $\div 10 = 1.203$

$7,029 \div$ __10^4__ $= 0.7029$ __7,640__ $\div 10^4 = 0.764$

C. Solve the word problems.

A local restaurant bought 10 pounds of beef at $53.20. What is the price of beef per pound?	$5.32
A box of 100 pencils sells at $12.00. Jason bought 25 pencils and paid $10. What was his change?	$7
A supermarket sells 20 pounds of potatoes at $38.60. How much does 2 pounds of potatoes cost?	$3.86
Joan's car can drive 100 miles on 6 gallons of gas. How many gallons of gas does it use per mile?	0.06 gallons

Today they do the same, but the opposite. This is similar to lesson 100 in that they are working with powers of ten again. This time they are dividing. Make sure they know that means the decimal point is going to be moving left.

When you divide, the number gets smaller. When the decimal point moves to the left, the number gets smaller. It changes ten into one, 10.0 into 1.00.

The same rules apply about counting the decimal places and the number of decimal places equaling the exponent number. Dividing by 10^4 means moving the decimal point four times to the left. That may mean realizing the invisible decimal point at the end of a whole number. It may also mean that they need to add zeros onto the front of a number. Here's an example.

$34 \div 10^4 = 0.0034$

Lesson 103

LESSON 103 Dividing decimals

A. Here are the steps for dividing decimals.

```
              7.8
0.06 | 0.468  ⇨  6 | 46.8
                     42
   Move both         4 8
decimal points       4 8
   2 places            0
to the right.
```

To solve 0.468 ÷ 0.06:
1. Move the decimal points in the divisor and dividend the same number of places to the right to make the divisor a whole number.
2. Ignore the decimal points and divide as usual.
3. Place a decimal point in the quotient directly above the decimal point in the dividend.

B. Divide the decimals.

```
      7              8.3             590              13
0.9 | 6.3      0.7 | 5.81     0.04 | 23.6     0.62 | 8.06
```

```
      9              8.3              37             550
0.5 | 4.5      0.6 | 4.98     0.26 | 9.62     0.13 | 71.5
```

```
      8              2.6             180              84
0.8 | 6.4      1.2 | 3.12     0.42 | 75.6     0.06 | 5.04
```

LESSON 103 Practice

A. Divide the decimals.

```
      9              2.4             180              48
0.3 | 2.7      0.6 | 1.44     0.07 | 12.6     0.06 | 2.88
```

```
      6              9.3              14             180
0.6 | 3.6      0.4 | 3.72     0.23 | 3.22     0.53 | 95.4
```

```
      4              1.4             130              48
0.7 | 2.8      1.8 | 2.52     0.48 | 62.4     0.12 | 5.76
```

B. Solve the word problems.

Carol is making a game board. Its area is 388.8 square inches, and one side is 18 inches long. How long is the other side?	21.6 inches
Carol wants to cover the board with 3.6-inch square tiles. How many tiles will she need?	30 tiles
Carol decided to put a ribbon stripe along the perimeter of the board. How many inches of ribbon will she use?	79.2 inches

The next step is dividing decimals. When we multiply decimals, we add the number of decimal places together. Dividing is the opposite of multiplying, so naturally, they can subtract the number of decimal places to find where the decimal point goes in the answer.

That's not how they are taught in the lesson, though, but I will show you below. On their lesson page it shows the traditional method. The divisor is what you are dividing by and the dividend is what you are dividing into. You move the decimal point over in the divisor until there are no decimal places, until it's a whole number. You move the decimal point in the dividend the same number of places. That may mean adding on some zeros. The decimal point goes directly above into the answer.

With the subtraction method, you divide and then place the decimal point. Here are a few from the first line on the lesson page:

6.3 ÷ 0.9 = 1 decimal place – 1 decimal place = 0 decimal places in the answer
(You divide 63 by 9 normally and then don't move the decimal point.)

5.81 ÷ 0.7 = 2 decimal places – 1 decimal place = 1 decimal place in the answer
(You divide normally, and then add a decimal place; the decimal point moves one to the left.)

23.6 ÷ 0.04 = 1 decimal place – 2 decimal places = -1 decimal places
Add 1 place value to the answer. The answer to 236 ÷ 4 = 59, so the answer is 590.
(You divide normally and then the decimal point moves one to the right.)

Lesson 104

LESSON 104 Dividing decimals

A. Here's an example of dividing decimals where there is a remainder.

```
                    1.5
0.6 ) 0.9  ⇨  6 ) 9.0
                    6
Move both          3 0
decimal points     3 0
1 place            ___
to the right.        0
```

To solve 0.9 ÷ 0.6:
1. Move the decimal points as before.
2. Ignore the decimal points and divide as usual.
3. If there is a remainder, keep adding zeros to the right of the dividend and continue to divide.
4. Place a decimal point in the quotient where appropriate.

B. Divide the decimals.

```
       268.9              11.54              82.05
0.03 ) 8.067       0.45 ) 5.193       0.68 ) 55.794


       34.86              44.25              202.7
0.05 ) 1.743       0.18 ) 7.965       0.42 ) 85.134
```

LESSON 104 Practice

Divide the decimals.

```
      1.5            8.6            120             2
0.8 ) 1.2     0.7 ) 6.02    0.34 ) 40.8    0.61 ) 1.22


      4.5            0.8            52             96
0.6 ) 2.7     3.2 ) 2.56    0.45 ) 23.4    0.08 ) 7.68


       8.05            126             558
0.32 ) 2.576   0.54 ) 68.04    0.77 ) 429.66


       27.6            9.25            50.8
0.55 ) 15.18   0.42 ) 3.885    0.31 ) 15.748
```

This lesson is on dividing decimals. You might want to ask your child why when you multiply whole numbers the answer is bigger but when you multiply decimals the answer is smaller. It's also the opposite for division. When you divide whole numbers, the answer is always smaller. When you divide decimals, the answer is always bigger. Why?

The answer is that when you are multiplying whole numbers you are getting many of many things. When you are multiplying decimals, you are getting part of a part. Taking half of a half is going to leave you with something smaller. For division think of a square shape made up of 50 blocks. When you divide by a whole number, you are saying something like how many chunks of ten blocks fit into that square. The answer is 5, smaller than 50. The square divided by one is 50. Anything smaller than one, like a decimal, will result in a bigger answer. Think about it. A decimal is a small number. Think about asking how many times a half of a block would fit into the big square. The answer would be twice as many as the regular sized block. Can you see how a decimal makes the answer larger? Since it's smaller, more of them will fit in.

Fractions, Decimals, and Percents

Lesson 105

LESSON 105 Converting fractions to decimals

A. A decimal is a special way of writing a fraction whose denominator is a power of 10. Here are some examples. Fill in the numerators.

$0.7 = \dfrac{7}{10}$ $0.53 = \dfrac{53}{100}$ $0.029 = \dfrac{29}{1000}$

$2.3 = \dfrac{23}{10}$ $4.09 = \dfrac{409}{100}$ $5.103 = \dfrac{5103}{1000}$

B. One way to convert a fraction to a decimal is to find an equivalent fraction whose denominator is a power of 10. Then write the equivalent fraction as a decimal. Here are some examples of using this method. Complete the examples.

$\dfrac{3}{5} = \dfrac{6}{10} = 0.6$ $\dfrac{31}{25} = \dfrac{124}{100} = 1.24$

$\dfrac{58}{20} = \dfrac{29}{10} = 2.9$ $\dfrac{24}{75} = \dfrac{8}{25} = \dfrac{32}{100} = 0.32$

C. Convert the fractions to decimals.

$\dfrac{1}{2} = 0.5$ $\dfrac{51}{50} = 1.02$

$\dfrac{4}{5} = 0.8$ $\dfrac{63}{75} = 0.84$

$\dfrac{9}{25} = 0.36$ $\dfrac{58}{200} = 0.29$

$\dfrac{17}{20} = 0.85$ $\dfrac{136}{250} = 0.544$

LESSON 105 Practice

A. Write each decimal as a fraction with a power of 10 in the denominator.

$0.9 = 9/10$ $0.07 = 7/100$ $0.217 = 217/1000$

$6.5 = 65/10$ $3.29 = 329/100$ $1.403 = 1403/1000$

B. Convert the fractions to decimals.

$\dfrac{5}{2} = 2.5$ $\dfrac{39}{75} = 0.52$

$\dfrac{7}{5} = 1.4$ $\dfrac{45}{50} = 0.9$

$\dfrac{6}{4} = 1.5$ $\dfrac{11}{20} = 0.55$

$\dfrac{24}{15} = 1.6$ $\dfrac{53}{25} = 2.12$

$\dfrac{16}{80} = 0.2$ $\dfrac{72}{200} = 0.36$

$\dfrac{37}{50} = 0.74$ $\dfrac{96}{300} = 0.32$

Did you know? The name Google came from misspelling the word 'googol', which is a very large number. A googol is the number 1 followed by 100 zeros.

They are going to be looking at the relationship between fractions and decimals today and converting fractions into decimals.

They should first read the numbers at the top of the page in part A and fill in the blanks to see how they read the fractions and the decimals the same. That's because they are the same. They have the same value. They are just different ways of writing the same number.

In Lesson 106 they will be converting fractions into decimals with division, but today, they are just finding equivalent fractions that make it easy to write the decimal. That means they are going to be finding equivalent fractions with a denominator of 10, 100, or 1000. A fraction with a denominator of 1000 is equal to a number with three decimal places. (Three zeros = three decimal places.) There are examples for them on the page.

Lesson 106

LESSON 106 Converting fractions to decimals

A. A **fraction** is a division expression where the numerator is divided by the denominator. To convert any fraction to a decimal, simply divide the numerator by the denominator. On the right is an example of using long division to convert fractions to decimals.

$$\frac{5}{8} = 5 \div 8 \Rightarrow 8 \overline{\smash{)}5.000} = 0.625$$

$$\begin{array}{r} 0.625 \\ 8 \overline{\smash{)}5.000} \\ \underline{4\ 8} \\ 20 \\ \underline{16} \\ 40 \\ \underline{40} \\ 0 \end{array}$$

B. Convert the fractions to decimals. Round off your answers to 3 decimal places. (Rounding off decimals to 3 decimal places means rounding to the nearest thousandth.)

$\frac{3}{8} = 0.375$ $\frac{38}{4} = 9.5$ $\frac{14}{25} = 0.56$ $\frac{49}{35} = 1.4$

$\frac{3}{7} = 0.429$ $\frac{14}{3} = 4.667$ $\frac{10}{11} = 0.909$ $\frac{42}{16} = 2.625$

LESSON 106 Practice

Convert the fractions to decimals. Round off decimals to 3 decimal places.

$\frac{9}{4} = 2.25$ $\frac{33}{6} = 5.5$ $\frac{53}{20} = 2.65$ $\frac{44}{80} = 0.55$

$\frac{7}{8} = 0.875$ $\frac{41}{5} = 8.2$ $\frac{15}{40} = 0.375$ $\frac{30}{48} = 0.625$

$\frac{5}{9} = 0.556$ $\frac{20}{7} = 2.857$ $\frac{25}{15} = 1.667$ $\frac{33}{28} = 1.179$

Today they are going to convert more fractions into decimals. This time by dividing. They can remember that fractions are just a way to write a division problem. They need to pay attention to make sure they are dividing the denominator into the numerator.

Then they just need to divide like they have been. They will need to place a decimal point and zero or zeros after the numerator in order to divide. They have an example on their page.

In part B they are asked to round some of their answers. If the answer goes to a fourth decimal place, they just need to know if that digit is going to be five or more. If so, they will round the digit in the thousandths place up one. Otherwise, they just cut the decimal off at that point. Here's an example from the lesson.

$3 \div 7 = 0.4285\ldots$ They can stop there and round and write their answer as 0.429.

Lesson 107

They are going to be working in the opposite direction today. They are going to write the decimals as fractions. To do this they just need to read the decimal. If it's thousandths, then it is written over 1000 as the denominator. To read the decimal, they just need to count those decimal places. If there are three decimal places; that's three zeros; that's thousandths.

There are examples in their lesson. Here's one for you from their lesson.
$2.75 = 2\,^{75}/_{100} = 2\,\tfrac{3}{4}$

They must reduce and simplify the fractions. Any whole number will stay the same between the fraction and the decimal.

Lesson 108

LESSON 108 Converting decimals to fractions

A. Converting decimals to fractions is simply a matter of using appropriate denominators. Fill in the denominators to convert each decimal to a fraction.

$$0.4 = \frac{4}{10} = \frac{2}{5} \qquad 10.56 = 10\frac{56}{100} = 10\frac{14}{25}$$

$$3.5 = 3\frac{5}{10} = 3\frac{1}{2} \qquad 0.072 = \frac{72}{1000} = \frac{9}{125}$$

B. Convert the decimals to fractions. Simplify your answers.

$$0.2 = \frac{1}{5} \qquad\qquad 1.44 = 1\frac{11}{25}$$

$$3.1 = 3\frac{1}{10} \qquad\qquad 7.94 = 7\frac{47}{50}$$

$$0.04 = \frac{1}{25} \qquad\qquad 0.002 = \frac{1}{500}$$

$$0.48 = \frac{12}{25} \qquad\qquad 0.035 = \frac{7}{200}$$

$$4.25 = 4\frac{1}{4} \qquad\qquad 1.875 = 1\frac{7}{8}$$

$$6.15 = 6\frac{3}{20} \qquad\qquad 4.025 = 4\frac{1}{40}$$

LESSON 108 Practice

Convert the decimals to fractions. Simplify your answers.

$$0.3 = \frac{3}{10} \qquad\qquad 4.05 = 4\frac{1}{20}$$

$$2.8 = 2\frac{4}{5} \qquad\qquad 0.54 = \frac{27}{50}$$

$$3.2 = 3\frac{1}{5} \qquad\qquad 1.88 = 1\frac{22}{25}$$

$$4.3 = 4\frac{3}{10} \qquad\qquad 0.125 = \frac{1}{8}$$

$$0.22 = \frac{11}{50} \qquad\qquad 7.008 = 7\frac{1}{125}$$

$$0.65 = \frac{13}{20} \qquad\qquad 0.325 = \frac{13}{40}$$

$$1.49 = 1\frac{49}{100} \qquad\qquad 9.504 = 9\frac{63}{125}$$

$$7.75 = 7\frac{3}{4} \qquad\qquad 8.027 = 8\frac{27}{1000}$$

They are doing the opposite today, converting decimals into fractions. Again, they just have to read it to do it. If the decimal is four tenths, then they write the fraction four tenths.

The number of zeros equals the number of decimal places. 0.004 is four thousandths. There are three digits after the decimal point, three decimal places. The denominator is 1000, one with three zeros.

Lesson 109

LESSON 109 Converting fractions to repeating decimals

A. Some fractions are converted to decimals where a digit or a group of digits repeats without ending. Such decimals are called **repeating decimals**, and are represented by putting a horizontal bar above the repeating digit(s). Here are some examples.

$$\frac{1}{3} = 0.3333... = 0.\overline{3} \qquad \frac{2}{11} = 0.181818... = 0.\overline{18}$$

$$\frac{1}{6} = 0.1666... = 0.1\overline{6} \qquad \frac{1}{7} = 0.\overline{142857}$$

B. Convert the fractions to decimal. If necessary, use a bar to indicate the repeating digit(s).

$$\frac{2}{3} = 0.\overline{6} \qquad \frac{1}{9} = 0.\overline{1} \qquad \frac{14}{16} = 0.875 \qquad \frac{50}{66} = 0.7\overline{5}$$

$$\frac{5}{6} = 0.8\overline{3} \qquad \frac{7}{11} = 0.\overline{63} \qquad \frac{29}{37} = 0.\overline{783} \qquad \frac{54}{80} = 0.675$$

LESSON 109 Practice

Convert the fractions to decimal. If necessary, use a bar to indicate the repeating digit(s).

$$\frac{4}{3} = 1.\overline{3} \qquad \frac{1}{8} = 0.125 \qquad \frac{1}{11} = 0.\overline{09} \qquad \frac{4}{33} = 0.\overline{12}$$

$$\frac{7}{6} = 1.1\overline{6} \qquad \frac{4}{18} = 0.2\overline{2} \qquad \frac{9}{12} = 0.75 \qquad \frac{27}{20} = 1.35$$

$$\frac{9}{4} = 2.25 \qquad \frac{8}{12} = 0.\overline{6} \qquad \frac{41}{90} = 0.45\overline{5} \qquad \frac{31}{99} = 0.\overline{31}$$

They are going back to dividing fractions today to come up with decimals. This time it's a specific kind of decimal, the repeating decimal. They will divide until they find the repeating pattern. Then they draw a line over that part of the decimal. The line shows that those digits repeat.

A repeating decimal is one where the same digits repeat over and over infinitely. Those numbers are expressed more precisely as fractions. Today they are mostly learning to recognize the notation of a repeating decimal.

Lesson 110

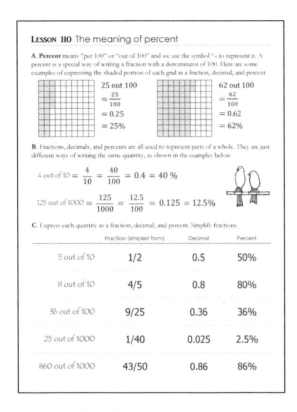

LESSON 110 The meaning of percent

A. Percent means "per 100" or "out of 100" and we use the symbol % to represent it. A percent is a special way of writing a fraction with a denominator of 100. Here are some examples of expressing the shaded portion of each grid as a fraction, decimal, and percent.

25 out 100
$= \frac{25}{100}$
$= 0.25$
$= 25\%$

62 out 100
$= \frac{62}{100}$
$= 0.62$
$= 62\%$

B. Fractions, decimals, and percents are all used to represent parts of a whole. They are just different ways of writing the same quantity, as shown in the examples below.

4 out of 10 $= \frac{4}{10} = \frac{40}{100} = 0.4 = 40\%$

125 out of 1000 $= \frac{125}{1000} = \frac{12.5}{100} = 0.125 = 12.5\%$

C. Express each quantity as a fraction, decimal, and percent. Simplify fractions.

	Fraction (simplest form)	Decimal	Percent
5 out of 10	1/2	0.5	50%
8 out of 10	4/5	0.8	80%
36 out of 100	9/25	0.36	36%
25 out of 1000	1/40	0.025	2.5%
860 out of 1000	43/50	0.86	86%

LESSON 110 Practice

Express each quantity as a fraction, decimal, and percent. Simplify fractions.

	Fraction (simplest form)	Decimal	Percent
1 out of 10	1/10	0.1	10%
7 out of 10	7/10	0.7	70%
6 out of 10	3/5	0.6	60%
5 out of 100	1/20	0.05	5%
75 out of 100	3/4	0.75	75%
90 out of 100	9/10	0.9	90%
8 out of 1000	1/125	0.008	0.8%
45 out of 1000	9/200	0.045	4.5%
192 out of 1000	24/125	0.192	19.2%
560 out of 1000	14/25	0.56	56%

Did you know? 111111111 x 111111111 = 12345678987654321

This is a simple lesson showing the relationship between fraction, decimal, and percent. We've just looked at how fractions and decimals are two expressions of the same thing.

Percent is also a similar expression. Percent shows the part of one hundred. So it's the same as having the number with one hundred as its denominator or with two digits after the decimal point. 5% is 0.05, 5/100.

There are illustrations and examples on their page. They are just to rewrite the expressions in all three formats.

For instance, 5 out of 10, is 5/10 or ½, 0.5, and 50%. It's not five percent. That would be 0.05. Percent is two decimal places, so it takes 0.50 and turns it into 50%. To find the percent you move the decimal point over two places.

Fractions, Decimals, and Percents

Lesson 111

LESSON 111 Converting decimals to percents

A. To convert a decimal to a percent, multiply the decimal by 100 and add the % sign. This is equivalent to moving the decimal point 2 places to the right. Convert the decimals below.

0.5 = 50%	0.01 = 1%	0.002 = 0.2%
0.8 = 80%	0.03 = 3%	0.005 = 0.5%
0.2 = 20%	0.98 = 98%	0.074 = 7.4%
2.2 = 220%	4.12 = 412%	3.102 = 310.2%

B. Express each quantity as a decimal and percent.

	Decimal	Percent	Work area
7 out of 10	0.7	70%	
9 out of 20	0.45	45%	
26 out of 50	0.52	52%	
8 out of 100	0.08	8%	
14 out of 200	0.07	7%	
55 out of 500	0.11	11%	
752 out of 1000	0.752	75.2%	

LESSON 111 Practice

A. Convert the decimals to percents.

0.9 = 90%	0.05 = 5%	0.003 = 0.3%
0.1 = 10%	0.62 = 62%	0.016 = 1.6%
1.6 = 160%	3.02 = 302%	5.208 = 520.8%
3.7 = 370%	7.15 = 715%	6.734 = 673.4%
0.5 = 50%	2.36 = 236%	0.008 = 0.8%
4.2 = 420%	0.01 = 1%	1.059 = 105.9%

B. Express each quantity as a decimal and percent.

	Decimal	Percent	Work area
1 out of 10	0.1	10%	
7 out of 20	0.35	35%	
5 out of 100	0.05	5%	
12 out of 500	0.024	2.4%	
9 out of 1000	0.009	0.9%	
274 out of 1000	0.274	27.4%	

They are going to be working with percents today. A percent is a part of one hundred. 0.12 is twelve hundredths. It is also twelve percent.

To convert from a decimal to a percent the decimal point moves two places to the right. Here are some examples.

0.50 becomes 50%

0.04 becomes 4%

1.2 becomes 120%

3.925 becomes 392.5%

Lesson 112

LESSON 112 Converting percents to decimals

A. To convert a percent to a decimal, divide the percent by 100 and drop the % sign. This is equivalent to moving the decimal point 2 places to the left. Convert the percents below.

3% = 0.03	10% = 0.1	0.3% = 0.003
1% = 0.01	40% = 0.4	7.5% = 0.075
5% = 0.05	28% = 0.28	200% = 2
9% = 0.09	59% = 0.59	54.7% = 0.547

B. To find a percent of a number, convert the percent to either a fraction or a decimal. Then multiply the fraction or decimal by the number. The following examples show why you can use either fractions or decimals. Complete the second example.

$$50\% \; of \; 20 = \frac{50}{100} \, of \, 20 = \frac{50}{100} \times 20 = 0.5 \times 20 = 10$$

$$40\% \; of \; 45 = \frac{40}{100} \, of \, 45 = \frac{40}{100} \times 45 = 0.4 \times 45 = 18$$

C. Calculate the percent of each number.

20% of 5		7% of 150	
	1		10.5
9% of 50		50% of 80	
	4.5		40
10% of 20		55% of 60	
	2		33

LESSON 112 Practice

A. Convert the decimals to percents.

2% = 0.02	11% = 0.11	0.6% = 0.006
7% = 0.07	55% = 0.55	7.2% = 0.072
3% = 0.03	32% = 0.32	100% = 1
5% = 0.05	29% = 0.29	240% = 2.4

B. Calculate the percent of each number.

3% of 70		6% of 220	
	2.1		13.2
5% of 65		5% of 180	
	3.25		9
10% of 50		4% of 675	
	5		27
11% of 15		22% of 90	
	1.65		19.8
20% of 90		70% of 40	
	18		28

Today they are moving in the opposite direction and converting from percents to decimals.

The decimal point will be moving in the opposite direction. It will move two places to the left. Here are some examples.

30% becomes 0.30 or 0.3

2% becomes 0.02

683% becomes 6.83

They are going to be multiplying by percents as well, which just means multiplying by a decimal. The examples show that you can multiply by a fraction as well, but I think it's much simpler to multiply by the decimal.

25% of 10 is 0.25 x 10 = 2.5

"Of" is always a clue word that you need to multiply.

Lesson 113

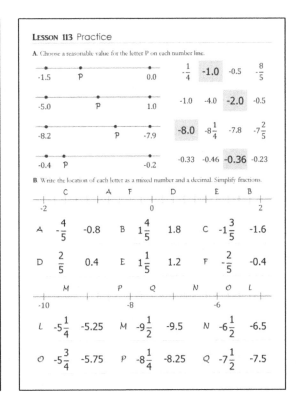

They are going to be working with negative fractions and decimals today. These work just like negative whole numbers, the larger negative number goes to the left on the number line; it's the smaller number.

They have seen similar pages to this before with numerous number lines. Each number line has them filling in both decimals and fractions. They need to not get confused by all the numbers. When the decimal is already filled in for a mark on the number line, they just need to fill in the fraction. They can convert the decimal to figure out what fraction goes there.

Where there are no fractions or decimals already given, they need to count up the number of divisions on the number line to see what part of the whole they are looking at. If there are ten divisions, then three of those lines is three tenths. 0.3 and 3/10.

Lesson 114

LESSON 114 Ordering numeric expressions

A. You can compare numbers expressed as fractions, decimals, and percents since they are just different ways of writing the same quantity. To compare these different numeric expressions, first convert them to the same form and then compare their values. Here are some examples of using this method. Complete the examples using <, >, or =.

$$\frac{1}{8} \quad ? \quad 0.12 \quad \Rightarrow \quad 0.125 \; > \; 0.12 \quad \text{or} \quad \frac{1}{8} \; > \; \frac{12}{100}$$

$$5.4\% \quad ? \quad 0.54 \quad \Rightarrow \quad 0.054 \; < \; 0.54 \quad \text{or} \quad 5.4\% \; < \; 54\%$$

B. Order each set of numbers from least to greatest.

0.85, 2.3, 50%
$$50\%, \; 0.85, \; 2.3$$

0.4, 23%, 16%
$$16\%, \; 23\%, \; 0.4$$

9%, 1.3, 72%
$$9\%, \; 72\%, \; 1.3$$

4.8, 30%, 2.5
$$30\%, \; 2.5, \; 4.8$$

$\frac{3}{5}$, 0.4, 20%
$$20\%, \; 0.4, \; \frac{3}{5}$$

0.8, $\frac{5}{4}$, 25%
$$25\%, \; 0.8, \; \frac{5}{4}$$

$\frac{3}{8}$, 0.125, 62%
$$0.125, \; \frac{3}{8}, \; 62\%$$

$\frac{11}{20}, \frac{3}{2}$, 50%
$$50\%, \; \frac{11}{20}, \; \frac{3}{2}$$

LESSON 114 Practice

Order each set of numbers from least to greatest.

1.5, 0.5, 15%
$$15\%, \; 0.5, \; 1.5$$

7%, 0.02, 0.05
$$0.02, \; 0.05, \; 7\%$$

2.4, 13%, 0.17
$$13\%, \; 0.17, \; 2.4$$

0.4, 32%, 28%
$$28\%, \; 32\%, \; 0.4$$

1.8, 2.1, 90%
$$90\%, \; 1.8, \; 2.1$$

2.4, 20%, 1.5
$$20\%, \; 1.5, \; 2.4$$

$\frac{9}{4}$, 2.3, 15%
$$15\%, \; \frac{9}{4}, \; 2.3$$

1.2, $\frac{9}{10}$, 85%
$$85\%, \; \frac{9}{10}, \; 1.2$$

0.72, $\frac{71}{10}$, 7%
$$7\%, \; 0.72, \; \frac{71}{10}$$

$\frac{9}{20}, \frac{13}{10}$, 50%
$$\frac{9}{20}, \; 50\%, \; \frac{13}{10}$$

$\frac{1}{2}, \frac{2}{5}$, 10%
$$10\%, \; \frac{2}{5}, \; \frac{1}{2}$$

$\frac{7}{25}$, 65%, 30%
$$\frac{7}{25}, \; 30\%, \; 65\%$$

They will be working with fractions, decimals, and percents today. They will be ordering numbers, finding which is greater, which is less.

To compare the numbers it's easiest to put them in the same format, to compare fractions to fractions and decimals to decimals, percents to percents.

Here's the first from the lesson page.

0.85, 2.3, 50% In percents that's 85%, 230%, 50%. Then it's easy to order them.

To find the percent, you move the decimal point over two places to the right.

Here's another example.

3/5, 0.4, 20% That's 0.6, 0.4, 0.2 in decimals.

I doubled 3 and 5 to get six tenths. That's easy to write as a decimal. To turn the percent into a decimal, I moved the decimal back over to the left two places.

Fractions, Decimals, and Percents

Lesson 115

LESSON 115 Numbers as fractions, decimals, and percents

A. Improper fractions and mixed numbers are converted to decimals greater than 1 and percents greater than 100%, as shown in the examples below.

$$\frac{6}{5} = 1\frac{1}{5} = 1.2 = 120\% \qquad \frac{19}{8} = 2\frac{3}{8} = 2.375 = 237.5\%$$

B. Convert between fractions, decimals, and percents. Simplify fractions and round off decimals to 3 decimal places, if necessary.

Fraction	Decimal	Percent	Work area
$\frac{5}{6}$	0.833	83.3%	
17/25	0.68	68%	
3 1/2	3.5	350%	
7/8	0.875	87.5%	
$\frac{11}{9}$	1.222	122.2%	
9/40	0.225	22.5%	
$7\frac{3}{4}$	7.75	775%	
123/250	0.492	49.2%	

LESSON 115 Practice

Convert between fractions, decimals, and percents. Simplify fractions and round off decimals to 3 decimal places, if necessary.

Fraction	Decimal	Percent	Work area
$\frac{2}{3}$	0.667	66.7%	
3/4	0.75	75%	
$\frac{4}{9}$	0.444	44.4%	
41/50	0.82	82%	
1 16/25	1.64	164%	
$\frac{11}{12}$	0.917	91.7%	
19/50	0.38	38%	
$\frac{16}{7}$	2.286	228.6%	
8 13/50	8.26	826%	
9/200	0.045	4.5%	

They are going to continue converting between fractions, decimals, and percents. They can turn back in their workbook if they need a reminder of how to find fractions or decimals.

They will be using some mixed numbers this time. 5.1 as a percent is 510%. 64.5% as a decimal is 0.645. The decimal point is moving two places to the right to make the percent and two places to the left to make the decimal.

Lesson 116

LESSON 116 Identifying percent, whole, and part

A. Percent problems have three components: **percent, whole** (total amount), and **part** (partial amount). The part is what you get when you take the percent of the whole. The percent equation states this relationship: percent · whole = part.

B. Percent problems often ask you to find the unknown component among the three. The first step is always to identify the three components in a problem. Here are some real world examples. Identify the percent, whole, and part in each situation. Use the letter a to represent the unknown component.

	Percent	Whole	Part
Mia has 20 crayons, and 15% of them are broken. How many crayons are broken?	15%	20	a
Danny got 48 questions correct out of 50 in a test. What percent was that?	a	50	48
Sam spent 50% of his money to buy a book at $15. How much money did Sam have at first?	50%	a	15
Terry bought a box of 60 apples, and 15 of them were bad. What percent was that?	a	60	15
Josh bought a shirt at 12% off the regular price of $24. How much did he save?	12%	24	a
Kelly read 4 books last month. It was 80% of what Eli read. How many books did Eli read?	80%	a	4

C. Write the percent equation, percent · whole = part, for each situation above.

Mia's crayons	Danny's test	Sam's money
15% · 20 = a	a% · 50 = 48	50% · a = 15

Terry's apples	Josh's saving	Eli's books
a% · 60 = 15	12% · 24 = a	80% · a = 4

LESSON 116 Practice

A. Write the percent equation for each situation. Use the letter a to represent the unknown.

Six percent of 50 apples are bad. How many apples are bad?	6% · 50 = a
Fifteen percent of 40 crayons are broken. How many crayons are broken?	15% · 40 = a
In a math club, 22 of 40 kids are boys. What percentage are boys?	a% · 40 = 22
Stacey got 24 questions correct out of 25 in a test. What percent was that?	a% · 25 = 24
Eighty percent of 150 kids attended the baseball game. How many kids were at the game?	80% · 150 = a
The dinner bill was $40, and Mr. Kim left $7 as a tip. What percent was the tip?	a% · 40 = 7
Paul saved $800 for a trip and actually spent $600. What percent did he spend?	a% · 800 = 600
Ron's new laptop was $960 plus 7% sales tax. How much sales tax did he pay?	a% · 960 = a

B. What number am I? Use the clues to solve each riddle.

I am a percent. In fraction form, I am equivalent to three quarters minus two eighths. What number am I?	50%
I am a percent less than 100%. As a decimal, I have two digits in total and my tenths digit is the square of 3. What number am I?	90%
I am a fraction. My numerator is 8 less than my denominator. In percent form, I can be written as 60%. What number am I?	12/20
I am a decimal with 2 digits in total. As a percent, I'm between 200% and 300%. The sum of my digits is 5. What number am I?	2.3

They will be setting up for word problems today. They need to figure out the three components to each question: the percent, the total amount, and the partial amount. One of them will be unknown. If they are confused, label that as a question mark to make it clear that's what they don't know and are looking for. In their workbook, it's letter A, as in the answer they are looking for.

They will be finding the percent of a total to get the partial amount. Sometimes, for instance, the percent won't be known. They need to write the equation to set up what they know and what they need to find out.

They will all have the structure of percent x total = partial amount. They just need to fill in the numbers for each separate equation, each separate question.

Lesson 117

LESSON 117 Types of percent problems

A. There are three types of percent problems depending on which of the three components is missing. Regardless of the type, to solve percent problems, you first identify the percent, whole, and part. Then use the percent equation, percent · whole = part, to find the unknown. Let's look at each type of problem and how to solve it.

Find the part:	Find the percent:	Find the whole:
What is 20% of 80?	36 is what percent of 90?	6 is 30% of what number?
Percent = 20%	Percent = Unknown	Percent = 30%
Whole = 80	Whole = 90	Whole = Unknown
Part = Unknown	Part = 36	Part = 6
20% × 80 = Part	Percent × 90 = 36	0.3 × Whole = 6
0.2 × 80 = Part	Divide both sides by 90.	Divide both sides by 0.3.
16 = Part	Percent = 36/90	Whole = 6/0.3
	= 0.4 = 40%	= 20

B. Solve the percent problems.

What is 40% of 900?

360

15 is what percent of 120?

12.5%

19 is 20% of what number?

95

Find 16% of 240.

38.4

16 is what percent of 64?

25%

90% of what number is 135?

150

LESSON 117 Practice

Solve the percent problems.

Find 75% of 300.

225

33 is 30% of what number?

110

12 is what percent of 60?

20%

What is 50% of 112?

56

70% of what number is 147?

210

49 is what percent of 350?

14%

What 5.5% of 1400?

77

35 is what percent of 125?

28%

45 is what percent of 500?

9%

44 is 25% of what number?

176

They will be setting up equations today again, but this time they need to find that missing number. There are examples on the page of how to figure it out each time.

First they need to write their equation. Then they need to figure out which type of problem it is. Then they can follow the example on the page for that type of problem.

They need to remember that OF means to multiply. IS means an equal sign. WHAT is the ?, the unknown. Here's an example from their lesson.

16 "is" "what" percent "of" 64?
16 = ?   x 64

The example shows you divide 16 by 64 and end up with ¼ or 0.25, so 25%.

Lesson 118

LESSON 118 Word problems: percents

A. To solve word problems involving percents, first identify the percent, whole, and part. Then use the percent equation, percent · whole = part, to find the unknown and finally what is being asked. Here is an example of using this strategy.

A TV originally cost $350. If the price of the TV increases by 10%, what is the new price?   **$385**

Identify the percent, whole, and part:
Percent = 10%,
Whole = $350
Part = Price increase
    = 10% × $350
    = 0.1 × $350 = $35

Find what is being asked:
New price
= Original price + Increase
= $350 + $35
= $385

B. Solve the word problems.

$8.00 candy bars are now on sale for 30% off. What will be the candy bars price now?   **$5.60**

The dinner bill was $42, and Emma left a 20% tip. How much did Emma pay for the dinner?   **$50.40**

A video game costs $50. It's on sale for $44. What percent of the price is discounted?   **12%**

Cammy bought a jacket at $11. The price was 80% off its regular price. What was the original price?   **$55**

Max's new laptop was $980 plus 7% tax. How much did Max pay for his laptop?   **$1,048.60**

Michael earns $48,000 per year, and he pays 25% for income tax. What is his annual income after tax?   **$36,000**

Jessica saved $180. Denise saved 90% of Jessica's amount. How much money did Denise save?   **$162**

The gym membership fee is $55 per month. If Alex signs up for one whole year, she'll receive 15% off the total annual cost. What will be her actual cost for one year?   **$561**

LESSON 118 Practice

Solve the word problems.

Lucy bought a pair of shoes at 10% off the regular price of $45. How much did she pay?   **$40.50**

The dinner bill was $58, and Sam left a 15% tip. How much did Sam pay for the dinner?   **$66.70**

Sophia bought a computer game at 12% off the regular price of $35. How much did she save?   **$4.20**

Kelly read 40% of a novel, and she now has 108 pages left. How many pages does the novel have?   **180 pages**

There are 25 children in Josh's book club. Twelve of them wear glasses. What percent of the book club wear glasses?   **48%**

Stacey bought a table at 35% off the regular price. She paid $81.90 for the table. What was the regular price?   **$126**

Walter's rent was $520 per month. Starting this month, it went up by 4%. What will be his rent payment now?   **$540.80**

A shoe store has a sale on sneakers for 40% off. If the sale price of a pair is $39, what is the original price?   **$65**

Laura solved 25 decimal problems and got 23 problems correct. What percent of the problems did she get correct?   **92%**

A pair of socks sells for $12. The sales tax is 6%. Tylor bought 5 pairs of socks. How much did he pay in total?   **$63.60**

The population of Daniel's city was 50,000 two years ago. The population grew by 4% last year and then dropped by 4,000 this year. What is the population of Daniel's city this year?   **48,000**

Our homeschool group includes 25 high school students, 32 middle school students, and 23 elementary students, and 55% of the students are girls. How many boys are in our group?   **36 boys**

This is the final page in this section of the book. They are going to be doing the same thing but with word problems. They need to do the same thing: set up their equation and find what they are missing.

After they find the answer, they should read the question again. There may be another step to the problem. For instance, if the question was about what the sale price is if it's 30% off, then after they find what 30% is, they need to subtract that off the original total cost.

If they get something wrong that's not just a little mistake, have them go back and read the question again and make sure they answered the right question.

Lesson 119

LESSON 119 Introduction to ratios

A. A **ratio** is a comparison of two numbers. A ratio of two numbers a and b can be written in three ways: a:b, a to b, and a/b. The ratio a:b means that for every a units of one quantity there are b units of another quantity. Write each ratio below in three ways.

	Using a colon	In words	As a fraction
There are 5 apples and 8 bananas. What is the ratio of apples to bananas?	5:8	5 to 8	5/8
There are 7 girls and 9 boys at the park. What is the ratio of boys to girls?	9:7	9 to 7	9/7
Max has $8. Laura has $11. What is the ratio of Laura's money to Max's money?	11:8	11 to 8	11/8
Sam has 6 blue pens and 7 red pens. What is the ratio of blue pens to all pens?	6:13	6 to 13	6/13
In the words "Easy Peasy," what is the ratio of vowels to consonants?	6:3	6 to 3	6/3

B. Write each ratio using a colon and as a fraction.

What is the ratio of the number of nickels in a dollar to the number of quarters in a dollar?	20:4	20/4
Jessica has 15 pennies, 11 nickels, 7 dimes, and 14 quarters. What is the ratio of pennies to dimes?	15:7	15/7
What is the ratio of the number of sides in a pentagon to the number of sides in a hexagon?	5:6	5/6
What is the ratio of the number of seconds in a minute to the number of hours in a day?	60:24	60/24
A rectangle is 5 inches wide and 8 inches long. What is the ratio of the perimeter to the area of the rectangle?	26:40	26/40
Terry bought a box of 40 apples, and 15 of them were bad. What is the ratio of bad apples to good apples?	15:25	15/25

LESSON 119 Practice

A. Write each ratio in three different ways.

	Using a colon	In words	As a fraction
There are 9 peaches and 12 bananas. What is the ratio of peaches to bananas?	9:12	9 to 12	9/12
Mia has 16 blue pens and 7 red pens. What is the ratio of red pens to blue pens?	7:16	7 to 16	7/16
There are 14 girls and 25 boys at the park. What is the ratio of girls to boys?	14:25	14 to 25	14/25
Ron saved $22. Max saved $30. What is the ratio of Max's savings to Ron's savings?	30:22	30 to 22	30/22
A farm has 6 cows, 7 pigs, and 25 chickens. What is the ratio of pigs to all animals?	7:38	7 to 38	7/38

B. Write each ratio using a colon and as a fraction.

Mike solved 17 fraction problems and 15 decimal problems. What is the ratio of decimal problems to all problems?	15:32	15/32
What is the ratio of the number of faces in a cube to the number of faces in a pyramid?	6:5	6/5
A rectangle is 8 inches wide and 4 inches long. What is the ratio of the perimeter to the area of the rectangle?	24:32	24/32
Kate has 12 pennies, 7 nickels, 18 dimes, and 3 quarters. What is the ratio of dimes to all coins?	18:40	18/40
Penny used 5 cups of flour, 4 tablespoons of butter, 2 teaspoons of cinnamon, and 3 cups of sugar to bake cookies. What is the ratio of sugar to flour?	3:5	3/5
Paul bought a pair of socks at $15, a hat at $13, and a shirt at $24. What is the ratio of the money spent on a pair of socks to the total money spent?	15:52	15/52

We've moved into a new category today, ratios and proportions. This is all about comparing two things to each other. For example, there are six of these compared to seven of the other. There are half as many as the other. There are twice as many of these. "To" and "as" are some of the key words to ratios and proportions.

They will be using the word "to" today to write ratios, but they will also be writing them with colons and as fractions. They are all ways of saying the same thing.

If there are 3 apples and 4 oranges in a fruit bowl, there are 3 apples to 4 oranges. We can also write that as 3:4 and ¾.

This is a little confusing because they've always learned that the denominator is showing the total number and the top is the part of the whole. This would be 3/7 if it were showing the number of apples compared to the total number of fruit. But we're not looking for that. Apples and oranges aren't the same thing. The apples aren't part of the oranges. That's not what we're saying with our ratio fractions.

The ratio of apples to oranges is 3/4 and the ratio of oranges to apples is 4/3. We say that the ratio of oranges to apples is "four to three."

Lesson 120

LESSON 120 Simplifying ratios

A. One way to simplify ratios is to write them as fractions and simplify the fractions to the lowest terms. Then you can write the simplified fractions as ratios with a colon. Here are some examples of using this method. Complete the second example.

$$12:20 = \frac{12}{20} = \frac{3}{5} = 3:5 \qquad 35:42 = \frac{35}{42} = \frac{5}{6} = 5:6$$

B. Simplify each ratio.

18:27 = 2:3	24:28 = 6:7
16:32 = 1:2	42:54 = 7:9
27:15 = 9:5	20:56 = 5:14
60:90 = 2:3	44:72 = 11:18
72:84 = 6:7	33:88 = 3:8

42:210 = 1:5

24:108 = 2:9

LESSON 120 Practice

Simplify each ratio.

8:14 = 4:7	10:16 = 5:8
9:15 = 3:5	12:27 = 4:9
6:27 = 2:9	32:28 = 8:7
14:98 = 1:7	44:55 = 4:5
25:45 = 5:9	24:28 = 6:7
33:39 = 11:13	42:56 = 3:4

90:315 = 2:7

64:200 = 8:25

8:2 (5 and 3) or 16:14 (15 and 1)

This lesson will look familiar. They are going to be simplifying ratios. This is just like reducing fractions. Reducing fractions works because you are just finding an equivalent fraction. You do that by multiplying or dividing by one, which doesn't change the value of the fraction. You do that by using a fraction like 3/3 or 5/5 where the numerator and denominator are the same. All of those fractions equal one. That's just what they will be doing here. They will divide the numerator and denominator by the same number.

But, let me just show you that this works with ratios as well.

There are two circles and four squares. The ratio of circles to squares is two to four. For every two circles there are four squares. We can divide both two and four by two and get ½. Is it true that for every one circle there are two squares? Yes, the ratio of circles to squares is 1 to 2. That's a more descriptive ratio, one more easily understood, than if you had say, 47 circles and 94 squares.

Lesson 121

LESSON 121 Simplifying ratios

A. You can simplify ratios just as you simplify fractions: divide both numbers by their greatest common divisor (GCD) or keep dividing both sides by a common divisor until you can't divide them any further. The following examples use the strategy of 'keep dividing' to reach the simplest form of a ratio. Complete the second example.

$\div 3 \big(\; 63 : 84 \; \big) \div 3$
$= 21 : 28$
$\div 7 \big(\; = 3 : 4 \; \big) \div 7$

$\div 4 \big(\; 128 : 200 \; \big) \div 4$
$= 32 : 50$
$\div 2 \big(\; 16 : 25 \; \big) \div 2$

B. Equivalent ratios are just like equivalent fractions. Ratios are equivalent if they can be simplified to the same ratio. To find equivalent ratios, multiply or divide both sides by the same number. Write at least three equivalent ratios for each ratio below.

4:5   Answers will vary.   20:50 _____

5:7 _____   60:90 _____

C. Simplify each ratio.

12:60   36:54   96:42
= 1:5   = 2:3   = 16:7

30:75   22:88   99:30
= 2:5   = 1:4   = 33:10

84:156   25:150   80:400
= 7:13   = 1:6   = 1:5

LESSON 121 Practice

A. Circle all ratios that are equivalent to the first one in each row.

12:15	4:5	36:45	3:5	45/36	5:4	24:30
36:27	12:6	4 to 3	16:12	5:4	72:54	6/8
40:32	20/18	10:8	4:5	15:12	44:36	5:4
44:66	22:33	3:2	11:22	2 to 3	4:6	55:77
25:50	1:2	12:25	5/10	4:10	10:20	2:5

B. Simplify each ratio.

45:50   54:72   58:20
= 9:10   = 3:4   = 29:10

42:63   75:21   16:64
= 2:3   = 25:7   = 1:4

54:108   48:132   44:121
= 1:2   = 4:11   = 4:11

105:375   320:608   125:350
= 7:25   = 10:19   = 5:14

They are going to be continuing to practice reducing fractions, namely simplifying ratios. These are written with the colon, but they will do the same thing, divide each side by the same number.

This idea of doing the same thing to each side is the basis of algebra. That's how they will work equations, by doing the same to each side. It's an important concept that you can keep things equal by treating them equally. (Maybe it's a good life lesson as well.)

Here's an example from the practice page.

54:72

I could divide each side by two seeing that they are both even, but I can also see that they are both multiples of nine, so I will divide each side by nine and get 6:8. I still have even numbers, so I will divide each side by two and get 3:4.

This is just like reducing a fraction. Remember that 54:72 could also be written 54/72.

Lesson 122

LESSON 122 Word problems: equivalent ratios

A. To solve word problems involving ratios, first identify the known ratio and the unknown ratio. Then use their relationship to find the unknown and finally what's being asked. Here is an example of using this strategy.

Jenny is having a party. She wants to prepare 1 pie for every 6 guests. If 24 guests are coming, how many pies does she need?

4 pies

Identify the known and unknown ratios:
Known = Pie : Guests = 1:6
Unknown = Pie : Guests = x : 24
Two ratios should be equivalent, so we need to find x that makes 1:6 = x : 24.

Find what is being asked:
$1:6 = x:24$ or $\frac{1}{6} = \frac{x}{24}$
$\frac{1}{6} = \frac{1 \times 4}{6 \times 4} = \frac{4}{24}$
Therefore, $x = 4$.

B. Solve the word problems.

At a market, 5 tomatoes were being sold for $2. Peter bought $10 worth of tomatoes. How many tomatoes did he buy?
25 tomatoes

Sandy can solve 24 division problems every 20 minutes. How many problems can she solve in 10 minutes?
12 problems

Ella planted 30 roses, 27 daisies, and 15 violets in her garden. For every 9 daisies, how many roses did Ella plant?
10 roses

In a zoo, the ratio of adults to children is 5 to 7. If there are 125 adults in the zoo, how many children are there?
175 children

A recipe calls for 3 cups of milk for every 2 cups of flour. Sarah used 4 cups of flour. How many cups of milk did she use?
6 cups

A book club has 30 members, and the ratio of boys to girls is 2:1. How many boys are in the book club?
20 boys

Sam drew a rectangle whose length to width ratio was 3 to 2. If the width of the rectangle was 10 inches, what was its area?
150 sq in

A recipe calls for 2 cups of vegetables, 3 cups of chicken stock, and 2 teaspoons of salt to make 4 servings of soup. How many teaspoons of salt is used for every cup of vegetables?
1 teaspoon

LESSON 122 Practice

A. The table shows what Lisa planted in her garden. Use the table to answer the questions.

Plants in Lisa's Garden

Plant	# of plant
Peppers	20
Broccoli	18
Lettuce	30
Beets	12

For every 10 pepper plants, how many beet plants are there?
6 plants

For every 6 broccoli plants, how many lettuce plants are there?
10 plants

What is the ratio of pepper plants to all plants?
20:80 or 1:4

B. Solve the word problems.

Adam can solve 15 fraction problems every 18 minutes. How many problems can he solve in 6 minutes?
5 problems

A restaurant makes cakes to pies in the ratio of 4 to 5. If the restaurant makes 35 pies, how many cakes does it make?
28 cakes

A recipe calls for 6 bananas to make 4 servings of banana pudding. How many bananas will be used to make 12 servings?
18 bananas

The ratio of boys to girls in a library is 5 to 6. If there are 20 boys in the library, how many girls are there?
24 girls

In a grocery, apples and pears are sold in the ratio of 6:7. If the grocery sells 49 pears, how many apples are sold?
42 apples

A math club has 35 members, and the ratio of boys to girls is 3:4. How many girls are in the math club?
20 girls

Mark drew a rectangle whose length to width ratio was 4 to 5. If the width of the rectangle was 15 inches, what was its perimeter?
54 inches

Eight candies are sold at $2. Brian bought 40 candies and paid with $20. How much change did he receive?
$10

Larry's car uses 5 gallons of gas to travel 110 miles. How many miles can Larry drive on one gallon of gas?
22 miles

The example on the page is showing that there is a one pie to six guest ratio, 1:6. There will be 24 guests, so they need to figure out how many pies they will need. This is a typical problem and useful in real life. ☺

The equivalent ratios are 1:6 = x:24. X is the unknown quantity. It just means the number you don't know. I like to use a ?.

$$\frac{1}{6} = \frac{?}{24}$$

In the next lesson they will learn to solve this with cross multiplying. Right now they just need to think about equivalent fractions, equivalent ratios. 24÷6 = 4, so 6 was multiplied by 4 to get to 24. 1 x 4 = 4, so ? = 4 They need to make four pies.

The most important thing in setting up these problems is to make sure they are comparing apples to apples and oranges to oranges, so to speak. The same thing should be on the same side of the colon. In this problem it's #of pies : #of people to #of pies : #of people.

Here's the set up for the first couple word problems.

5:2 = x:10   ? tomatoes

24:20 = x:10   ? problems

Lesson 123

LESSON 123 Understanding proportions

A. A **proportion** is an equation that states two ratios are equal. It can be written in two ways: in colon form, $a:b = c:d$, or in fraction form, $a/b = c/d$. Here are some examples.

$$3:4 = 15:20 \quad \text{or} \quad \frac{3}{4} = \frac{15}{20} \qquad 5:2 = 25:10 \quad \text{or} \quad \frac{5}{2} = \frac{25}{10}$$

B. A proportion is true if its ratios are equal. One way to determine if a proportion is true or false is to simplify the ratios and compare them, as shown in the example below.

$$\frac{6}{9} = \frac{12}{30} \Rightarrow \frac{6}{9} = \frac{2}{3} \quad \text{but} \quad \frac{12}{30} = \frac{2}{5} \Rightarrow$$ The ratios are not equal, so the proportion is false.

C. Another way to determine if a proportion is true or false is to cross multiply the ratios and compare the cross products. Cross multiplying means to multiply diagonally across the equal sign, and cross products are the products found by cross multiplication. A proportion is true if the cross products are equal. Here is an example of using this method.

$$\frac{6}{15} \times \frac{10}{25} \Rightarrow \begin{array}{l} 6 \cdot 25 = 150 \\ 15 \cdot 10 = 150 \end{array} \Rightarrow$$ The cross products are equal, so the proportion is true.

D. Determine whether each proportion is true or false. Show why.

$6:7 = 12:14$	True		$32:40 = 10:8$	False
$5:2 = 20:15$	False		$8:14 = 16:28$	True
$\frac{9}{8} = \frac{15}{10}$	False		$\frac{24}{40} = \frac{16}{30}$	False
$\frac{18}{24} = \frac{6}{8}$	True		$\frac{14}{18} = \frac{35}{45}$	True

LESSON 123 Practice

A. Determine if each proportion is true or false. Show why.

$5:9 = 15:45$	False		$15:10 = 12:8$	True
$7:4 = 63:36$	True		$21:49 = 7:14$	False
$\frac{15}{45} = \frac{24}{64}$	False		$\frac{32}{40} = \frac{20}{25}$	True
$\frac{63}{36} = \frac{28}{16}$	True		$\frac{12}{44} = \frac{24}{66}$	False
$\frac{18}{54} = \frac{33}{99}$	True		$\frac{45}{40} = \frac{54}{48}$	True
$\frac{36}{48} = \frac{27}{36}$	True		$\frac{24}{30} = \frac{70}{54}$	False

B. Write a proportion for each situation. Write ratios using a colon.

Two bags of apples at $8; x bags of apples at $40.	$2:8 = x:40$
4 free throws in 10 seconds; 20 free throws in y seconds.	$4:10 = 20:y$
255 miles on 10 gallons of gas; z miles on 5 gallon of gas.	$255:10 = z:5$
80 miles per hour; 300 miles in n hours.	$80:1 = 300:n$
23 out of 25 problems; k out of 100 problems.	$23:25 = k:100$

This lesson is introducing proportions, but you can let your child know they just used proportions in Lesson 122. A proportion is just two equal ratios. That's exactly what they were finding in Lesson 122.

Two equivalent fractions are in proportion to each other. That makes sense. If a rectangle has sides of 2 and 4 and another has sides of 3 and 6, they are in proportion to each other. They are different sizes, but their ratios of width to length are the same. One would look like a smaller version of the other.

Scale models and scale drawings are smaller versions of the real thing. They are made with the same proportions. The artists just find the equivalent fractions, the equivalent ratios, in other words the proportion.

There's a neat trick demonstrated in part C today, cross multiplying. You can always cross multiply like that; it's not something special about proportions. It has to do with algebra and doing the same thing to each side. The example is $^6/_{15} = {}^{10}/_{25}$. When you multiply each side by 25, the 25 on the right disappears because you just made $^{25}/_{25}$ which equals 1. The same thing happens on the other side when you multiply each side by 15. That's really what you are doing in order to keep the equation equal by treating each side equally, but since we know that always happens, we just think about it as cross multiplying. It's a nifty trick that will come in handy.

Lesson 124

LESSON 124 Solving proportions

A. Solving a proportion means finding the value of a **variable**, an unknown represented by a letter, which makes the proportion true. One way to solve a proportion is to find the appropriate equivalent ratio, as shown in the example below. Complete the example.

$$\frac{6}{15} = \frac{x}{40} \Rightarrow \frac{6}{15} = \frac{2}{5} = \frac{16}{40} \Rightarrow x = 16$$

B. Solve each proportion (or solve for x).

$\frac{20}{25} = \frac{x}{20}$ x = 16 $\frac{30}{x} = \frac{66}{77}$ x = 35

$\frac{x}{27} = \frac{72}{81}$ x = 24 $\frac{40}{25} = \frac{32}{x}$ x = 20

$\frac{12}{18} = \frac{14}{x}$ x = 21 $\frac{x}{36} = \frac{24}{54}$ x = 16

$\frac{21}{x} = \frac{36}{60}$ x = 35 $\frac{15}{21} = \frac{x}{49}$ x = 35

C. Write a proportion and solve it to answer each question.

Six apples are sold at $5.25. How much do 18 apples cost?

$15.75

Angie drove 55 miles per hour for 4 hours. How many miles did she drive?

220 miles

Six cans of soda cost $2.50. How many cans of soda can you buy for $25?

60 cans

Josh drove 156 miles at 52 miles per hour. How many hours did he drive?

3 hours

LESSON 124 Practice

A. Solve each proportion.

$\frac{3}{5} = \frac{x}{45}$ x = 27 $\frac{36}{28} = \frac{9}{x}$ x = 7

$\frac{8}{x} = \frac{64}{72}$ x = 9 $\frac{x}{55} = \frac{4}{5}$ x = 44

$\frac{12}{42} = \frac{20}{x}$ x = 70 $\frac{x}{40} = \frac{12}{96}$ x = 5

$\frac{25}{x} = \frac{45}{54}$ x = 30 $\frac{32}{24} = \frac{x}{21}$ x = 28

$\frac{24}{26} = \frac{x}{39}$ x = 36 $\frac{27}{x} = \frac{36}{40}$ x = 30

B. Write a proportion and solve it to answer each question.

A recipe calls for 2 cups of milk to make 24 cookies. Sarah baked 36 cookies. How many cups of milk did she use?

3 cups

A rectangle #1 is 5 inches long and 6 inches wide. A similar rectangle #2 is 20 inches long. What is the width of #2?

24 inches

Stacey bought a shirt for $25. The sales tax is 8% ($8 per $100). How much sales tax did she pay?

$2

Mia has 20 crayons, and 15% (or 15 per 100) of the crayons are broken. How many crayons are broken?

3 crayons

They will solve proportions today. While they could cross multiply and then divide, that's not going to be the simplest way for how it's set up. They are encouraged to reduce the fraction and then find the equivalent fraction for the new ratio.

In Lesson 125, the next lesson, they will be solving similar problems by cross multiplying, so you don't need to show them that today even though that would be the typical way to quickly solve proportions. However, these are using bigger numbers today with the intention that the student would reduce the ratios first.

Here's the first one from the lesson.

$$\frac{20}{25} = \frac{x}{20}$$

$^{20}/_{25}$ reduces to $^4/_5$ by dividing both by 5. The new denominator, 5, times four = 20, so the numerator needs to be multiplied by four as well. 4 x 4 = 16 That's the new numerator, the X, what we are looking for.

Lesson 125

LESSON 125 Solving proportions

A. You can solve a proportion using **cross multiplication**: if a/b = c/d, then a·d = b·c. After cross multiplying, you divide both sides of the equation by the number in front of the variable to find its value. Here are the steps for using this method.

Cross multiply.　　　　Divide.　　　　Simplify.

$$\frac{x}{9} = \frac{5}{6} \Rightarrow 6 \cdot x = 9 \cdot 5 \Rightarrow \frac{6 \cdot x}{6} = \frac{9 \cdot 5}{6} \Rightarrow x = 7\frac{1}{2}$$

B. Solve each proportion. Simplify your answers and write as mixed numbers, if necessary.

$\dfrac{5}{6} = \dfrac{x}{20}$　　$x = 16\dfrac{2}{3}$　　　　$\dfrac{3}{x} = \dfrac{12}{25}$　　$x = 6\dfrac{1}{4}$

$\dfrac{x}{25} = \dfrac{9}{45}$　　$x = 5$　　　　$\dfrac{40}{25} = \dfrac{8}{x}$　　$x = 5$

$\dfrac{4}{21} = \dfrac{x}{18}$　　$x = 3\dfrac{3}{7}$　　　　$\dfrac{x}{4} = \dfrac{13}{22}$　　$x = 2\dfrac{4}{11}$

$\dfrac{x}{50} = \dfrac{7}{30}$　　$x = 11\dfrac{2}{3}$　　　　$\dfrac{12}{x} = \dfrac{8}{42}$　　$x = 63$

$\dfrac{5}{28} = \dfrac{20}{x}$　　$x = 112$　　　　$\dfrac{9}{30} = \dfrac{x}{16}$　　$x = 4\dfrac{4}{5}$

LESSON 125 Practice

Solve each proportion. Simplify your answers and write as mixed numbers, if necessary.

$\dfrac{3}{4} = \dfrac{x}{9}$　　$x = 6\dfrac{3}{4}$　　　　$\dfrac{x}{6} = \dfrac{4}{5}$　　$x = 4\dfrac{4}{5}$

$\dfrac{7}{x} = \dfrac{9}{10}$　　$x = 7\dfrac{7}{9}$　　　　$\dfrac{8}{15} = \dfrac{x}{6}$　　$x = 3\dfrac{1}{5}$

$\dfrac{x}{12} = \dfrac{3}{8}$　　$x = 4\dfrac{1}{2}$　　　　$\dfrac{16}{10} = \dfrac{8}{x}$　　$x = 5$

$\dfrac{8}{36} = \dfrac{x}{9}$　　$x = 2$　　　　$\dfrac{9}{x} = \dfrac{15}{21}$　　$x = 12\dfrac{3}{5}$

$\dfrac{3}{x} = \dfrac{18}{45}$　　$x = 7\dfrac{1}{2}$　　　　$\dfrac{x}{14} = \dfrac{5}{42}$　　$x = 1\dfrac{2}{3}$

$\dfrac{21}{28} = \dfrac{12}{x}$　　$x = 16$　　　　$\dfrac{18}{63} = \dfrac{x}{14}$　　$x = 4$

They are cross multiplying today to find X, the missing value of the proportion. I wouldn't be opposed to you allowing them to use a calculator on something like this to multiply and then divide.

This is algebra they are doing. They are finding the unknown in an equation by doing the same thing to each side of the equation. This is how these types of problems are solved.

6/15 = x/40
40 * 6 = 15x　 (Multiply each side by 15 and 40. 15/15 = 1 and 40/40 = 1)
240 = 15x
240/15 = x　　(Same thing happens here. Divide each side by 15. 15/15 = 1)
16 = x

It really is a useful type of equation to understand how to solve quickly. They don't have to write out all those steps. They would just write the third and last lines if they were figuring this out on paper. I used an * instead of x for showing multiplication because once you starting using X to mean an unknown, it's too complicated to use X for multiplication as well.

Lesson 126

<table>
<tr><td>

LESSON 126 Finding unit rates

A. A **rate** is a ratio of two quantities with different units. A **unit rate** is a rate with a denominator of 1. Unit rates are often written with a slash (/) or the word "per." Here is an example of a rate and its unit rate written in three different ways.

$$\frac{120\ miles}{3\ hours} = \frac{40\ miles}{1\ hour}\ \ or\ \ 40\ miles/hour\ \ or\ \ 40\ miles\ \textbf{per}\ hour$$

B. To find a unit rate, first write the rate as a fraction. Then divide both sides of the rate by the denominator. Here is an example of converting a rate to a unit rate.

I can walk 18 miles in 4 hours. ⇨ $\frac{18\ miles}{4\ hours} = \frac{18 \div 4}{4 \div 4} = 4.5\ miles/hour$

C. Find a unit rate to represent each situation.

Buy 4 tickets at $126. How much per ticket?

Run 35 miles every 7 days. How many miles per day?

$31.50/ticket   5 miles/day

Type 675 words in 15 minutes. How many words per minute?

Need 3 eggs to bake 24 cookies. How many cookies per egg?

45 words/minute   8 cookies/egg

D. Solve the word problems. You may use a calculator.

Mia can swim 20 meters per minute. If she swims 30 minutes each day, how many days will it take her to swim 9,000 meters?   **15 days**

Sam is painting 1,200 square feet of wall space. Paint costs $26 per gallon, and one gallon covers 300 square feet. How much would it cost Sam to paint the entire wall space?   **$104**

Jake had a road trip across the United States during the summer. He drove 5,850 miles for 18 days at an average speed of 65 miles per hour. How many hours did he drive per day?   **5 hours**

</td><td>

LESSON 126 Practice

A. Find a unit rate to represent each situation.

2 inches of rain in 4 hours. How many inches per hour?

216 miles on 9 gallons of gas. How many miles per gallon?

0.5 inch/hour   24 miles/gallon

20 video lessons over 5 days. How many lessons per day?

195 heartbeats in 3 minutes. How many heartbeats per minute?

4 lessons/day   65 heartbeats/minute

5 laps in 15 minutes. How many minutes per lap?

150 customers during 6 hours. How many customers per hour?

3 minutes/lap   25 customers/hour

B. Solve the word problems. You may use a calculator.

Ana can type 45 words per minute. If she types 20 minutes each day, how many days will it take her to type 4,500 words?   **5 days**

A bakery bakes 3 trays of cookies every 2 hours. Each tray holds 36 cookies. How many cookies does the bakery bake in 6 hours?   **324 cookies**

A company has 4 factories. Each factory produces 8 cars per hour. All factories operate 8 hours a day and 5 days a week. How many cars does the company produce in 4 weeks?   **5,120 cars**

Kim has completed 16 worksheets of 25 math problems each in 20 days. On average it took her 3 minutes per problem. How many hours per day did she spend on math problems?   **1 hour**

Max is driving for 4.5 hours today. He wants to drive at a speed of 56 miles per hour. His car can go 28 miles per gallon of gas. How many gallons of gas does he need for his journey?   **9 gallons**

</td></tr>
</table>

This lesson is on a particular use of proportions. They come in handy! The example is about miles per hour. See if your child can write sixty miles per hour as a ratio and figure out how long it would take to go forty miles.

$$60:1 = 40:\ ?$$
$$60? = 40$$
$$? = 40/60 = 4/6 = 2/3\ of\ an\ hour$$

Of course, it would be smart to use 60 minutes instead of one hour. Then what happens?

$$60\ miles:60 minutes = 40\ miles:\ ?$$
$$1/1 = 40/?$$
$$? = 40\ minutes$$

They will be setting up proportion word problems again today. They need to make sure that they are keeping the same thing on the same side of the ratio. The trick to the lesson today is the word per. 60 miles per hour is 60 to 1. $3 per ticket is 3 to 1.

Here's the first question from the lesson. 4:126 = 1:? This is 4? = 126. ? = 126 ÷ 4.

Lesson 127

LESSON 127 Finding unit prices

A. A unit price is a price per unit. It is often used to compare the prices of different sizes (or brands) of the same product. One way to find a unit price is to use a proportion.

A 3-pound bag of sugar for $3.60 ⟹ $\frac{\$3.60}{3 \; pounds} = \frac{x}{1 \; pound}$ ⟹ $x = \frac{\$3.60}{3} = \$1.20$

B. A shortcut method to find a unit price is simply to divide the price by the quantity. Here is an example of comparing unit prices to determine the better buy.

A 2-pound bag of flour for $1.40   or   A 5-pound bag of flour for $2.50

$\frac{\$1.40}{2 \; pounds} = \$0.70/pound$ $\frac{\$2.50}{5 \; pounds} = \$0.50/pound$ ⟵(circled)

C. Find the unit price of each item. Determine the better buy for each pair.

2 pounds of beef for $10.90	or	4 pounds of beef for $18.80
$5.45/pound		$4.70/pound
12 inches of ribbon for $3	or	36 inches of ribbon for $7.20
$0.25/inch		$0.20/inch
1 gallon of paint for $26	or	5 gallons of paint for $150
$26/gallon		$30 /gallon
A dozen eggs for $1.80	or	Two dozen eggs for $4.80
$0.15/egg		$0.20/egg
6 bottles of soda for $5.40	or	12 bottles of soda for $12.00
$0.90/bottle		$1/bottle

LESSON 127 Practice

A. Find the unit price of each item. Circle the better buy between each pair.

2 kilograms of rice for $6.90	or	5 kilograms of rice for $18.00
$3.45/kilogram		$3.60/kilogram
8 ounces of honey for $5.20	or	16 ounces of honey for $9.60
$0.65/ounce		$0.60/ounce
10 meters of wire for $15	or	50 meters of wire for $80
$1.50/meter		$1.60/meter
2 cucumbers for $1.10	or	15 cucumbers for $7.50
$0.55/each		$0.50/each

B. Go to a grocery store. Write the price and unit price as well as the measurements (for example, 4 ounces) for five different products. At home see if you can take the product price and measurements and come up with the same unit price as the store.

	The information on the tag			Your calculation
Product name	Price	Measurements	Unit price	Unit price

The lesson today is a practical one on being a smart shopper. What's the better bargain? They will figure it out by finding the unit price, a use of proportions. The unit price is the price per one of whatever it is. This will be similar to setting up problems with "per" in them. Today they are finding the price per unit.

Let's say there is a box with ten little bags of chips in it. It costs $7. One bag of chips costs $.75. Is it cheaper to buy the box or ten little bags? You figure it out by finding the unit price, the cost of one of the bags in the box.

$7:10 = ? : 1
      7 = 10?
  7/10 = ?
$0.70 = ?

While proportions can help you set up the problem, because the unit we're looking for is just one, what they really end up doing is just dividing the total cost by the number of units. 10 units for $7 is $7 divided by 10, which gives us 70 cents for each bag.

They need to remember to answer the question. Which is the better buy? The box is the better buy in my example because 70 cents is less than 75 cents.

Lesson 128

LESSON 128 Converting units

A. Proportions can be used to convert between different units. Here is an example of using a proportion to convert feet to inches. Complete the example.

There are 12 inches in 1 foot. How many inches are in 8 feet?

$$\frac{12\ inches}{1\ foot} = \frac{x\ inches}{8\ feet} \Rightarrow 1 \cdot x = 12 \cdot 8 \Rightarrow x = 96$$

B. Another way to convert units is to multiply ratios called **conversion factors**. Conversion factors are relationships between two units. The goal is to cancel out the units you don't want and leave the units you do. Here are some examples of using conversion factors to convert units. Complete the examples.

There are 1000 meters in 1 kilometer. What is 5800 meters in kilometers?

$$5800\ \cancel{meters} \times \frac{1\ kilometer}{1000\ \cancel{meters}} = 5.8 \quad kilometers$$

What is 10 m/s (meters per second) in km/h (kilometers per hour)?

$$\frac{10\ \cancel{meters}}{1\ \cancel{second}} \times \frac{1\ kilometer}{1000\ \cancel{meters}} \times \frac{3600\ \cancel{seconds}}{1\ hour} = 36 \quad km/h$$

C. Convert each unit as indicated.

There are 5,280 feet in a mile. What is 2.5 miles in feet?	What is 60 mph (miles per hour) in fps (feet per second)?
13,200 feet	**88 fps**
There are 1,609 meters in a mile. What is 3218 meters in miles?	What is 440 fps (feet per second) in mph (miles per hour)?
2 miles	**300 mph**
One inch is 2.54 centimeters. What is 5 inches in centimeters?	What is 180 mph (miles per hour) in m/s (meters per second)?
12.7 centimeters	**80.45 m/s**

LESSON 128 Practice

Convert each unit as indicated.

What is 1,200 meters in kilometers?	What is 1.2 miles in feet?
1.2 km	**6,336 feet**
What is 804.5 meters in miles?	What is 8 inches in centimeters?
0.5 mile	**20.32 cm**
What is 1,320 feet in miles?	What is 0.04 kilometer in meters?
0.25 mile	**40 m**
What is 22.86 centimeters in inches?	What is 0.3 mile in meters?
9 inches	**482.7 m**
There are 3 feet in 1 yard. What is 15 feet in yards?	There are 100 centimeters in 1 meter. What is 75,000 centimeters in kilometers?
5 yards	**0.75 km**
What is 50 m/s (meters per second) in km/h (kilometers per hour)?	What is 72 mph (miles per hour) in m/s (meters per second)?
180 km/h	**32.18 m/s**
What is 360 km/h (kilometers per hour) in m/s (meters per second)?	What is 4,400 fps (feet per second) in mph (miles per hour)?
100 m/s	**3,000 mph**

They are going to be applying this same lesson again; this time with converting units. There are two different types of examples on the page. The first is what they've done before. They just need to make sure to keep their proportions straight. The example shows inches to feet and inches to feet. They can't flip flop the numerator and denominators in the ratios. The inches need to either both be on the top or the bottom.

The second example shows multiplying. That's the difference between the two examples. The first set up has an equals sign between them. The second has a multiplication sign between them.

In the second example they are taking advantage of the most fun thing with this type of multiplication, crossing things out. In the example they are finding 5800 meters in kilometers. They multiply 5800 meters by 1 kilometer/1000 meters. They cross off meters as 1. That's weird because they are words, but whenever the numerator and denominator are the same, that equals one. Meters/meters just disappears the way 15/15 and 40/40 did in a previous lesson.

What they don't do in the example, but your child can do is cross off more things. I love crossing things off in these types of problems. Makes them so easy. They can cross off two zeros in 5800 and two zeros in 1000. They can then just divide 58 by 10 by moving the decimal point over one place.

In the last example, they could cross of all the zeros in 10, 3600, and 1000.

Lesson 129

LESSON 129 Converting units of length

A. Here are the conversion charts for units of length.

Customary units of length:

1 mile (mi) = 1,760 yards (yd)
1 mile (mi) = 5,280 feet (ft)
1 yard (yd) = 3 feet (ft)
1 foot (ft) = 12 inches (in)

Customary to metric:

1 mi = 1.61 km
1 yd = 0.91 m
1 ft = 30.48 cm
1 in = 2.54 cm

Metric units of length:

1 kilometer (km) = 1000 meters (m)
1 meter (m) = 100 centimeters (cm)
1 centimeter (cm) = 10 millimeters (mm)

Metric to customary:

1 km = 0.625 mi
1 m = 1.1 yd
1 cm = 0.033 ft
1 cm = 0.396 in

B. Convert each unit as indicated. Round off decimals to 2 decimal places, if necessary.

12 yd ⇨ ft
36 ft

5.8 km ⇨ m
5,800 m

98 in ⇨ ft and in
8 ft 2 in

0.037 m ⇨ mm
37 mm

52 ft ⇨ yd and ft
17 yd 1 ft

468,000 cm ⇨ km
4.68 km

2 yd ⇨ cm
182 cm

10 m ⇨ ft
33 ft

200 ft ⇨ m
60.96 m

8 km ⇨ mi
5 mi

LESSON 129 Practice

Convert each unit as indicated. Round off decimals to 2 decimal places, if necessary.

4 ft 6 in ⇨ in
54 in

0.7 m ⇨ mm
700 mm

2.5 mi ⇨ yd
4,400 yd

2 m 4 cm ⇨ cm
204 cm

58 in ⇨ ft and in
4 ft 10 in

1290 m ⇨ km
1.29 km

76 ft ⇨ yd and ft
25 yd 1 ft

8,300 mm ⇨ m
8.3 m

6 mi ⇨ m
9,660 m

5 km ⇨ mi
3.13 mi

0.5 in ⇨ mm
12.7 mm

60 cm ⇨ in
23.76 in

500 yd ⇨ km
0.46 km

30 m ⇨ ft
99 ft

20,000 in ⇨ km
0.51 km

7 km ⇨ mi
4.38 mi

They are going to be converting units again today. The key is in setting up the proportion. I'll set up the first several on the page to help you out.

12 yd : ? feet = 1 yd : 3 ft Cross multiply to get 36ft.

5.8 km : ? m = 1 km : 1000 m   They just need to cross multiply 1000 x 5.8 and then just move the decimal point over three places to get 5800 meters.

98 in : ? ft = 12 in : 1 ft
   98in = 12in?
  8 2/12 = 8 ft and 2 in
There are twelve inches in a foot, so two leftover just represents two inches.

0.037 m : ? mm = 1 m : 1000 mm   Cross multiply (and move the decimal point three places) to get 37mm.

52 ft : ? yd = 3 ft : 1 yd
   52ft = 3?
   17 yd 1 ft   (The remainder 1 is 1 foot.)

Lesson 130

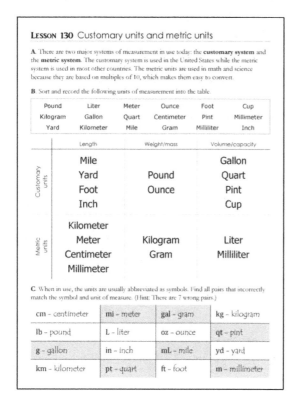
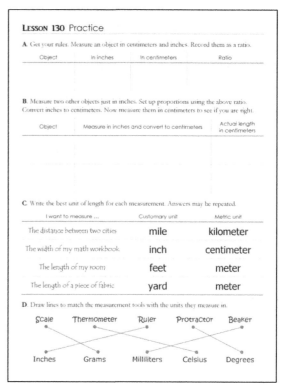

This is a different kind of lesson today. They need to know the measurements and their abbreviations. Some measurements are "customary," the kind used in America and almost nowhere else in the world. And there are metric units, the kind everyone else around the world uses, the kind that make sense and are easy to use.

I think it's fine to let them look up any they aren't sure about, but they could also do research in your kitchen to see measurements. If they ask you an answer, don't tell them, send them to find the answer. Boxes and drink containers in your kitchen will likely list both types of measurements, but they will show what measurement is used for weights or for volume. Drinks are measured in volume. Boxes and bags are measured by weight.

Lesson 131

LESSON 131 Converting between metric units

A. The metric system is a decimal-based system, meaning the units are defined in multiples of 10 from the base unit. The prefixes are used to indicate which multiple of 10 is being used. As a result, converting between metric units is the same as switching between prefixes, which is simply moving the decimal point. The table below shows metric prefixes, symbols, and their meanings. The most common base units are the meter, gram, and liter.

Divide by 10s or move the decimal point to the left.

Prefix	Kilo-	Hecto-	Deka-	Base unit	Deci-	Centi-	Milli-
Symbol	k	h	da	-	d	c	m
Meaning	1000	100	10	1	0.1	0.01	0.001

Multiply by 10s or move the decimal point to the right.

B. Make your own chart for commonly used metric units. Convert each unit to the other units to show how many are in each other. The first one is done for you!

1 km = 1,000 m = 100,000 cm = 1,000,000 mm
1 m = 0.001 km = 100 cm = 1,000 mm
1 cm = 0.00001 km = 0.01 m = 10 mm
1 mm = 0.000001 km = 0.001 m = 0.1 cm

1 kg = 1,000 g = 1,000,000 mg
1 g = 0.001 kg = 1,000 mg
1 mg = 0.000001 kg = 0.001 g

1 kL = 1,000 L = 1,000,000 mL
1 L = 0.001 kL = 1,000 mL
1 mL = 0.000001 kL = 0.001 L

LESSON 131 Practice

A. Convert each unit as indicated.

0.5 kg =	500	g	0.17 m =	170	mm
45 cm =	450	mm	0.08 km =	8,000	cm
0.89 L =	890	mL	3,360 mg =	3.36	g
2300 g =	2.3	kg	0.00027 kL =	270	mL
620 cm =	6.2	m	500,000 mm =	0.5	km

B. Which is longer, heavier, or larger in each pair?

810 mm or 8.1 cm   120 kL or 1,200 L
240 mL or 2.4 L   0.09 m or 900 mm
300 mg or 30 g   180 cm or 0.018 m
0.05 m or 5 mm   0.17 kg or 17,000 g

C. Solve the word problems.

Emma runs 300 meters per day to stay fit. How many kilometers does she run in 4 weeks?	8.4 km
Sunny had a ribbon 2.5 m long. She cut some off and 85 cm was left. How much did Sunny cut off?	1.65 m
One bucket holds 2.5 liters of water. Walter needs 5 buckets of water for his garden. How much water does he need in liters?	12.5 L
Joan had a cold. She took 4 ml of medicine, 3 times a day, for 5 days. How much medicine did she take?	60 mL
Peter bought a 2 kg bag of flour. He used 460 grams of it to bake cookies and 780 grams to bake pies. How much flour does he have left?	760 g

---

They are converting units once again; this time just using metric units. That means they are just multiplying and dividing powers of ten. The metric unit is just about place value. The decimal point just moves to the right or to the left.

The chart on their page moves from the largest to the smallest unit of measurement. They should check to make sure their answer makes sense, that they moved the right way. If they are moving from a larger measurement to a smaller measurement, the number of units should go up. For instance, one meter is one hundred centimeters. Meters > Centimeters so 1 < 100.

The first one they are asked to do is convert from 1 meter. 1 meter is the base unit. You have to move three place values to the left to get to kilometer (on the chart on their page), so you move the decimal point three places to the left; it's one thousandth of a kilometer. 1 m = 0.001 km A millimeter is three place values to the right of meters, so the decimal place moves over three times to the right to get from meter to millimeters. A meter is 1000 millimeters.

Of course, they could also set up proportions if they need help figuring out how to get from one measurement to another.

Lesson 132

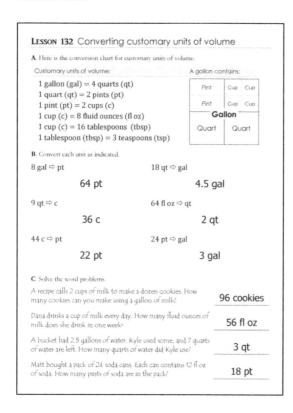

They are doing the same thing today with customary units. No more easy moving of the decimal point. They will have to set up proportions to keep straight the conversions.

The first one they have to do is change 8 gallons into pints. One gallon = four quarts we can see on the chart on their page. That means that 8 gallons is 32 quarts (by multiplying 4 x 8). Then they can set up the proportion 32 qt : ? = 1 qt : 2 pt Cross multiply to get the answer.

They could set that up a number of ways. They don't have to set up proportions. Proportions are handy to make sure you are working the in the right direction, multiplying where you should be multiplying and dividing where you should be dividing. Sometimes it can get confusing in conversions which way you are going. Proportions make it clear as long as you are comparing same things: gallons to gallons, cups to cups, etc.

Ratios and Proportions

Lesson 133

LESSON 133 Converting customary units of weight

A. Here are the conversion charts for units of weight.

Customary units of weight:
1 ton (t) = 2,000 pounds (lb)
1 pound (lb) = 16 ounces (oz)

Customary to metric:
1 t = 907.2 kg
1 lb = 453.59 g

B. Convert each unit as indicated.

6 lb ⇨ oz   96 oz
0.02 t ⇨ oz   640 oz
64 oz ⇨ lb   4 lb
8,000 lb ⇨ t   4 t
0.7 t ⇨ lb   1,400 lb
32,000 oz ⇨ t   1 t
5 t ⇨ kg   4,536 kg
6 lb ⇨ g   2,721.54 g

C. Solve the word problems.

Stacey bought four dozen cookies. Each cookie weighs 1.5 ounces. How many pounds of cookies did she buy?   4.5 lb

Daniel bought a cake that weighed 4 pounds and cut it into 8 equal pieces. How many ounces does each piece weigh?   8 oz

A book store found that the average weight of their books was 12 ounces. What will be the weight of 2,000 books in pounds?   1,500 lb

A farmer packaged 2 tons of his beans into 200 2-pound bags and 300 5-pound bags and sold them to a local grocery. How many pounds of the beans does he have left after that?   2,100 lb

---

LESSON 133 Practice

A. Convert each unit as indicated. Round off decimals to 2 decimal places, if necessary.

4.1 lb ⇨ oz   65.6 oz
0.1 t ⇨ oz   3,200 oz
72,000 oz ⇨ t   2.25 t
2 lb ⇨ g   907.18 g
8 lb ⇨ kg   3.63 kg
152 oz ⇨ lb   9.5 lb
32 oz ⇨ g   907.18 g
0.062 t ⇨ lb   124 lb
2 t ⇨ kg   1,814.4 kg
400 lb ⇨ t   0.2 t

B. Solve the word problems.

A pack of 12 pencils weighs 1 pound 2 ounces. How many ounces does each pencil weigh?   1.5 oz

Sam's cat weighs 6 pounds 8 ounces. Laura's cat weighs 12 ounces less than Sam's cat. How much does Laura's cat weigh?   5 lb 12 oz

Jim harvested 9 tons of corn and loaded it into trucks that can carry 6,000 pounds each. How many trucks did he load?   3 trucks

Mark put 128 candies equally into 8 boxes. Each candy weighs 4 ounces. How many pounds does each box weigh?   4 lb

---

They are converting units once again. They are using weights and using both metric and customary measurements.

Here are the word problems set up for you. They can be set up in different ways, but this will be the outcome. They can convert and then do the math or do the math and then convert the measurements. Let them do whatever makes sense to them.

4 x 12 x 1.5 ounces

4/8 = ½ pound = 8 oz. OR   4 x 16 / 8 ounces

2000 x 12 / 16 pounds (They can divide 12 by 16 first to get pounds and then multiply or multiply first to get the total number of ounces and then divide by 16 to get pounds.)

4000 (That's 2 tons) – 200 x 2 – 300 x 5

Lesson 134

LESSON 134 Converting temperatures

A. The most commonly used temperature scales are the **Fahrenheit** scale (°F) and the **Celsius** scale (°C). The United States mainly uses the Fahrenheit scale while most of the world uses the Celsius scale.

B. Here are the formulas to convert between Fahrenheit and Celsius temperatures.

Fahrenheit to Celsius

$$°F = \frac{5}{9}°C + 32$$

Celsius to Fahrenheit

$$°C = \frac{9}{5}(°F - 32)$$

C. Convert Fahrenheit to Celsius and Celsius to Fahrenheit. Round off decimals to 1 decimal place, if necessary.

Human body: 98.6°F	Summer at South Pole: -18°F
37°C	-27.8°C
Room temperature: 20°C	Winter at South Pole: -60°C
68°F	-76°F
Water's freezing point: 0°C	Summer day on Mars: 70°F
32°F	21.1°C
Water's boiling point: 212°F	Summer night on Mars: -73°C
100°C	-99.4°F

LESSON 134 Practice

Convert each temperature. Round off decimals to 1 decimal place, if necessary.

Absolute zero: -273°C	Steel's melting point: 2500°F
-459.4°F	1,371.1°C
Dog's body: 102°F	Summer at North Pole: 32°F
38.9°C	0°C
Chicken's body: 41.7°C	Winter at North Pole: -40°C
107.1°F	-40°F
Earth's core: 10,800°F	Hottest weather recorded: 134°F
5,982.2°C	56.7°C
Surface of sun: 5,505°C	Coldest weather recorded: -89.2°C
9,941°F	-128.6°F

Did you know? There is another temperature scale used in scientific measurements: the **Kelvin** scale (K). It is named in honor of the Scottish physicist who first defined it. Its zero point, 0 K, is defined to coincide with the coldest physically possible temperature, called absolute zero, at which nearly all molecules stop moving. The temperature of absolute zero is 0 K = -459.67°F = -273.15°C.

This is a different kind of conversion today. They are converting temperatures. There are formulas for doing this, which are on their page. The F or C is their "x", their ?, their unknown quantity. They will be given one temperature. They will plug that into its spot in the equation and do the math. The answer will give them the other temperature.

Here's an example. x + 3 = ? If I tell you that x = 4, then you plug that in to get 4 + 3 = 7, and you know that ? = 7.

Here's the first example from the page. 98.6°F We are looking for Celsius.

9/5 (F   – 32) = C
9/5 (98.6 – 32) = 9/5 (65.6) = 118.08 rounds to 118.1°C
This part is 65.6 times 9 divided by 5 or divided by 5 and then times 9.

Lesson 135

They are converting one last time. They can do actual measurements to figure out how long their foot is, etc., or they can just estimate. This is supposed to be a little bit of a fun converting activity.

Lesson 136

LESSON 136 Understanding exponents

A. An exponent or power represents repeated multiplication of the same number. The expression b^n means the number b is multiplied n times, as shown in the examples below.

$$2^4 = 2 \cdot 2 \cdot 2 \cdot 2 = 16 \qquad (-3)^3 = (-3) \cdot (-3) \cdot (-3) = -27$$

B. Any non-zero number raised to the power of 0 is 1: $b^0 = 1$. The example below demonstrates this **zero exponent rule** by following the pattern of powers.

$$2^4 \xrightarrow[\text{power by 1}]{\text{divide by 2}} 2^3 \xrightarrow[\text{power by 1}]{\text{divide by 2}} 2^2 \xrightarrow[\text{power by 1}]{\text{divide by 2}} 2^1 \xrightarrow[\text{power by 1}]{\text{divide by 2}} 2^0$$
$$= 16 \quad \text{decrease the} \quad = 8 \quad \text{decrease the} \quad = 4 \quad \text{decrease the} \quad = 2 \quad \text{decrease the} \quad = 1$$

C. A negative power of a number means how many times the number is divided by itself. It is equal to the reciprocal of its positive power of the number: $b^{-n} = 1/b^n$. The example below demonstrates this **negative exponent rule** by following the pattern of powers.

$$8^1 \xrightarrow[\text{power by 1}]{\text{divide by 8}} 8^0 \xrightarrow[\text{power by 1}]{\text{divide by 8}} 8^{-1} \xrightarrow[\text{power by 1}]{\text{divide by 8}} 8^{-2}$$
$$= 8 \quad \text{decrease the} \quad = 1 \quad \text{decrease the} \quad = 1/8 \quad \text{decrease the} \quad = 1/8^2$$

D. Fill in the missing numbers to simplify and evaluate each expression.

$$2^{-5} = \frac{1}{2^5} = \frac{1}{32} \qquad 5^3 \cdot 5^{-5} = \frac{5^3}{5^5} = \frac{\cancel{5} \cdot \cancel{5} \cdot \cancel{5}}{\cancel{5} \cdot \cancel{5} \cdot \cancel{5} \cdot 5 \cdot 5} = \frac{1}{25}$$

$$1/3^{-3} = 3^3 = 27 \qquad (-7)^3 / (-7)^4 = \frac{-7 \cdot -7 \cdot -7}{-7 \cdot -7 \cdot -7 \cdot -7} = -\frac{1}{7}$$

E. Evaluate each expression.

$$7^0 \cdot 3^4 = 81 \qquad\qquad (-5)^3 \cdot 2^3 = -1{,}000$$
$$8^2 \cdot 2^{-5} = 2 \qquad\qquad 8^{-1} \cdot (-4)^2 = 2$$
$$9^{-2} \cdot 3^7 = 27 \qquad\qquad 6^3 \cdot (-3)^{-3} = -8$$
$$10^4 / 5^3 = 80 \qquad\qquad 1^9 / (-7)^{-2} = 49$$

LESSON 136 Practice

A. When evaluating expressions with exponents, cancel as many common factors as possible to simplify the expressions before you jump into multiplication. Here are some examples. Fill in the missing numbers.

$$3^{-2} = \frac{1}{3^2} = \frac{1}{9} \qquad 7^5 \cdot 7^{-4} = \frac{7^5}{7^4} = \frac{7 \cdot 7 \cdot 7 \cdot 7 \cdot 7}{7 \cdot 7 \cdot 7 \cdot 7} = 7$$

$$1/10^{-3} = 10^3 = 1{,}000 \qquad (-9)^4 / 9^6 = \frac{-9 \cdot -9 \cdot -9 \cdot -9}{9 \cdot 9 \cdot 9 \cdot 9 \cdot 9 \cdot 9} = \frac{1}{81}$$

$$(-5)^5 / (-10)^4 = \frac{-5 \cdot -5 \cdot -5 \cdot -5 \cdot -5}{-10 \cdot -10 \cdot -10 \cdot -10} = -\frac{5}{16}$$

$$8^3 \cdot 2^{-4} \cdot 3^4 \cdot 9^{-2} = \frac{8^3 \cdot 3^4}{2^4 \cdot 9^2} = \frac{8 \cdot 8 \cdot 8 \cdot 3 \cdot 3 \cdot 3 \cdot 3}{2 \cdot 2 \cdot 2 \cdot 2 \cdot 9 \cdot 9} = 32$$

B. Evaluate each expression.

$$3^4 = 81 \qquad\qquad (-2)^6 = 64$$
$$2^{-2} = 1/4 \qquad\qquad (-1)^9 = -1$$
$$10^5 = 100{,}000 \qquad\qquad (-4)^0 = 1$$
$$10^{-2} = 1/100 \qquad\qquad (-10)^{-3} = -1/1{,}000$$
$$6^0 \cdot 8^2 = 64 \qquad\qquad 1 / 4^{-2} = 16$$
$$2^2 \cdot 5^2 = 100 \qquad\qquad (-1)^8 / 7^0 = 1$$
$$9^8 / 9^6 = 81 \qquad\qquad 10^3 \cdot (-2)^3 = -8{,}000$$
$$20^4 / 2^4 = 10{,}000 \qquad\qquad 2^9 \cdot (-2)^{-9} = -1$$

$$3^2 = 4 + 5 \; (3 \text{ squared} = 4 + 5)$$

They are moving onto their last section today, and it's a short one. It's on exponents. They have been introduced to exponents as meaning that you multiply the number by itself over and over again as many times as is shown by the exponent.

There are several examples on their page. Today's lesson goes beyond that introduction and shows that a number to the zero power equals one and that a number to a negative power means you divide by that number that many times.

It would be nice to look at their page together. Parts B and C show moving to smaller exponents. In part D look at the second example with five to the third times five to the negative fifth power. They can write in 5 * 5 * 5 in the numerator. Then they can cross off the three fives in the numerator and three fives in the denominator below. Crossing out is fun! Show them this please! 5/5 = 1, making it disappear. That just leaves 1 over 5 * 5 or 25.

Lesson 137

LESSON 137 Patterns in zeros

A. Powers of 10 are often used to avoid writing many zeros in very large and small numbers. Write each number as the product of a whole number and a power of 10.

$12{,}000{,}000 = 12 \cdot 10^6$ $\qquad$ $0.00000005 = 5 \cdot 10^{-8}$

$900{,}000{,}000 = 9 \cdot 10^8$ $\qquad$ $0.0000000076 = 76 \cdot 10^{-10}$

B. Multiplying powers of 10 is the same as adding the exponents while dividing powers of 10 is the same as subtracting the exponents, as shown below. Fill in the blanks.

$10^2 \cdot 10^3 = 100 \times 1{,}000 = 100{,}000 = 10^5$ $\qquad$ $2 + 3 = 5$

$10^3 / 10^5 = \dfrac{1{,}000}{100{,}000} = \dfrac{1}{100} = \dfrac{1}{10^2} = 10^{-2}$ $\qquad$ $3 - 5 = -2$

$10^9 \cdot 10^{-6} = 10^9 / 10^6 = 10^3$ $\qquad$ $9 + (-6) = 3$

$10^7 / 10^{-3} = 10^7 \cdot 10^3 = 10^{10}$ $\qquad$ $7 - (-3) = 10$

C. Evaluate each expression. Write your answers as a power of 10.

$10^7 \cdot 10^3 = 10^{10}$ $\qquad$ $10^8 / 10^4 = 10^4$

$10^{-2} \cdot 10^6 = 10^4$ $\qquad$ $10^{-7} / 10^3 = 10^{-10}$

$10^{-4} \cdot 10^{-5} = 10^{-9}$ $\qquad$ $10^4 / 10^{-9} = 10^{13}$

D. Multiplying and dividing large and small numbers becomes easy when the numbers are expressed as powers of 10. Rewrite and evaluate each expression using powers of 10. Write your answers as the product of a whole number and a power of 10.

$80{,}000 \times 0.0000003 = (8 \cdot 10^4) \cdot (3 \cdot 10^{-7}) = 24 \cdot 10^{-3}$

$0.000007 \times 0.00005 = (7 \cdot 10^{-6}) \cdot (5 \cdot 10^{-5}) = 35 \cdot 10^{-11}$

$42{,}000{,}000 \div 0.0006 = (42 \cdot 10^6) / (6 \cdot 10^{-4}) = 7 \cdot 10^{10}$

LESSON 137 Practice

A. Evaluate each expression. Write your answers as a power of 10.

$10^3 \cdot 10^5 = 10^8$ $\qquad$ $10^5 \cdot 0.0001 = 10$

$10^{-9} \cdot 10^7 = 10^{-2}$ $\qquad$ $0.00001 \cdot 10^{-2} = 10^{-7}$

$10^8 / 10^2 = 10^6$ $\qquad$ $10^3 / 0.000001 = 10^9$

$10^{-3} / 10^6 = 10^{-9}$ $\qquad$ $0.0001 / 100{,}000 = 10^{-9}$

B. Evaluate each expression. Use mental math if you can. Write your answers as the product of a whole number and a power of 10.

$(7 \cdot 10^{-3}) \cdot (5 \cdot 10^6) = 35 \cdot 10^3$

$(-3 \cdot 10^6) \cdot (2 \cdot 10^{-4}) = -6 \cdot 10^2$

$(24 \cdot 10^{-4}) / (4 \cdot 10^2) = 6 \cdot 10^{-6}$

$(15 \cdot 10^8) / (-5 \cdot 10^3) = -3 \cdot 10^5$

C. Rewrite and evaluate each expression using powers of 10. Write your answers as the product of a whole number and a power of 10.

$4{,}000 \times 0.000007 = (4 \cdot 10^3) \cdot (7 \cdot 10^{-6}) = 28 \cdot 10^{-3}$

$200{,}000 \times 800{,}000 = (2 \cdot 10^5) \cdot (8 \cdot 10^5) = 16 \cdot 10^{10}$

$0.00006 \times 0.00009 = (6 \cdot 10^{-5}) \cdot (9 \cdot 10^{-5}) = 54 \cdot 10^{-10}$

$3{,}500{,}000 \div 50{,}000 = (35 \cdot 10^5) / (5 \cdot 10^4) = 7 \cdot 10$

$0.000009 \div 300{,}000 = (9 \cdot 10^{-6}) / (3 \cdot 10^5) = 3 \cdot 10^{-11}$

$560{,}000 \div 0.000007 = (56 \cdot 10^4) / (7 \cdot 10^{-6}) = 8 \cdot 10^{10}$

Both weigh the same.

Today they will be adding and subtracting exponents to find their answer. They will be using powers of ten today, which means they are using place value. 10^6 means the number is getting bigger; the decimal point is moving 6 places to the right. 10^{-6} means the number is getting smaller; the decimal point is moving 6 places to the left.

To multiply the same number with different powers, you just need to add the exponents. They can see this in action in this example from the previous lesson.

To figure out $5^3 * 5^{-5}$ they just need to combine the exponents. $3 - 5$ is -2, which is the answer, 5^{-2}.

To divide the same number with different powers, you do the opposite, you subtract the exponents.

Lesson 138

LESSON 138 Exponent rules

A. When simplifying expressions with exponents, you can use properties of exponents called "**Exponent Rules**." The following table summarizes the exponent rules. Complete the table with your own examples that demonstrate the rules.

	Rule	Example
Zero exponent	$x^0 = 1, x \neq 0$	Answers will vary.
Negative exponent	$x^{-n} = \dfrac{1}{x^n}, x \neq 0$	
Product of powers	$x^m x^n = x^{m+n}$	
Quotient of powers	$\dfrac{x^m}{x^n} = x^{m-n}, x \neq 0$	
Power of a power	$(x^m)^n = x^{m \cdot n}$	
Power of a product	$(xy)^n = x^n y^n$	
Power of a quotient	$\left(\dfrac{x}{y}\right)^n = \dfrac{x^n}{y^n}, y \neq 0$	

B. Circle all expressions that are equivalent to the first one in each row.

$4^3 \cdot 4^{-6}$	$4^{-3} \cdot 4^6$	$\dfrac{4^3}{4^6}$	$(4^{-3})^2$	$4^{-6} \cdot 4^3$	4^{-3}
$(a^{-3}b^3)^2$	$\left(\dfrac{b^3}{a^3}\right)^2$	$(ab)^6$	$\left(\dfrac{b}{a}\right)^6$	$\dfrac{a^6}{b^6}$	$a^{-6}b^6$
$\dfrac{9x^8y^{-1}}{(3xy)^2}$	x^6y^{-3}	$\left(\dfrac{x^2}{y}\right)^3$	$(x^2y)^{-3}$	$3x^6y^3$	$\dfrac{x^6}{y^3}$

LESSON 138 Practice

A. Evaluate each expression using the exponent rules.

$5^{-7} \cdot 5^9 = 25$ $(7^{-2})^3 \cdot 7^5 = 1/7$

$3^8 \cdot 9^{-4} = 1$ $(4 \cdot 6)^2 \cdot 4^{-3} = 9$

$\dfrac{(2 \cdot 7)^6}{2^3 \cdot 7^5} = 56$ $\dfrac{(4 \cdot 5)^6 \cdot 5^2}{16^3 \cdot 25^3} = 25$

B. Simplify each expression. Write your answers in positive exponents.

$(a^2)^3$ $m^7 m^{-4}$ $(p^3q^4)^6$

$= a^6$ $= m^3$ $= p^{18}q^{24}$

$(2n^{-5})^2$ $r^5 r^{-7} r^6$ $(3x^{-2}y)^{-3}$

$= \dfrac{4}{n^{10}}$ $= r^4$ $= \dfrac{x^6}{27y^3}$

$\dfrac{b^9}{b^5}$ $\dfrac{k^5}{(k^2)^5}$ $\dfrac{8p^5q^2r^2}{4p^3q^7r^2}$

$= b^4$ $= \dfrac{1}{k^5}$ $= \dfrac{2p^2}{q^5}$

$\left(\dfrac{s^2t^4}{st}\right)^3$ $\dfrac{(5h^2)^3}{5^4h^5}$ $\dfrac{(9xy^3z)^2}{9y^4z^3}$

$= s^3t^9$ $= \dfrac{h}{5}$ $= \dfrac{9x^2y^2}{z}$

They are going to be looking at formulas today. These are rules for exponents, things that are always true. They are written with X because they hold true for any number they put in there.

That's the first thing they are asked to do, write in their own examples. They can substitute any number in for X, except for 0 in several cases. That's what it means when it shows that $x \neq 0$. They can pick any number but zero to substitute in for X to be their example. Where there is an X and a Y, they can substitute in any two numbers for X and Y.

Then they are asked to use those rules to figure out which of the exponent expressions equals the first in the line. You can tell them that there are three in each line if you want to encourage them to keep looking if they don't find them all.